America is in the middle of a great spiritual battle. Our weapons are spiritual. In *American Amnesia*, Jerry Newcombe fights back against the atheistic deconstruction of America with historic, Biblical truth. God will prevail.

— JOSEPH FARAH
Founder and Chief Executive Officer
WND.com, WND Books, WND Films

You can't have a nation built on freedom and personal responsibility without heaven's core principles and a rule of law. The Biblical worldview is where we were founded as a nation and where we should return to as a nation. I am pleased to recommend Dr. Jerry Newcombe's new book, *American Amnesia* because he speaks the truth in love.

— STAR PARKER
Syndicated Columnist & President of CURE

Jerry Newcombe is one of the foremost Christian commentators on American culture and government today. His modern insights are uniquely combined with his knowledge and understanding of America's history, making his commentaries especially important reading for anyone who wants to keep our nation free and prosperous. As Benjamin Franklin once told a Philadelphia matron, our Founders established a free republic. Keeping that republic free is our challenge as Americans today, and Newcombe has an important and unique understanding of that challenge. This book should be required reading for all politicians and for any citizens interested in keeping America true to the values and goals on which our nation was founded.

— DAVID GIBBS III,
President and General Counsel,
National Center for Life and Liberty

Jerry Newcombe is one of the most consistent voices defending the foundational significance of Biblical Christianity and the Judeo-Christian tradition for understanding the American experiment in Liberty. I highly commend this book given its clarity, coherence, and insightful commentary on contemporary culture and the controversies that flame in the public square. If you care about America and the Christian's vital role in civil society, read this book with care and pass it on to many others as well!

— Dr. Peter A. Lillback
Co-author of George Washington's Sacred Fire*;*
President, The Providence Forum;
President, Westminster Theological Seminary, Philadelphia

One well-accepted truism is that "ideas have consequences." True also is that those ideas are "culturally-codified" by the choices we make. Said another way: "Ideas have little consequence until you act upon them." This reality is exemplified by the rise, and some say the ongoing decline, of Western Civilization, based upon its initial embrace and subsequent rejection of absolute truth.

In antiquity, Procurator Pontius Pilate responded to Christ's claim of having come to "testify to the truth" with the now-clichéd response: "What is truth?" In our day, such rhetorical argumentation has been replaced by the very real and deadly consequences of denying that truth.

It is this latter-day reality that Dr. Jerry Newcombe explores in a powerful series of essays titled *American Amnesia*. In them, Newcombe's trenchant analysis helps us make important connections between the active rejection of God's truth and a culture that seems to be on moral life support. In doing so, Newcombe proves the Churchillian axiom: "The farther you look back, the farther forward you can see."

— Frank Wright, Ph.D.
President & CEO, D. James Kennedy Ministries

Endorsements for
AMERICAN AMNESIA

Newcombe writes to the heart, both the heart of the issue he's addressing and, more importantly, right to the heart of the reader. Highly recommended!

— CAROLE ADAMS
Founder and Board Member, Stone Bridge School;
President, Foundation for American Christian Education,
Chesapeake, Virginia

Jerry Newcombe's new book is not only must reading, but a timeless tool to help discover God's solutions to the urgent dilemmas of our day. Jerry weaves into his writing his lifelong study of history with Biblical insights. It is much like a recipe book—not for food, but for successful decision making on real culture-changing, life-changing issues.

— MARSHALL FOSTER
Founder and President of World History Institute

Jerry Newcombe's book *American Amnesia* is a "must-read" for Americans frustrated with the evil machinations of the political Left in America and the passivity of many Americans—especially Christians—toward this rising evil.

— DONALD MCALVANY
Intelligence News Writer, Author, and Missionary

What happens when a nation forgets about God? We can see that in history, and we are seeing it here in America. Jerry Newcombe brings together a collection of his columns that remind us of our history and focus on our current political debates. And a key element has been the attack on religious liberty in general and attacks on Christianity in particular. American Amnesia reminds us of the heavy price we pay when we forget about God.

— KERBY ANDERSON,
President, Probe Ministries; host, Point of View radio talk show

AMERICAN AMNESIA

AMERICAN AMNESIA

Is America Paying the Price for Forgetting God, the Source of Our Liberty?

JERRY NEWCOMBE, D.Min.

Be aware —
Part of D. James Kennedy!
(Second Reformation Movement)

Nordskog Publishing inc.

VENTURA, CALIFORNIA

AMERICAN AMNESIA:
IS AMERICA PAYING THE PRICE FOR FORGETTING GOD,
THE SOURCE OF OUR LIBERTY?
by Jerry Newcombe, D.Min.

© 2018 by Jerry Newcombe, D.Min.

ISBN: 978-1-946497-99-4
Library of Congress Control Number: 2018956223

Editing and Production:
Ronald W. Kirk, Theological Editor
Michelle Shelfer (benediction.biz), Managing Editor
Cheryl Geyer, Assistant Editor
Nikola Dimitrov (thefourinonegospelofjesus.com), Proofreader

Printed in the United States of America by Versa Press.

Published by

2716 Sailor Avenue, Ventura, California 93001
1-805-642-2070 • 1-805-276-5129
NordskogPublishing.com

MEMBER

CHRISTIAN SMALL
PUBLISHERS ASSOCIATION

I'd like to dedicate this book to my wife of thirty-eight years,

KIRSTI NEWCOMBE.

I have thirty-eight years of empirical proof that I married a saint. She's put up with me all these years.

TABLE OF CONTENTS

Part II

RENEWING OUR ROLE AS ACTIVE CITIZENS

Part III

RECOVERING OUR RELIGIOUS LIBERTY
IN THE FACE OF A MILITANT SECULARISM

PROLOGUE

by Colonel John Eidsmoe

Journalism has been called the first rough draft of history, and my friend Jerry Newcombe is both journalist and historian par excellence. *American Amnesia* is a timely compilation of Jerry's columns, articles, interviews, and other writings over the years.

Journalism is a high calling—or at least it was. There was a time when journalists were committed to ferreting out the truth and reporting the facts as clearly, fully, and accurately as possible. But that commitment rested on two basic assumptions: 1) absolute, objective truth exists; and 2) with diligent effort it is possible to find the truth, or at least come close.

But with the rise of postmodernism and its denial that objective truth exists, a new view of journalism has arisen as well. If objective truth doesn't even exist, the new school asks, why should seeking and reporting objective truth be our goal? Instead, the goal of much of modern journalism is to make news, not report news; to report it first, not report it best; and as much as possible, to center the news around the journalists themselves.

The Left rewrites history to fit its current politically correct narrative, hoping no one will notice because Americans have a short political/historical memory—in short, American amnesia. And to make sure no one remembers, we see a current drive to take down monuments, historical markers, and any reminders that there was a time past during which people thought differently.

That's nothing new. New civilizations have often destroyed the records of the old. The Spanish conquistadors destroyed the writings of the conquered Aztecs, believing they were formulas for devil worship—but the Aztecs had destroyed the writings of the Toltecs who preceded them, and so on. Muslims, Nazis, communists, and conquerors of every sort have tried to consolidate their control by burning books and eliminating memories of the past. By controlling people's memory of the past, they shape people's view of the present and the future. Remember Winston Smith, the protagonist officer of the Ministry of Truth in George Orwell's classic *1984*, as he explains: "If the Party could thrust its hand into the past and say of this or that event, it never happened—that, surely, was more terrifying than mere torture and death? . . . And if all others accepted the lie which the Party imposed—if all records told the same tale—then the lie passed into history and became truth. 'Who controls the past,' ran the Party slogan, 'controls the future: who controls the present controls the past'" (Orwell 1945).

But once in a while someone stands up and interrupts the politically correct narrative by saying, "That's not the way it happened! I know; I was there. I saw it."

That's why Jerry's book is so necessary today—as an antidote to American amnesia. Kaepernick's NFL anthem caper, the communist USSR, the Charlottesville riots, the Ferguson riots, the mess of Obamacare, the SPLC-inspired shooting at Family Research Council— Jerry provides the truth on these important stories, not the politically correcct version of truth. Then he relates it to the Bible and American history, and his first draft journalism becomes history.

That's one reason God gave us the gift of freedom of speech and freedom of the press, and a reason our founding fathers chose to protect those freedoms in the Bill of Rights. As irritating as the media can be at times, a free press is a check on tyranny. And today even those freedoms are under attack by the radical Left who would subordinate them to political correctness.

As you read these entries in *American Amnesia*, your reactions may vary: "Oh yes, I remember that!" "Really? I didn't know that!" or maybe sometimes, "I don't agree with Jerry on that; I remember it differently." But you'll learn a lot, you'll remember a lot, and you'll think a lot.

And you'll be reminded of the true source of America's greatness: our Biblical heritage.

JOHN A. EIDSMOE, COLONEL (MS), MISSISSIPPI STATE GUARD
Senior Counsel, Foundation for Moral Law
Pastor, Association of Free Lutheran Congregations

FOREWORD

HAS AMERICA LOST ITS MEMORY?

by William J. Federer

John F. Kennedy wrote in the Introduction to *The American Heritage New Illustrated History of the United States* (Dell Publishing Co., 1960): "History, after all, is the memory of a nation."

Pulitzer Prize-winning historian Arthur M. Schlesinger, Jr., wrote in an op-ed titled "Folly's Antidote" (*The New York Times*, January 1, 2007): "History is to the nation as memory is to the individual."

Have you ever met an individual who has lost their memory? Maybe they have Alzheimer's? They cannot remember who you are, or who they are. Someone could easily take things away from them.

Do we have national Alzheimer's? Have we lost our collective memory? Yes, in a sense, we are suffering from American amnesia. Here we are, the most prosperous nation in world history, with more individual liberty and opportunity than any previous people, and yet we forgot how we got here.

As a result, our freedoms are being taken right out of our hands.

Is this by accident or on purpose?

There is actually a socialist–communist tactic called "deconstruction," where you separate a people from their past, get them into a neutral position where they do not remember where they came from, then you can easily brainwash them into whatever future you have planned for them. It is like cultural gene-therapy.

It mirrors a sales technique. If I were a toothpaste salesman, the first thing I would do is say negative things about the toothpaste you are currently using—"You are using that old stuff—it will dry out your gums and eat the enamel off your teeth!" "Yikes"—you are repulsed by it.

Now I have you in a neutral position, where you are open-minded—"What are all the toothpastes out there nowadays?" Then I can give you my pitch for this brand-new, tartar-control, breath-freshener toothpaste.

This technique is applied nationally. First, students are taught negative things about the country's founders—"They took land from Indians, sold people into slavery, and were chauvinists." "Yikes"—students are repelled by them.

Now, students are in a neutral position where they are open-minded to other belief systems. Then students can be given the pitch for socialism, the LGBT agenda, or even Islam, being peer-pressured, intimidated, and ridiculed into accepting the guilt of "white privilege" and the reprograming indoctrination of common-core curriculum.

Just as a car has to go from drive into neutral before it can go into reverse, this process has taken place in Western Civilization. Look at Europe. It has gone:

- from a Judeo-Christian *past*
- into a Secular-Free-Sex *present*
- now Europe is entering an Islamic *future*

History is not prophetic, but it is predictive. Winston Churchill stated: "The farther back you can look, the farther forward you are likely to see."

Patrick Henry observed: "I know of no way of judging the future but by the past."

For centuries, Europe was Catholic, with many cities having Jewish neighborhoods. In 1517, the Protestant Reformation began.

Then Europe had a secular French Revolution. As head of France's Committee of Public Safety, Robespierre began the Reign of Terror in 1793. He put a prostitute in Notre Dame Cathedral, covered her with a sheet, and declared her the goddess of reason. Paris sent its military to the Vendée, a rural Catholic area. Soldiers killed over three hundred thousand men, women, and children including priests, nuns, and those who did not comply with the official secular edicts.

Napoleon spread this new French secularism across Europe, effectively cutting cultural ties with the Judeo-Christian *past*.

Europe then drifted into a secular *present*, with its non-religious atheistic, free-sex, and LGBT agenda.

Now, Europe is entering an Islamic *future*, with: "Mohammed" as the number one name given to newborns in London, Brussels, and Milan; Paris surrounded by five million Muslims in over seven hundred neighborhoods; women raped on streets in Germany, Sweden, and Denmark; trucks being driven into crowds.

African Archbishop Robert Sarah of Guinea told the Synod of Bishops in Rome, October 12, 2015:

> Like two apocalyptic beasts,...on the one hand...atheistic secularism,... on the other, Islamic fundamentalism.... We find ourselves between gender ideology and ISIS.... Two major threats.... Disintegration in the secularized West through quick and easy divorce, abortion, homosexual unions, euthanasia, etc. (cf. the LGBT lobby) On the other hand,... Islam, which legitimizes polygamy, female subservience, sexual slavery, child marriage etc. (cf. Al Qaeda, ISIS, Boko Haram).[1]

Italian Archbishop Carlo Liberati stated (*Breitbart*, January 14, 2017):

> We have a weak Christian faith.... Seminaries are empty.... Italy and Europe live in a pagan and atheist way, they make laws that go against God and they have traditions that are proper of paganism.... All this paves the way to Islam.... Europe will soon be Muslim.

This drive–neutral–reverse process has been successful in fundamentally transforming Europe, and it is advancing to the point of no return in America.

Consistent with this is the practice of fundamentalist Muslims, who upon entering an "infidel" country, destroy museums, libraries,

---

1. Romeo Hontiveros, "Cardinal Sarah urges Synod to reject liberal agenda pushed by organizers in blistering speech, interview," *Pagadian Diocese*, October 15, 2015, pagadiandiocese.org.

statues, artwork, and artifacts linking the conquered people to their past.

In the article "ISIS Burns Books at Mosul Libraries," (*Breitbart*, February 5, 2015), it was reported:

> The Islamic State continues to purge anything they deem to defy Islam.... They raided the Central Library of Mosul to destroy all non-Islamic books. "These books promote infidelity and call for disobeying Allah," announced a militant to the residents. "So they will be burned." Militants targeted the library at the University of Mosul. They burned science and culture textbooks in front of the students.... Extremists started wrecking the collections of other public libraries,... particularly heavy damage to... the Mosul Museum Library with works dating back 5,000 years.

This is similar to the first emperor of China, Qin Shi Huangdi, who conquered kingdoms to unify China in 221 BC, then destroyed all books linking them to the past. *The Basic Annals of the First Emperor of Qin* reported that Chancellor Li Si told the Emperor in 213 BC:

> I, your servant, propose that all historians' records other than those of Qin's be burned.... If anyone under heaven has copies of the *Classics of History* [Shu Jing],... they shall deliver them to the governor... for burning. Anyone who dares to discuss the *Classics of History* shall be publicly executed. Anyone who uses history to criticize the present shall have his family executed.... Anyone who has failed to burn the books after thirty days of this announcement shall be subjected to tattooing and be sent to build the Great Wall.[2]

In 1933, the Nazi leader Adolf Hitler burned books by Jewish authors, including Einstein. Jewish poet Heinrich Heine prophetically penned in 1822: "Where they burn books, they will, in the end, burn human beings too."

Poet Carl Sandburg cautioned: "When a nation goes down,... one condition may always be found; they forgot where they came from."

More familiar, perhaps, is the statement of Harvard Professor George Santayana, who warned: "Those who cannot remember the past are condemned to repeat it."

---

2. Sima Qian, *Records of the Grand Historian*, 94 BC.

Any hope of preserving America's freedoms is dependent upon Americans rediscovering their history—regaining their corporate memory—and realizing how truly rare their liberties are. This is why I highly recommend Dr. Jerry Newcombe's book *American Amnesia: Is America Paying the Price for Forgetting God, the Source of Our Liberty?* In this one volume, the reader will get a lifetime of wisdom. Dr. Newcombe's decades of study and research are distilled into this powerfully insightful and inspiring book. Lest we forget.

WILLIAM J. FEDERER
Best-selling author and speaker, AmericanMinute.com

AN INTRODUCTION:
OUR FREEDOM IS WORTH PRESERVING

I live in Florida. Sometimes we will see a sign on the highway declaring a "Silver Alert." It refers to someone on the highway who has lost their memory and should not be behind the wheel of a car—but they are driving anyway, to society's potential peril. In America, we have a problem of collective amnesia. We have been blessed by God perhaps more than any other nation before us. But in the process of being blessed, we have forgotten God.

We do have Alzheimer's as a nation. We have forgotten the hand of God that helped us become a nation. Read the 1606 charter to the first permanent British North American settlement, that of Jamestown, written long before we were a nation: "We, greatly commending, and graciously accepting of, their Desires for the Furtherance of so noble a Work, which may, by the Providence of Almighty God, hereafter tend to the Glory of His Divine Majesty, in propagating of Christian Religion to such People as yet live in Darkness and miserable Ignorance of the true Knowledge and Worship of God..."

Consider the example of the Fundamental Orders of Connecticut, 1639: "Forasmuch as it hath pleased the Almighty God by the wise disposition of his divine providence...for our souls and our Successors and such as shall be adjoined to us at any time hereafter, enter into Combination and Confederation together, to maintain and preserve the liberty and purity of the gospel of our Lord Jesus which we now profess, as also the discipline of the Churches, which according to the truth of the said gospel is now practiced amongst us." We see the Christian faith playing a pivotal role here. These quotes are typical of the early charters in colonial America, where the Christian faith was front and center.

I don't want to be unkind, but I can't help but feel that those who seek to cut us off from our roots are like termites. They burrow into a beautiful building and eat away at it until it is a hollowed-out shell of what it once was.

We see a pattern in the Bible: God redeems His people, then they thank Him. For a while. Then they prosper, and they forget Him. So He sends a punishment, and they call out to Him. They repent. Then He relents, and they thank Him for His deliverance. And the cycle begins all over again. God says that we should trust in Him. He declares in Psalm 81:10, "I am the Lord your God, who brought you up out of Egypt. Open wide your mouth and I will fill it."

The famous Frenchman Alexis de Tocqueville came to America in the early 1830s. He noted that religion played an important role in society—as a restraining force. "The main business of religions is to purify, control, and restrain that excessive and exclusive taste for well-being which men acquire in times of equality, but I think it would be a mistake for them to attempt to conquer it entirely and abolish it." (de Tocqueville, *Democracy in America,* 1838).

When I consider how precious my grandchildren are and I contemplate what kind of world I want them to grow up in, I must express my concern overall about the direction of America at this present time. At the same time, it is astounding to think that if genuine revival happens, America's best days could truly be ahead of us.

America needs to wake up, like someone who has long been asleep. Like Rip Van Winkle, it's time to wake up. One of the great challenges of our time is that while the church is a mile wide, it appears to be an inch deep. There are millions of professing Christians but many of them lack solid Biblical discernment. The world will not get its act together. It basically cannot. But the church can and so far doesn't seem willing to do so. But, as Dr. Richard Land would put it, may God give us the grace that we would have a great revival (a renewal of the church), a great awakening (where many unsaved would come to faith in Jesus), and a society-transforming reformation that results.

What follows is a collection of essays that I have written in the last several years. These focus on God and government, on the American experiment, and on church and state matters. Thanks to my brother, Rick, the founder and long-time head of Creators Syndicate, who encouraged me in 2010 to write a weekly column. I'm grateful to D. James Kennedy Ministries, and the excellent editing of these columns by John Rabe, Susie Dzuro, and Dr. Karen Gushta. I'm thankful for the various outlets that run these columns, including *WorldNetDaily*, *Townhall*, *Christian Post*, *Newsmax*, and so on. And I'm grateful to the publisher of this book, Jerry Nordskog (the other Jerry N.) and to his excellent staff—Ron Kirk, Michelle Shelfer, Kyle Shepherd, Cheryl Geyer, and Nikola Dimitrov. Special thanks also go out to my extraordinary webmaster, Michael ("Mike at the Mic") Schlote. I also give thanks for my wife Kirsti and her constant encouragement and feedback. And finally, I want to thank my Lord and Savior Jesus Christ, by Whose grace beat all our hearts and to Whom we shall all give an account one day. Only because of His death and resurrection and trusting in Him can anyone be saved.

JERRY NEWCOMBE, D.MIN.
July 31st, in the Year of Our Lord, 2018

PART I

REMEMBERING OUR NATION'S JUDEO-CHRISTIAN ROOTS

1

COLUMBUS DAY OR INDIGENOUS PEOPLES' DAY?

Originally published on October 8, 2014

Political correctness infects virtually every aspect of our culture, our thinking, our heritage.

When I grew up (and I was born in 1956), Christopher Columbus was a great hero. Now, to some, he has become a villain. He is blamed for many unjustifiable things, most of which followed in the wake of his voyage. Meanwhile, most of us have lost the Christian side of Columbus.

Just days ago, the Seattle School Board voted unanimously to replace Columbus Day, a federal holiday, with "Indigenous Peoples' Day," celebrated on the same day in support of the people allegedly plundered and wiped out by Columbus and his heirs.

Contrast this view of Columbus, which has gained currency recently, with a statement by one of the nation's first great historians, George Bancroft (1800–1891). His six-volume series (final version, 1888) on the history of the United States was a standard for a couple of generations. When I began to study America's roots in earnest years ago, I invested in getting those six volumes. What a treasure trove. Although Bancroft was a nineteenth-century Unitarian, at least he didn't edit out the G-word (*God*), the C-word (*Christian*), or the B-word (*Bible*) in his quotes. Bancroft said that Columbus's voyage was certainly "the most memorable maritime enterprise in the history of the world."

Modern authors George Grant (*The Last Crusader*) and John Eidsmoe (*Columbus & Cortez*) confirm Bancroft's excellent information with their own scholarship on the explorer and his Christian faith.

In 1892, the City of Chicago elaborately honored Columbus on the 400th anniversary of his voyage. I understand that the genesis of the Museum of Science and Industry (a phenomenal place) came out of that anniversary celebration. But jump forward a hundred years to 1992. By then the politically correct elites in our culture had already begun reviling. Columnist Gary Wills captured that sentiment well, saying: "A funny thing happened on the way to the quincentennial observation of America's discovery: Columbus got mugged."

It is true that Spanish and Portuguese explorers who followed Columbus's voyage greedily sought gold, not God, in the New World. They significantly mistreated the indigenous peoples here, especially in South America. But should we lay all the blame at the feet of the Genoan sailor? Listen to what Columbus himself wrote to King Ferdinand and Queen Isabella of Spain on February 15, 1493, during his return voyage: "I forbade that they [the Indians] should be given things so worthless as pieces of broken crockery and broken glass, and lace points.... I gave them a thousand good, pleasing things which I had bought, in order that they might be fond of us, and furthermore might become Christians and be inclined to the love and service of Their Highnesses and of the whole Castilian nation [Spain], and try to help us and to give us of the things which they have in abundance and which are necessary to us" (Federer 2000, 113).

In 1505 he finished writing his *Book of Prophecies*, where he laid out the Christian motivation of his enterprise. He viewed his voyage as helping to hasten the Second Coming. He took to heart these words of Jesus Christ: "And this gospel of the kingdom will be preached in all the world as a witness to all the nations, and then the end will come" (Matthew 24:14).

Although a sinful man like all of us, he still stands as a hero. Why did he persevere for at least seven years requesting funding for his voyage? Why did he suffer repeated rejections of his proposal and even ridicule? Why did he defy death and risk mutiny to sail west into unknown waters? He tells us in his own words: "It was the Lord who put into my mind (I could feel His hand upon me) to sail to the Indies. All who heard of my project rejected it with laughter, ridiculing me. There is no question that the inspiration was from the Holy Spirit, because

He comforted me with rays of marvelous illumination from the Holy Scriptures" (Federer 2000, 120).

Under Columbus' leadership, the sailors on the three ships began each day of the voyage with a prayer:

> Blessed be the light of day,
> And the Holy Cross, we say;
> And the Lord of Verity
> And the Holy Trinity.
> Blessed be th' immortal soul
> And the Lord who keeps it whole
> Blessed be the light of day
> And He who sends the night away. (Moore 2008)

Columbus named the places he landed in a way reflective of his Christian faith. These include the first island (in the Bahamas), *San Salvador* ("Holy Savior"). Other lands he named are *Trinidad* ("Trinity"), *Vera Cruz* ("True Cross"), and *Navidad* ("Christmas").

He was a study in endurance. I've heard that he repeatedly wrote in his journal, "And this day we sailed on." Of course, even the missionary enterprise itself is suspect in our day, when each of us is expected to invent and live by "our own truth." But Columbus was a man, like all great men, who believed in real truth—and worked as hard as he could to spread it far and wide.

Although politically incorrect today, Christopher Columbus is still a hero in my book.

2

AMERICA HAS CHRISTIAN ROOTS: GIVE THANKS TO THE SOURCE OF OUR NATIONAL GREATNESS

Originally published on November 23, 2016

Why do people from many other countries try to come to America—even in some cases, risking their lives to do so? What is the source of this nation's greatness?

I think the single biggest thing that makes this country so great is that our founding document—the Declaration of Independence (upon which the Constitution is predicated)—says that our rights come from God. What God has given to us, no man can take away.

John F. Kennedy said as much in his Inaugural Address, explaining that the fundamental beliefs "for which our forebears fought are still at issue around the globe—the belief that the rights of man come not from the generosity of the state but from the hand of God."

But long before 1776, if you look at the original charters and founding documents of America, we see over and over the mention of God and the Christian faith—so much so that when the Supreme Court quoted many of those documents in the *Trinity* decision in 1892, they concluded with the words, "...this is a Christian nation."[1] The Supreme Court marshaled a very rich argument, documenting in detail our nation's rich Judeo-Christian heritage. I assembled an appendix for my book *The Book that Made America: How the Bible Formed Our Na-*

---

1. *Church of the Holy Trinity v. the United States.* No. 143. Supreme Court of the United States 143 U.S. 457, 36 L.Ed. 226, 12 S.Ct. 511, 29 February, 1892. Decided.

tion built primarily on that *Trinity* decision (Newcombe 2009). The facts are on our side.

For example, in the Mayflower Compact, the Pilgrims explained why they came here. They wrote: "In the name of God, Amen. We whose names are underwritten...having undertaken a voyage for the glory of God and the advancement of the Christian faith..."

Since the Pilgrims cast a long and positive shadow over so much of the future founding of the nation (even Thanksgiving is derived from them), you could say America began "in the name of God, Amen." The Pilgrims saw their establishment in the New World as guided by the hand of God, by His Providence. The Biblical concept of covenant gave rise to our two key founding documents, the Declaration of Independence and the Constitution.

When our founding fathers first met in the First Continental Congress in 1774, they decided to open in prayer. Congress has been praying ever since. In fact, the founders created chaplains for our national and state legislatures, and the military as well.

If they thought that such religious activities violated their key principle that there would be no national denomination in America, they would not have created the chaplaincy system. Of course, all the original chaplains, decade upon decade, were Christian ministers.

Because of the Christian roots of America, people of all faiths or no faith are welcome here, though not to the purposeful undermining of our Christian institutions. The founders wanted religion to be voluntary, not forced, but they wanted it to flourish. Freedom *of* religion gives freedom to all—including nonbelievers. Freedom *from* religion leads to state-sanctioned atheism and leads to non-freedom. Even the atheists fared badly in the failed Soviet Union if they happened to disagree with the atheists in charge. Trotsky is an example.

1. George Washington said, "Of all the dispositions and habits which lead to political prosperity, religion and morality are indispensable supports." That's from his Farewell Address in 1796.[2] He made that statement in a nation where 99.8 percent of the people professed to be Christians.

---

2. George Washington, *George Washington's Farewell Address* (New York: Firework Press, 2015).

2. Several years ago, *Time* magazine wrote, "Ours is the only country deliberately founded on a good idea. That good idea combines a commitment to man's inalienable rights with the Calvinist belief in an ultimate moral right and sinful man's obligation to do good. These articles of faith, embodied in the Declaration of Independence and in the Constitution, literally govern our lives today."[3]

3. President Eisenhower said in 1955, "Without God, there could be no American form of Government, nor an American way of life. Recognition of the Supreme Being is the first—the most basic—expression of Americanism."[4]

4. Ronald Reagan said, "America needs God more than God needs America. If we ever forget that we are one nation under God, then we will be a nation gone under."[5]

So in today's highly secular age, where ideological forces seek to banish any mention of God from the public square, we should never forget that God has been central to America's greatness.

This Thanksgiving, as we see the need for the healing of the American soul and a need for America to return to God, at least we should be grateful for what He has done in our past. People are dying—in some cases, literally—to get into this country, so that perhaps they too can enjoy what we often take for granted every single day: freedom, which is a gift from our Christian forebears.

---

3. Ezra Bowen, "Looking to Its Roots," *Time*, May 25, 1987.
4. *New York Herald Tribune*, Feb 21, 1955.
5. Ronald Reagan, at Dallas Prayer Breakfast, Aug 23, 1984.

3

WHAT'S IN YOUR WALLET?

Originally published on October 16, 2013

Virtually not a week goes by without some sort of lawsuit or complaint against a reference to God or Jesus in the public arena. Oftentimes these lawsuits or complaints run along the lines of, "I'm offended," and that settles it. So the Ten Commandments have to go. God has to be chiseled out.

Yet our national motto remains "In God We Trust." It has been since 1956. These words are chiseled in stone above the Speaker's platform in the House of Representatives. Anyone can see by a review of U.S. money how God's hand helped create and sustain this nation—all of it declares, "In God We Trust." What's in your wallet? Many reminders of our nation's godly heritage.

Stephen McDowell, cofounder of the Providence Foundation, explains: "You pull out your dollar [and] you see George Washington's picture, the father of our country who is a Christian man who reflected it in his actions and in his words."

For instance, in his Circular to the States (June 8, 1783), Washington said to all the governors that we could never hope to be a happy nation unless we learned to humbly imitate Jesus, whom he called "the Divine Author of our blessed religion."[1]

During his first Inaugural Address, he said, "No people can be bound to acknowledge and adore the Invisible Hand which conducts the af-

---

1. George Washington, "Circular Letter to the States," *George Washington's Mount Vernon,* mountvernon.org/library.

9

fairs of men more than those of the United States. Every step by which
they have advanced to the character of an independent nation seems to
have been distinguished by some token of providential agency."[2]

The same concept of gratitude to God for His help can be seen on
the back of the dollar bill. On the left, we see in Latin this phrase: *annuit coeptis*, meaning, "He has favored our undertakings." As in, God
has helped us win our independence.

As Stephen McDowell notes, "God has blessed our undertakings
because the founders believe that God and His providence had overseen
the birth of this nation and that is reflected there. . . . There are many
miracles God did during the American Revolution, but the greatest
miracle was that thirteen sovereign, independent states could gather
together to unite to work together as one. John Adams said it was like
making thirteen clocks strike together in unison."

Go back to the wallet and pull out a five-dollar bill, and we see
Abraham Lincoln. During the dark days of the Civil War, on March
30, 1865, our sixteenth president called for a national day of fasting
and prayer. He reminded the country, "We have been the recipients of
the choicest bounties of Heaven. We have been preserved, these many
years, in peace and prosperity. We have grown in numbers, wealth and
power, as no other nation has ever grown. But we have forgotten God."
When a group of black citizens gave him a Bible in 1864, President Lincoln said, "In regard to this great book, I have but to say, it is the best
gift God has given to men. All the good the Savior gave to the world
was communicated through this book. But for it we could not know
right from wrong."

If we pull out a ten-dollar bill we see Alexander Hamilton, who was
the first Secretary of the Treasury, under George Washington. Hamilton had attended the Constitutional Convention in 1787 and later
wrote to a friend, James Bayard: "Let an association be formed to be
denominated 'The Christian Constitutional Society,' its object to be
first: The support of the Christian religion. Second: The support of the
United States." His death in a duel that he did not want to participate
in ended that plan.

---

2. George Washington, "First Inaugural Address," *George Washington's Mount Vernon*,
mountvernon.org/library.

If we pull out a twenty-dollar bill we see Andrew Jackson, our seventh president. He said that the Bible is the "rock upon which our republic rests."

On the fifty-dollar bill is the face of Ulysses S. Grant. Although he seemed to have a serious problem with drinking, even he apparently made his peace with God by the end of his life. He once declared of the Bible, "To the influence of this Book are we indebted for all the progress made in true civilization, and to this must we look as our guide in the future. 'Righteousness exalteth a nation: but sin is a reproach to any people.'"

Finally, a one-hundred-dollar bill has the face of Benjamin Franklin, a man who apparently was not an orthodox Christian. Yet even he saw the importance of Christianity in society. He did not believe it was wrong for public officials to pray. In fact, he encouraged it. Franklin called for prayer at the Constitutional Convention (June 28, 1787), saying: "I have lived, Sir, a long time, and the longer I live, the more convincing proofs I see of this truth—that God Governs in the affairs of men. And if a sparrow cannot fall to the ground without His notice, is it probable that an empire can rise without His aid? We have been assured, Sir, in the Sacred Writings, that 'except the Lord build the House, they labor in vain that build it.' I firmly believe this; and I also believe that without his concurring aid we shall succeed in this political building no better than the Builders of Babel: We shall be divided by our partial local interests; our projects will be confounded, and we ourselves shall become a reproach and bye word down to future ages."[3]

Thankfully, a variation of Ben Franklin's request for prayer at the Convention was adopted, and they were able to successfully complete the Constitution.

What's in your wallet? One reminder after another that we are still one nation under God.

---

3. Benjamin Franklin, Epes Sargent, ed., *The Selected Works of Benjamin Franklin* (Boston: Phillips, Sampson & Co., 1855), 101.

4

PROVIDENCE AND THE PILGRIMS

Originally published on November 21, 2011

Every Thanksgiving is an annual reminder of our nation's Christian roots. The Pilgrims began the tradition, and Presidents Washington and Lincoln each helped it to become an official holiday. The details surrounding the Pilgrims were such that they had much to be grateful for. Here is just a sample.

The Pilgrims were a small congregation who secretly became a congregation in central England in 1606 when they formed a spiritual covenant with one another. Because of the persecution of those who would not conform with the Church of England, they emigrated to Holland for about eleven years. Eventually, they decided to come to British North America, to sail to the "Northern parts of Virginia," after the permanency of the Jamestown settlement, so that they could worship Jesus Christ in total freedom. I believe that specific details about their classic voyage and early settlement show us the Providence of God. He was watching out for them.

1) No Pilgrim died on the voyage over—a miracle in that day and age. But there was one man who died on the way over. Because the voyage was so difficult, the Pilgrims comforted themselves by singing the psalms to remind themselves of God's care. Yet this gained them the ire of some of the crewmembers. One crewmember, in particular, sneered that he looked forward to throwing overboard their shrouded corpses after they succumbed to routine illnesses, from which we can infer that death was common in those days on such voyages. This vile man was a

Pilgrim hater who cursed these "psalm-singing" religious nuts.

Gov. Bradford (their leader for decades) writes in his book *Of Plimouth Plantation*: "He would always be condemning them [the Pilgrims] …and cursing them daily with grievous execrations…but it pleased God before they came half seas over, to smite this young man with a grievous disease, of which he died…and so was himself the first that was thrown overboard."

He was the only known casualty of the whole voyage. Peter Marshall reports that the Pilgrims showed him love by honoring him in a service, thus putting into practice the Biblical admonition to "love your enemies."

2) Why did only one person die on that voyage? A little-known fact about the Mayflower helps answer the question. The Mayflower was normally a wine cargo boat, and the wine from previous voyages had soaked some of the beams and essentially acted as a disinfectant. "God works in mysterious ways…"

3) The Mayflower contended with some severe storms, yet they still made it over. In fact, the storms were so bad that some considered the possibility of turning back to England. Cotton Mather says, "They met with such terrible storms, that the principal persons on board had serious deliberations upon returning home again."

During one storm, catastrophe struck—the main beam of the mast cracked. Death was certain for the crew and passengers if they could not repair it. The whole Pilgrim adventure could easily have ended up on the bottom of the Atlantic. But one of the Pilgrims had a large iron screw on board—some historians argue that it was a jack for lifting roofs onto houses; others argue it was part of a printing press. Whatever it was, the main beam was secured with this large screw, and so the Mayflower was saved.

4) Storms blew the Pilgrims off course, which forced them to pen the immortal words of the Mayflower Compact that were composed in the cabin of the ship. If everything had gone as scheduled, if they had landed where intended, they likely would not have written that document, which was the first step toward the U.S. Constitution. Free people created their own free government under God—spelling out representative government.

The Mayflower Compact says, "In the name of God, Amen. We whose names are underwritten...having undertaken a voyage for the glory of God and the advancement of the Christian faith...do covenant and combine ourselves into a civil body politic" (Bradford 2008, 110).

Historians such as Dr. Donald Lutz, author of *The Origins of American Constitutionalism,* tell us that the Mayflower Compact, based on the Biblical concept of covenant, eventually morphs into "We the people" (after about a hundred other additional Biblically-based charters written by various Christian colonists to North America).

5) The Indians in the area where they landed were very hostile, yet as the late Dr. D. James Kennedy pointed out, most of them off the coast of Cape Cod had died off in a plague that swept through there a few years before the Pilgrims came. So the Pilgrims didn't have to contend with fierce Indians, which was a constant problem for other settlers in other regions.

The Pilgrims loved peace and were able to make friends with the remaining Indians. One of them they described as "a special instrument sent of God." His name was Squanto. Providentially, he spoke English, and he was a godsend to them. Peter Marshall tells us: "Now Squanto came and offered them his services. They were desperate. They had nothing to eat. They had no more idea how to live in this wilderness than to fly to the moon. Squanto taught them how to track eels in the wet flats when the tide went out, what berries were edible. All the Indian lore. Most important, he taught them how to plant the Indians' winter staple, corn, which Europeans had known nothing about."

So we can see just from these few examples that the hand of God was upon them, as they paved the way for a permanent settlement, a settlement where they could worship God freely as they saw fit and where they could live their lives in peace.

As Gov. Bradford put it, "Thus out of small beginnings greater things have been produced by His hand that made all things of nothing, and gives being to all things that are; and, as one small candle may light a thousand, so the light here kindled hath shone unto many, yea in some sort to our whole nation; let the glorious name of Jehovah have all the praise."

5

THE HISTORY OF THE THANKSGIVING HOLIDAY

Originally published on November 27, 2013

One of my favorite times of year is Thanksgiving. What a great tradition—where we gather together to recount the Lord's blessings. I love the statement from columnist Mark Steyn: "Speaking as a misfit unassimilated foreigner, I think of Thanksgiving as the most American of holidays." Consider its history as a holiday.

In 1619, a year before the Pilgrims even landed, Jamestown (the first permanent British settlement in North America) had the first Thanksgiving celebration. Captain John Woodlief declared on December 4, 1619: "We ordain that the day of our ship's arrival at the place assigned for plantation in the land of Virginia shall be yearly and perpetually kept holy as a day of Thanksgiving to Almighty God."

That colony, begun in 1607, had "starving times," so that by 1610, says historian John Eidsmoe in a television interview I once did with him for D. James Kennedy Ministries, "Of the more than five hundred colonists who had come to Jamestown, only sixty remained alive."

But, eventually—providentially—Jamestown survived, and because of its permanency, the Pilgrims, a small group of Christian separatists, decided to settle in what they called "the northern parts of Virginia." Hence, the voyage of the Mayflower in 1620, which they said was "for the glory of God and the advancement of the Christian faith" (Mayflower Compact). Storms blew them off course from their intended destination of Virginia. They took it as Providence and so remained near Cape Cod.

Of course, our American tradition of Thanksgiving goes back to these hearty souls who in 1621 celebrated a time of thanksgiving to God despite all the problems they had seen. They invited the Indians, with whom they had made a treaty of peace (that lasted over fifty years).

The Pilgrims' long-time leader was William Bradford. He wrote a great book that tells us all the details about the Pilgrim saga, entitled, *Of Plymouth Plantation.* The late Samuel Eliot Morison of Harvard put together my favorite version of *Of Plymouth Plantation* (1952/2001). In a footnote on p. 90 he says: "Edward Winslow's letter of 11 Dec. 1621 to a friend in England describing this 'First Thanksgiving' is printed in *Mourt's Relation,* pp. 60–5: 'Our harvest being gotten in, our Governor sent four men on fowling, that so we might after a more special manner rejoice together, after we had gathered the fruit of our labours. They four in one day killed as much fowl as, with a little help beside, served the Company almost a week. At which time, amongst other recreations, we exercised our arms, many of the Indians coming amongst us, and amongst the rest their greatest king, Massasoit with some 90 men, whom for three days we entertained and feasted. And they went out and killed five deer which they brought to the plantation and bestowed on our Governor and upon the Captain and others'" (Fiore 1985, 72).

Pilgrim expert Paul Jehle notes that the second Thanksgiving was in July, 1623, and it "was not a harvest festival, but a day of thanksgiving for answered prayer for rain."

On November 1, 1777, notes author and speaker Bill Federer, the Continental Congress declared the first National Day of Thanksgiving. They wrote, "The grateful feeling of their hearts...join the penitent confession of their manifold sins...that it may please God, through the merits of Jesus Christ, mercifully to forgive and blot them out of re-membrance...and...under the providence of Almighty God...secure for these United States the greatest of all human blessings, indepen-dence and peace" (Federer 2000, 147).

Some people today don't like the idea of Thanksgiving as a national holiday because it is inherently religious. (Thanksgiving was indeed when the Pilgrims gave thanks to God.) But consider this fact: the same Congress that gave us the First Amendment (which is often twisted today to drive out any religious expression in public) suggested that the new president declare a national day of thanksgiving to celebrate the peaceful establishment of our government. The president agreed, so on October 3, 1789, from the city of New York, George Washington issued a Proclamation of a National Day of Thanksgiving, in which he said, "Whereas it is the duty of all nations to acknowledge the Providence of Almighty God, to obey His will, to be grateful for his benefits, and humbly to implore His protection and favor; and Whereas both Houses of Congress have by their joint Committee requested me 'to recommend to the People of the United States a day of public thanksgiving' . . ."[1]

Dr. Peter Lillback, with whom I had the privilege to cowrite *George Washington's Sacred Fire*, noted that those who heard our first president would have understood that he referred to Jesus in this line from that proclamation: "And also that we may then unite in most humbly offering our prayers and supplications to the great Lord and Ruler of Nations, and beseech Him to pardon our national . . . transgressions . . ." Jesus is the Lord and Ruler of the nations, as seen in Revelation 12 (based on Psalm 2).

While Washington was the first president to declare a national day of Thanksgiving, President Lincoln was the first one to make Thanksgiving an annual holiday, and during FDR's days, Congress fixed the date as the fourth Thursday of each November.

At one of the darkest periods in American history, on October 3, 1863, President Lincoln, in conjunction with Congress, looked for the good things to thank the Lord for: "In the midst of a civil war of un-equaled magnitude and severity, which has sometimes seemed to for-eign states to invite and to provoke their aggression, peace has been pre-served with all nations, order has been maintained, the laws have been respected and obeyed, and harmony has prevailed everywhere, except in the theater of military conflict." And he added, "I do, therefore, invite my fellow citizens in every part of the United States, and those who are sojourning in foreign lands, to set apart and observe the last Thursday of November next as a day of Thanksgiving and Praise to our beneficent Father who dwelleth in the heavens."

As Americans, we have much to be thankful for.

---

1. George Washington, "Thanksgiving Proclamation, 3 October, 1789," founders.archives.gov.

6

ON THE ORIGINS OF THE THANKSGIVING HOLIDAY . . . TEACHING US TO GIVE THANKS IN ALL CIRCUMSTANCES

Originally published on November 20, 2012

How would you like to set yourself up for almost guaranteed disappointment? Despite how much good you do, if you expect gratitude from other human beings, you will often be let down.

On one occasion Jesus healed ten lepers, but only one came back to say thank you, and he was of a despised race. (He was a Samaritan. They were hated because they were half-breeds). In that day, to have leprosy was a kiss of death. Christ gave them a totally new lease on life, yet only one—10 percent—came back to thank Him.

If that's how they treated Jesus, why should we expect more? Unfortunately, ingratitude is often the norm. Fyodor Dostoyevsky once labeled man as "the ungrateful biped." "Give a man everything he wants," declared Immanuel Kant, "and at that moment, everything will not be everything."

Yet here we are on the eve of a new Thanksgiving—one of the best times of the year. It's great to be reminded of our nation's rich spiritual heritage—a national annual holiday (with an interesting history) has been set aside to thank God for His many blessings.

So often it's tempting to be thankless, as we think about all our problems, including the poor economy, the setback in Biblical morality in the culture at large, challenges for the future, etc. If we're tempted to hold back our thanksgiving during this season of Thanksgiving, we would do well to remember the difficulties faced by those who initiated the tradition.

The Pilgrims who founded Plymouth gave thanks and held their day of Thanksgiving—actually three days of Thanksgiving—after God had blessed them with their first harvest in November 1621. They did this despite the fact that nearly half their number had died within the first few months of arriving on these shores the winter before. Also, they expressed gratitude despite their meager harvest due to the communism imposed on them by their investors. The leader of the Pilgrims declared, "Therefore, I, William Bradford...governor of Plymouth, say—through virtue of vested power—ye shall gather with one accord, and hold in the month of November, thanksgiving unto the Lord."

Jump ahead to the first year of the new nation under the Constitution. As noted before, on October 3, 1789, from the city of New York (our nation's capital at the time), President George Washington issued a Proclamation of a National Day of Thanksgiving. Said Washington: "Whereas it is the duty of all nations to acknowledge the Providence of Almighty God, to obey His will, to be grateful for His benefits, and humbly to implore His protection and favor.... Now, therefore, I do recommend and assign Thursday, the twenty-sixth day of November next, to be devoted by the People of these United States to the service of that great and glorious Being, who is the beneficent Author of all the good that was, that is, or that will be; That we may then all unite in rendering unto Him our sincere and humble thanks."

While Washington was the first president to declare a national day of Thanksgiving, President Lincoln was the first one to make Thanksgiving an annual holiday. The Civil War was one of the darkest periods in American history. However, on October 3, 1863, President Lincoln (in conjunction with Congress) made his Thanksgiving Proclamation.

Said Lincoln: "The year that is drawing towards its close, has been filled with the blessings of fruitful fields and healthful skies. To these bounties, which are so constantly enjoyed that we are prone to forget the source from which they come, others have been added, which are of so extraordinary a nature, that they cannot fail to penetrate and soften even the heart which is habitually insensible to the ever watchful providence of Almighty God."

"Filled with blessings..."? With so many dead Americans on both sides of the conflict?

"Of fruitful fields..."? How many of those fields contained the mangled corpses of young soldiers from North and South?

"Healthful skies..."? How many of those skies had exploded with cannon fire or crackling rifle shots?

Lincoln went on to acknowledge the "civil war of unequaled magnitude and severity," yet despite it all, he looked for the good, even the fact that "harmony has prevailed everywhere except in the theatre of military conflict."

He ends, "I do, therefore, invite my fellow citizens in every part of the United States, and those who are sojourning in foreign lands, to set apart and observe the last Thursday of November next as a day of Thanksgiving and Praise to our beneficent Father who dwelleth in the heavens." As an American holiday, Thanksgiving was born in difficult circumstances.

Last year on Thanksgiving I ran a 10K in Miami with thousands of others. One of them blew me away with his positive attitude. He had no legs; he had his torso on a skateboard, and he used very thick gloves to pull his way through the six miles. I got to speak with this man briefly after the run, and I found out that he had been born that way. But he didn't let that impediment stop him. He has even participated in marathons, and he has an attitude of gratitude through it all.

The late Dr. D. James Kennedy, my long-time pastor, once called gratitude "the Christian's magic wand," because it can transform everything—above all, it transforms those who give thanks. Thanksgiving is a wonderful holiday—that should be celebrated year round.

7

THE PILGRIMS GAVE THANKS, DESPITE
A MULTITUDE OF DIFFICULTIES

Originally published on November 27, 2017

With the holiday of Thanksgiving recently past, it's good to consider what the Pilgrims endured and how they thanked God through it all.

I just finished reading a phenomenal book on the group of dissident Christians who founded Plymouth in 1620. Historian Rod Gragg wrote *The Pilgrim Chronicles: An Eyewitness History of the Pilgrims and the Founding of Plymouth Colony*. I thought I knew a lot about the Pilgrims, but this book added greatly to my knowledge.

The Pilgrims were one congregation that was born in mid-England around 1606, at a time when church meetings, apart from the Church of England, were illegal. Their goal was to worship Jesus in the purity of the Gospel as they understood it. The Bible (Geneva version) was the focus of their existence.

Because of persecution in England, they decided to immigrate to Holland, but even leaving the mother country was a problem. A sea captain betrayed them and several of their men ended up in an English jail. Around 1609 they were able to finally make it to Holland.

Initially, the Netherlands was good for them. At least they could worship without government interference. But over time, they saw that some of their children were following the ways of the worldly Dutch youth. Meanwhile, the permanency of the Jamestown settlement in the New World allowed them to explore the possibility of going to America to stay intact as a congregation and to be able to worship Jesus in peace.

They borrowed money and received permission from King James, who was glad to be rid of them, to sail to the "northern parts of Virginia," which at that time would have been about where New York Harbor is today.

The voyage of the Mayflower was treacherous. One storm was so fierce they almost ended up on the bottom of the Atlantic. When they finally came to the New World, they were 250 miles north of their target and unable to safely sail south. They made history by writing up a Christian agreement for self-government that they signed before disembarking. This Mayflower Compact was the first step in the eventual creation of the Declaration of Independence and the Constitution 150 years later.

Then came the hostile winter of 1620–1621, when illness, cold, and starvation killed about half of them. They slept mostly aboard the Mayflower, having little opportunity to build houses in the howling winter.

Of the eighteen women aboard the Mayflower, only four survived that winter. Half of the married men died. There were twenty-nine unmarried men. Of these, ten died and nineteen survived. The children had the best survival rate. All seven girls lived. Of the thirteen boys, three died and ten lived. Yet through it all, they trusted in God and gave Him thanks.

The spring came early in 1621, and the death toll came to a halt. Two friendly Indians who were able to speak English greeted them and helped them make peace with the Indians. From them, they learned how to plant corn and capture eels to survive. The Pilgrims enjoyed a great relationship with the Native Americans—including making a peace treaty brokered by Chief Massasoit that lasted over fifty years.

At harvest time in 1621, the Pilgrims gave thanks to God and enjoyed a three-day feast with the Indians. This was the beginning of our Thanksgiving celebration in America.

Gragg quotes John Pory, a scholar from England who served in the colony of Virginia and was on his way back to England. Having visited Plymouth in 1622, Pory wrote: "the reasons of their continual plenty for those 7 months in the year may be the continual tranquility of the place, being guarded on all sides from the fury of the storms, as also the abundance of food they find at low water. . . . Now as concerning the quality of the people, how happy were it for our people [in Virginia], if they were as free from wickedness and vice as these are in this place....As touching their correspondence with the Indians, they are friends with all their neighbors."

Gragg also quotes Pilgrim leader Edward Winslow, who said, "None will ever be losers by following us so far as we follow Christ." Gragg concludes, on the Pilgrims' settlement, "And they had succeeded. No one in America would be raiding their Sunday services to stop their worship. Neither would they be hauled off to jail because of their beliefs, nor ever again forced to flee their homes because of their faith. And the way of freedom they had blazed in the wilds of the New World would eventually become the path of liberty for countless people from around the world: people yearning for a new life, a new start, a new home—and who would find it as Americans" (Gragg 2014, 288).

8

THE PILGRIMS AND THE U.S. CONSTITUTION

Originally published on November 25, 2015

As we get ready to celebrate another Thanksgiving, there's one more thing to be grateful to God for: the U.S. Constitution and the political freedom it has brought. What many people don't realize is the link between the Pilgrims, authors of our Thanksgiving tradition, and our nation's founding document.

When the founding fathers sat down in Philadelphia in the summer of 1787 at the Constitutional Convention, they had almost one hundred fifty years of constitution making on American soil to draw from. And devout Christians of earlier generations, who used the Biblical concept of covenant as a model, were those who provided the precedents.

One such document was the Fundamental Orders of Connecticut of 1639, which was inspired by a sermon that examined principles of government from the Bible. This covenant, which mentions "the gospel of our Lord Jesus," was the first complete constitution written on American soil, and is the reason that to this day Connecticut is called "the Constitution State."

A covenant is an agreement before God, binding a community together. The Pilgrims, Puritans, and other dedicated Christians engaged in writing about one hundred various agreements for self-government, paving the way for the Constitution. The first of these American covenants was written by the Pilgrims before they even disembarked from the Mayflower, a month before they even set foot in Plymouth.

The Pilgrims had a charter from King James, who hated Christian dissenters and was glad they were leaving England to settle in "the northern parts of Virginia." But they were blown off course and providentially hindered from sailing south of Cape Cod—at least for the winter. As we saw before, storms blew the Mayflower off course and so the Pilgrims would be under no government's jurisdiction. Realizing this, some of their hired hands had a mind to strike out on their own and leave the colony before it even started. When the leaders learned of it, they knew it would be disastrous. So before disembarking, the Pilgrims decided to write up an agreement for self-government. It was a Biblical type of covenant, calling on God as a witness and committing them all to a common purpose.

The Mayflower Compact says: "In the name of God, Amen. We whose names are underwritten, the loyal subjects of our dread sovereign lord, King James... Having undertaken for the glory of God, and advancement of the Christian faith, and the honor of our king and country, a voyage to plant the first colony in the northern parts of Virginia; do by these present, solemnly and mutually in the presence of God and one another, covenant and combine ourselves together into a civil body politic, for our better ordering and preservation, and furtherance of the ends aforesaid."

This document signed on November 11, 1620, was a milestone in history and a major step in the process of the creation of America.

In *A History of the English-Speaking Peoples*, Winston Churchill calls the Mayflower Compact "one of the remarkable documents in history."

Paul Johnson, author of *A History of the American People*, points out that the Mayflower Compact was "the single most important formative event in early American history, which would ultimately have an important bearing on... the American Republic" (Johnson 1997).

The great nineteenth-century historian George Bancroft writes: "In the cabin of the Mayflower humanity recovered its rights, and instituted government on the basis of 'equal laws' enacted by all the people for 'the general good'."

Dr. Donald S. Lutz, professor of political science at the University of Houston and the author of *The Origins of American Constitutionalism*, points out that the Bible provided the concept of the covenant. I once interviewed him for the television special, *One Nation Under God*, hosted by D. James Kennedy. In reference to the Pilgrims, the Puritans, and early Christian settlers of British North America, Lutz told me: "These poor people came to the New World, they had the wrong technologies, their plows would not work, their houses that they constructed were inappropriate for the weather. All their technology was wrong, except for one technology they brought with them, which was the ability to use covenants to create communities. It was the perfect technology. It was the technology that mattered that allowed them to survive all up and down the coast."

Lutz speaks in his book of the importance of the "covenants that derive from the biblical tradition" in ultimately helping to frame the U.S. Constitution. And he adds, "When one reads the preamble, which begins 'We the people...,' it is difficult not to think of 'We whose names are [underwritten]' in the Mayflower Compact, the first political covenant in America."

The Constitution and those, like the Pilgrims, who helped pave the way toward its creation, are blessings to be grateful for this Thanksgiving season. Thus endeth the history lesson. Happy Thanksgiving.

9

A NATION IN NEED OF REPENTANCE AND
A NEW GREAT AWAKENING, PART 1

Originally published on December 17, 2012

Last week's tragic shooting in the picturesque town of Newtown, Connecticut, reminds us of how sorely our nation needs the gift of repentance and a new Great Awakening. We've become a nation in mourning because of the tragedy. Many of us have not stopped praying for the shooting victims and their families in the wake of this massacre. The tragedy of these little children, blown away before they have had much of a chance to live, is mind blowing. Satan must be having a field day with what is going on in modern America.

It seems like every week that goes by there's some new tragedy unfolding in this country.

I think part of the reason for this is that we have forgotten God. We have no fear of the reality of hell that awaits those who knowingly reject Christ. Jesus died for sinners, going to hell for us on the cross so we wouldn't have to go. But because there's no fear of God in the land, there's no fear of the consequences after death.

We kick God out of all of our institutions. Then we turn around and get mad at Him for not intervening when some madman goes on a killing rampage. This reminds me of the verse in Proverbs that says, "A man's own folly ruins his life, yet his heart rages against the Lord."

I've mentioned this before, but I'll never forget what a black Alabama pastor said to me one time when I interviewed him about a lawsuit that called into question the public display of the Ten Commandments. He

said, "All across America people should stand with...the Ten Commandments. Why? Because [before] they took prayer out of school, you
didn't hear about kids killing each other, about them bringing dope to
school, shooting the teachers, you didn't hear about that. You see what
I'm saying? That's what's wrong. We need more God fearing."

We are in great need of national revival. America was born in part
through the revival that swept through the colonies, what we now call
the First Great Awakening. Founding father John Adams said, "The
Revolution was effected before the War commenced. The Revolution
was in the mind and hearts of the people and change in their religious
sentiments of their duties and obligations."

In his book, *A History of the American People*, the great historian Paul
Johnson adds, "The Great Awakening was thus the proto-revolutionary
event, the formative movement in American history, preceding the political drive for independence, and making it possible" (Johnson 1997,
116). The Second Great Awakening in the early part of the nineteenth
century is responsible for helping to end the horrible scourge of slavery.

During the dark days of the Civil War, Abraham Lincoln proclaimed
April 30, 1863, as a national day of fasting and prayer. In his proclamation, he noted, "We have grown in numbers, wealth and power, as no
other nation has ever grown. But we have forgotten God." He went
on to say, "Intoxicated with unbroken success, we have become too
self-sufficient to feel the necessity of redeeming and preserving grace,
too proud to pray to the God that made us!" And his conclusion was,
"It behooves us then, to humble ourselves before the offended Power,
to confess our national sins, and to pray for clemency and forgiveness."

Aleksandr Solzhenitsyn, who spent about a decade in a Soviet gulag and who wrote massive award-winning books on the failed Soviet
Union, said this at Harvard in 1978: "More than half a century ago,
while I was still a child, I recall hearing a number of older people offer
the following explanation for the great disasters that had befallen Russia: Men have forgotten God; that's why all this has happened."

He went on to say, "Since then I have spent well-nigh fifty years
working on the history of our Revolution; in the process I have read
hundreds of books, collected hundreds of personal testimonies, and
have already contributed eight volumes of my own toward the effort of

clearing away the rubble left by that upheaval. But if I were asked today to formulate as concisely as possible the main cause of the ruinous Revolution that swallowed up some sixty million of our people, I could not put it more accurately than to repeat: Men have forgotten God; that's why all this has happened."

Today, America must stop forgetting God. We are in need of a great national revival—another Great Awakening. I believe we should all pray to that end, before it's too late. It's America's only real hope in the long run.

10

A NATION IN NEED OF TRUE REVIVAL, PART 2

Originally published on August 14, 2012

Poll after poll finds that millions of Americans feel that we are headed in the wrong direction as a nation. We are in serious need of serious change. In fact, a poll from just this month shows: "Twenty-seven percent (27%) of Likely U.S. Voters now say the country is heading in the right direction" (Rasmussen Reports, August 8, 2012).

We see killing among strangers and even within families. As of this writing, there have occurred at least three shooting massacres in the last four weeks. We see unprecedented government spending—all on the backs of future Americans. We see families splitting up. We see epidemic cheating. We see theft at unprecedented levels. We see a host of moral breakdowns in our time.

Although we desire for God to bless America, our first president noted this in his First Inaugural Address: "The propitious smiles of Heaven can never be expected on a nation that disregards the eternal rules of order and right which Heaven itself has ordained." How can God bless us, asked George Washington, when we violate the rules He Himself has given us?

We are clearly in great need of national revival. America was born in part through the revival that swept through the colonies, what we now call the First Great Awakening. That revival began in the 1730s with the preaching of Rev. Jonathan Edwards in Northampton, Massachusetts, and spread throughout the colonies, mostly through the work of the traveling evangelist George Whitefield.

Sarah Edwards, Jonathan's wife, said this about the impact of White-field's messages: "It is wonderful to see what a spell he casts over an au-dience by proclaiming the simplest truths of the Bible. . . . Our mechan-ics shut up their shops, and the day laborers throw down their tools to go and hear him preach, and few return unaffected."

Ben Franklin commented on the social effects of the revival. He said of Whitefield's preaching, "It was wonderful to see the change soon made in the manners of our inhabitants. From being thoughtless or in-different about religion, it seemed as if all the world were growing reli-gious, so that one could not walk through the town in an evening with-out hearing psalms sung in different families of every street" (Franklin 1916).

A key thing to note is that prior to the French and Indian War and to the Great Awakening, generally the thirteen separate colonies com-prising British North America did not communicate with each other. The first real phenomenon that began to unite them was this spiritual movement, up and down the Atlantic seacoast.

We've already noted how the First Great Awakening helped to push for independence in America.

The Second Great Awakening in the early part of the nineteenth century helped end the horrible scourge of slavery. Two-thirds of the members of the abolition society in 1835 were ministers of the Gospel. Also, churches ran the anti-slavery Underground Railroad.

Then, during the Civil War, as noted before, Abraham Lincoln pro-claimed April 30, 1863, as a national day of fasting and prayer. He said that we needed to repent of our pride and of forgetting God as a nation. And his conclusion was, "It behooves us then, to humble ourselves be-fore the offended Power, to confess our national sins, and to pray for clemency and forgiveness."[1]

The late Dr. D. James Kennedy once said this: "Many people are un-der the misconception that government will solve all our problems. But I believe that true change is going to take place when people through-out the nation begin to trust in Christ and in the God that made this nation great. And that will bring about a genuine revival. A revival that

---

1. Abraham Lincoln, "Appointing a Day of National Humiliation, Fasting and Prayer," *The Ameri-can Presidency Project*, presidency.ucsb.edu.

eventually moves to the halls of government. Not from the government down, but from the people up."[2]

God told Solomon the Wise something that certainly fit the theocracy of ancient Israel, and I think the principle applies to nations in general. Here is what He said so famously almost a thousand years before Christ: "If my people, who are called by my name, will humble themselves and pray and seek my face and turn from their wicked ways, then will I hear from heaven and will forgive their sin and will heal their land" (2 Chronicles 7:14).

This is America's only real hope for a real and positive change. May God give us the grace to more earnestly pray for this.

2. D. James Kennedy, "A Third Great Awakening," *D. James Kennedy Ministries*, djameskennedy.org.

11

HOW IS CALLING FOR NATIONAL REVIVAL "CONTROVERSIAL"?

Originally published on January 28, 2015

Louisiana Governor Bobby Jindal did something supposedly "controversial." He called for a national revival. As noted in a *Washington Post* article by Rosalind S. Helderman (January 24, 2015): "Skipping an Iowa event that drew a number of 2016 Republican presidential hopefuls in favor of a controversial Louisiana prayer rally, Louisiana Gov. Bobby Jindal (R) called for a national spiritual revival and urged event attendees to proselytize on behalf of their Christian beliefs."

According to Helderman, Jindal insisted this was a religious event, not a political one. The American Family Association founded the rally. Jindal said: "Let's all go plant those seeds of the gospel.... Share the good news with all whom we encounter." He added: "We can't just elect a candidate to fix what ails our country. We can't just pass a law and fix what ails our country.... We need a spiritual revival to fix what ails our country."

So, what makes the rally so "controversial"? Is it the liberal protesters outside the rally? For those aware of America's history, there should be nothing controversial about Governor Jindal's appearance at the rally. America was born as a result of a national revival, known as the First Great Awakening.

It began in the 1730s under the preaching of the humble and brilliant Jonathan Edwards. It spread from colony to colony through many itinerant preachers, but especially Rev. George Whitefield, a British evangelist who spoke to thousands in a day long before microphones. We've already seen some of the remarks, e.g., of Sarah Edwards and of Ben Franklin, on the impact of Whitefield's message. Many were repenting and turning to Christ.

Whitefield returned repeatedly to America. The great British historian Paul Johnson, author of *A History of the American People*, writes: "He returned again and again to the attack—seven continental tours in the thirty years from 1740—and all churches benefited from his efforts." All of this helped pave the way for the creation of the new nation.

The founders made it clear that our republic depended on the people's virtue and that religion was the means by which the people would be virtuous. You can see this in Washington's Farewell Address. You can also see it in this famous quote from John Adams: "Our Constitution was made for a moral and religious people. It is wholly inadequate to the government of any other."

Thomas Jefferson—who later in life privately held unorthodox beliefs, while regularly worshiping in orthodox services, which he supported financially—was a champion of religious freedom. So was his friend and compatriot James Madison, and therefore they were heroes among the evangelicals in their day. They lived in the Piedmont region of Virginia, which was a hotbed of revivalism and a part of what we now call the Second Great Awakening. That movement helped give birth to the abolition of slavery.

So, when modern leaders like Governor Jindal assert that America needs a new spiritual awakening, they are the ones in touch with our nation's history, not the modern intelligentsia that views the religious right as interlopers to an otherwise blissful secular state.

12

WHY DO SO MANY AMERICANS
HATE AMERICA?

Originally published on October 17, 2011

Occupy Wall Street protesters have, of course, spilled over to all sorts of communities throughout the U.S. *Drudge Report* recently highlighted a group from Portland, Oregon, Occupy Portland, which protested by playing their own rock 'n' roll song, proclaiming, "F—— the USA."

Why do so many Americans hate America?

I remember once reading about Reagan and Gorbachev in America. As I recall the story, the two leaders saw some protesters in the street uttering some sort of anti-American chant along the lines of "Down with the USA!" Reagan commented that he didn't agree with them, but at least they are free to voice their protests. Gorbachev responded by saying that you could find these kinds of protesters in his country too.

"Really?" replied the U.S. president.

"Sure," said Gorbachev, "You can find protesters in Moscow, chanting 'Down with the USA!'"

So, I get back to my question. Why do so many Americans hate America?

I guess it gets back to the sixties, when thousands hit the street to protest the Vietnam War, especially because some were concerned that the government would draft them to fight in a war they didn't believe in. As mistaken as it may have been for the U.S. to ever send any troops to Vietnam, it is true we didn't go there so we could occupy the country, take it over, and grab its resources. As is generally the pattern of U.S.

involvement in wars, we went for freedom's sake—either to defend ours or someone else's freedom. We went to protect innocent people from the terrors of communism (terrors in the killing fields when we pulled out that ended up worse than predicted by even the most ardent hawk.)

Why do so many Americans hate America?

Was it because of slavery at the beginning of our country's history? It was so wrong, but 600,000 men shed their blood to reverse this evil. Was it because of the mistreatment of blacks for so long? But surely we've made much progress in this area.

America is not perfect, but does it merit all the anti-American feeling from so many within its own borders?

I'm in Norway as I write this, and I find an intense love of country here and gratitude to be Norwegian. Of course, there are tens of millions of Americans who love their country too. But some quarters discourage the love of America. It seems not cool to love America if you are an American. How long would an American flag hoisted with pride at an Occupy Wall Street protest last? Not long, I would imagine.

The U.S. Constitution is actually the model of constitutions for scores of countries all over the world (including that of Norway). More inventions have come from America than any other. America has sent more missionaries to all corners of the earth than any other country. America is well represented among Nobel Peace Prize winners.

America's founders said that our rights come from the Creator. In 1955, President Eisenhower said, "Without God, there could be no American form of Government, nor an American way of life. Recognition of the Supreme Being is the first—the most basic—expression of Americanism."

Even when America doesn't live up to its creed that our Creator has endowed us with certain unalienable rights, it's still a good creed. As Dr. Martin Luther King Jr. said in his classic speech: "I still have a dream. It is a dream deeply rooted in the American dream. I have a dream that one day this nation will rise up and live out the true meaning of its creed: 'We hold these truths to be self-evident; that all men are created equal.'" Surely, we have made great advances since he uttered those words in 1963. Are we not the only major Western country that has elected a black man as president?

When you see the protesters at Occupy This & That, you would never realize that this country has a lot to offer. You would never realize all the opportunities available.

Think of the would-be immigrants who literally risk their lives to try and get here. Some will risk their lives to leave Cuba, going through shark-infested waters, to try to get here. Those that make it here often do well over time, through incredible hard work and dedication. This is the land of opportunity. The problem is, said one commentator, that often when opportunity comes knocking, it's dressed up in overalls and looks like hard work.

Meanwhile, if you read the press on the Occupy This & That protesters, you would think all of these protests are simply spontaneous and that they have nothing to do with big money. But isn't it true that George Soros money can be traced to the Canadian anti-consumerist group, AdBusters, which advertised (no pun intended) for protesters to come to Wall Street on September 17, 2011? That is when it all began.

So the Occupy This & That protesters, including Occupy Portland, can chant anti-American slogans all they want. But their dissent and their freedom to express it, however crudely, only highlights their God-given freedom in this land that they seem to hate so much.

13

JUST WHO IS REWRITING HISTORY?

Originally published in Summer 2010

Glenn Beck recently raved about a book on the faith of George Washington, helping to propel the book to #1 on Amazon for six days in a row. MediaMatters, funded by George Soros, accuses this book of being "revisionist history." But just who is rewriting history?

The book in question is near and dear to my heart because I cowrote it. The chief author of *George Washington's Sacred Fire* is Dr. Peter Lillback, president of Westminster Theological Seminary, who researched the subject for some twenty years before we met (Lillback 2006). We began to collaborate in late 2004 and finished the book in the early summer of 2006. The late Dr. D. James Kennedy launched the book through his television and radio outreach, Coral Ridge Ministries (now D. James Kennedy Ministries), where I have worked for twenty-five years now.

George Washington's Sacred Fire is not revisionist history. It's a rebuttal to revisionist history—all 1,200 pages of it (700 pages of text with 500 pages of appendices and endnotes). The goal of the book is to set the record straight about George Washington's faith. Since the early 1960s, many scholars have essentially called our first president a deist—someone who believes that there is a God, but that this God far removes Himself from the daily affairs of men and is not a prayer-answering God. However, an honest look at the facts of history shows that George Washington was a devout eighteenth-century Anglican. He believed the basics of that orthodox, Trinitarian faith, including regarding the substitutionary death of Jesus Christ on behalf of sinners and His bodily resurrection from the dead.

From what we can tell, he had an exemplary private prayer life, he read the Scriptures regularly, and he habitually used the 1662 *Book of Common Prayer* from the Church of England. This was a very orthodox book—more theologically sound than the average book available in a Christian bookstore today.

We believe that modern skeptics have read into Washington their own unbelief. They have remade Washington into their own image— even though:

He was clearly an avid Bible reader. His private and public writings overflow with Scriptural phrases and concepts. (We have an appendix in the book with dozens and dozens of Biblical phrases culled from Washington's own works. It is as if, if you cut the man, he bled Scripture.)

He was a committed churchman, attending regularly when it was convenient and inconvenient. He not only attended service, but he diligently served the church, primarily in his youth, as a lay leader. Throughout his life he generously donated money and material goods for the well-being of the church.

He was very quiet about his faith, attempting to practice his Christianity without public flourish, as Jesus commanded us in the Sermon on the Mount to pray in private. There are numerous accounts—too numerous to be dismissed—of people happening upon Washington in earnest, private prayer. His motto was "Deeds, not words."

He repeatedly encouraged piety, public and private. He insisted on chaplains for the military and legislature. He often promoted "religion and morality" and recognized these as essential for our national happiness. (When he referred to religion, in a day when 99.8 percent of the population professed to be Christian,[1] he was referring to Christianity, regardless of the particular denomination.)

He shunned excessive power, even though a lesser man would have seized it. He did not fight the King of England in order to become a new king, even though men wanted to make him king after he won the war. In this regard, Washington is a model Christian servant-statesman.

---

1. Benjamin Hart, "The Wall That Protestantism Built: The Religious Reasons for the Separation of Church and State," *Policy Review*, Fall 1988, 44.

These and many other indicators show that revisionists have completely misread George Washington and have completely misread the true nature of his spirituality. By so doing, they have presented a very truncated and deceptive picture of Washington the man.

Washington said that America will only be happy if we imitate "the Divine Author of our blessed religion." This is a direct reference to Jesus Christ. This was not an obscure letter. It is the climax of a critical farewell letter the Commander-in-Chief wrote to the governors of all the states at the end of the Revolutionary War. It is known as the Circular to the States, from June 1783. Furthermore, Washington wrote about the need to be a good Christian—using the word *Christian*—in several different letters and communiqués.

Because America began on a Christian base, people of all faiths (or no faith) are welcome here. That freedom is not necessarily offered by other worldviews, such as secular fundamentalism. But to the founders, like Washington, freedom of conscience was paramount. We have hundreds of pages of documentation of these things—much of it from George Washington himself.

In 1779, Delaware Indian chiefs asked Washington's advice on how they could better train their sons. He responded, "You do well to wish to learn our arts and ways of life, and above all, the religion of Jesus Christ" (Rhodehamel 1997, 351).

In light of these kinds of facts, just who is revising history here? Glenn Beck or George Soros?

14

GEORGE WASHINGTON WORSHIPED HERE

Originally published on August 12, 2015

It used to be a joke to see signs in historic places boasting, "George Washington slept here." But I think in a very real sense, a handful of churches could legitimately have a sign proclaiming, "George Washington worshiped here." His active Christianity reflects a key aspect of our nation's founding—the importance of the Judeo-Christian tradition.

George Washington was a committed churchgoer all his life, even when it was difficult to attend. His main church as a young man was Pohick Church in Lorton, Virginia, and as an older man, it was Christ Church in Alexandria. He also attended other churches throughout his life in other states.

At these churches you can see the *reredos*, a wall or altar decoration, displaying the words of the Lord's Prayer, the Apostles' Creed, and the Ten Commandments, so the worshipers could recite them aloud. I personally have visited many of these churches. Some people today claim that George Washington was not a Christian, but a deist. Yet the facts don't support that view.

As noted before, the book I wrote with Dr. Peter Lillback on the faith of our founding father documents beyond reasonable doubt that our first president was indeed an active Christian all his life. His adoptive granddaughter said that if you question his Christianity, you might as well question his patriotism.

But sadly, people do question his faith. One man sent me an email disputing my comments about the Christian faith of some of our founders, including Washington. He wrote, "George Washington stopped going to church when he was admonished by the vicar for not taking communion. That is very different than your story that he got out of the habit, but continued to attend church. He stopped attending church, period."

This man is wrong.

You can visit Mount Vernon today and see the red "chariot" (buggy) in which he rode to and from church. You can also visit the church itself, which he attended regularly during the last years of his life. The building is still standing and in use. It is Christ Church in Alexandria, an Episcopal church. That's where his funeral was held. You can see and even sit in his box pew, which he paid for by subscription.

As noted, Pohick Church in Lorton, Virginia, was Washington's main church home as a young man. He served the church as a vestryman—like an elder and a deacon rolled into one person. To become a vestryman you had to swear allegiance to the doctrines of the Anglican Church. As a surveyor, Washington even chose the exact location for that church building. His recommendation beat out that of fellow church member and founding father George Mason.

Other churches that you can visit where Washington worshiped, and where you can see his own box pews, and the reredos, include:

- Bruton Parish in Colonial Williamsburg, where he worshiped along with Patrick Henry and Thomas Jefferson when they served in the Virginia House of Burgesses
- Trinity Episcopal Church in Newport, Rhode Island
- Christ Church in Philadelphia, where he worshiped during the summer he presided over the Constitutional Convention, and
- St. Paul's Chapel in New York City, near Wall Street.

After his inauguration in 1789, Washington led everyone over to St. Paul's Chapel, where they participated in a two-hour Christian service to dedicate the new nation to the Lord. This service included Holy Communion. Eyewitnesses, such as Mrs. Alexander Hamilton, said Washington communed.

That leads me to the question of why he did not always attend communion. The answer is simple. He did at first, but during the war, as

Dr. Lillback points out, Washington was leading the troops in a rebellion against the human head of the Church of England—i.e., King George III—and so he could not celebrate common faith with the king in good conscience.

During the war, he worshiped at the Presbyterian Church in Morristown, New Jersey. To this day, they have a stained-glass window showing him participating in the Lord's Supper there.

Washington indeed got out of the habit and did not attend the Lord's Supper on a regular basis during the few times a year they offered it back then—but he did so on occasion. Washington confessed his faith in Jesus Christ and His atonement throughout his life, not only as a worshiper and communicant but also at various public times when he served as a vestryman, churchwarden, and sponsor in several baptisms.

Why does this matter? I think there is a battle over history. I think it's important to recognize what made this nation great in the first place, and I believe if you dig a little deeper you see the positive impact of the Christian faith on what is best in the creation of America and its freedoms.

To paraphrase President Woodrow Wilson, if we don't know what we were in the past, we don't know what we are in the present, and where we are going in the future.

15

IS PATRIOTISM UNCOOL?

Originally published on May 29, 2012

The Memorial Day parades and barbecues had barely begun when a TV host put his foot in his mouth, for which he has now profusely (and rightly) apologized. Chris Hayes, a host on the very liberal MSNBC cable channel, who is also the editor at large for *The Nation* magazine, said on the eve of Memorial Day that he feels "uncomfortable" with the notion that soldiers who've died are "heroes." He said this is because he fears promoting more unnecessary war. Or as he worded it, "it is so rhetorically proximate to justifications for more war."

Naturally, this comment created a firestorm, and the next day he wrote an apology, stating: "On Sunday, in discussing the uses of the word 'hero' to describe those members of the armed forces who have given their lives, I don't think I lived up to the standards of rigor, respect and empathy for those affected by the issues we discuss that I've set for myself. I am deeply sorry for that."

He added, "As many have rightly pointed out, it's very easy for me, a TV host, to opine about the people who fight our wars, having never dodged a bullet or guarded a post or walked a mile in their boots. Of course, that is true of the overwhelming majority of our nation's citizens as a whole."

Hayes's comment and apology make me wonder if it is unfashionable to be patriotic today. Maybe in some circles. At least among the elite.

On Memorial Day, President Obama spoke at Arlington about the shameful mistreatment of Vietnam veterans, who came back to an ungrateful country. Although that message is a few decades late, it certainly is welcome. Ever since the days of the Vietnam War, it seems as if there's a segment of America that thinks it's not cool to be patriotic. Maybe those folks experienced a short blip of patriotism right after 9/11. But just as quickly as church attendance increased right after that catastrophe, it subsided.

I think to some degree there's a link between love of God and love of country. Not that the two always go hand in hand. God bless Thomas More when he died as a martyr and said, "Tell the king [Henry VIII] I die as his good servant, but God's first." If it's an either/or situation— God or country—for me God must always come first.

But in the American experience, because our founders said our rights come from God, there is a sense in which love of God and love of country (when in the right) go hand in hand. To paraphrase George Washington from his Farewell Address, you have no right to call yourself a patriot if you subvert two key "pillars of human happiness." These were "religion and morality."

There's a brand-new book that shows that prayer and patriotism have gone hand in hand from the beginning of the republic—actually even slightly before. The book is *Endowed by Their Creator: A Collection of Historic American Military Prayers 1774–Present*. It was compiled by Marine Colonel Ronald Ray (Ray 2013). I spoke with him recently about the book, and he explained that he searched through musty old American military prayer books and hymnals, old and new. (Mostly old.) He went through seventy-four volumes, and he found that 73 percent of military prayers throughout our history have been offered in the name of Jesus. It's only recently that the prayers have become more politically correct.

The book has more than 280 uniquely American prayers from and for the military. Colonel Ray explains why he put it together: "Prayer is under attack in the military institution. As a Vietnam combat veteran, 34 years as a Marine officer, a former Defense official, and a lawyer, I spent 10 years collecting American military prayer books from before the nation's founding to the present day." He adds, "I did this research not as a man of the church, but as a military historian and a lawyer to make the case for the 'Military Necessity' of prayer, because there are 'no atheists in foxholes'."

The colonel is not pleased with an anti-religious component he finds among some in our government today. He notes, "I found that while over 70 percent of those serving today in the U.S. military self-identify as Christians, their chaplains are threatened and discouraged from praying in the name of their God, Jesus Christ, and leaders are officially prohibited from leading their troops in prayer—even in battle in this, One Nation Under God."

Here's an example of a prayer from his book. This one comes from the West Point Prayer Book, 1948: "Almighty God, who hast given us this good land for our heritage; We humbly beseech thee that we may always prove ourselves a people mindful of thy favor and glad to do thy will...through Jesus Christ our Lord. Amen."

In short, I hope it becomes cool once again to be patriotic. And yes, Mr. Hayes, you were correct to issue your apology. Those who have laid down their lives for their country are indeed heroes.

As Jesus said in a different context, "Greater love has no one than this, that he lay down his life for his friends."

16

LOOK WHAT THEY LEFT OFF THE
MARTIN LUTHER KING MEMORIAL

Originally published on October 26, 2011

Would the Baptist minister, the *Rev.* Dr. Martin Luther King Jr. be pleased with the recently unveiled 450-foot memorial in Atlanta dedicated to his memory? I doubt it, because they left God out. His niece, Dr. Alveda C. King, also doubts that he would be pleased. She is the president of King for America and is a lay spokesperson for the organization Priests for Life.

In a press release dated October 18, 2011, she said, "This missed opportunity to carve GOD's Name on the wall still presents another opportunity. Many people don't know that Uncle M. L. was a preacher of the Gospel of Jesus Christ. It stands to reason that they have never heard of his devotion to Jesus Christ and his message of God's agape love."

She added, "I wasn't consulted on the design of the site[. S]till I see this as a teaching moment to encourage people to read King's sermons." Indeed, it's not surprising to learn that, as a minister, Martin Luther King's writings and speeches are filled with Biblical texts. These include his reference to Amos 5:24, which says, "Let justice roll down like waters" (RSV).

I guess we've become a nation of Biblical illiterates. Therefore, many people don't even realize when the Bible is being quoted, as Dr. King quoted it in his "I Have a Dream" speech. He said, "I have a dream that one day every valley shall be exalted, and every hill and mountain shall be made low, the rough places will be made plain, and the crooked places will be made straight; 'and the glory of the Lord shall be revealed and all flesh shall see it together.'" These are quotes right out of the fortieth chapter of the book of Isaiah.

One of my reference books is a paperback from the year King died, 1968, entitled, *The Wisdom of Martin Luther King in His Own Words*. I hate to pop the liberals' bubble on this, but the book is filled with references to God and to Jesus. Reading it, I am all the more amazed that they would leave God out of the recent memorial. Just flipping through the book at random, here are some examples:

- "Let us hope there will be no more violence. But if the streets must flow with blood let it flow with our blood in the spirit of Jesus Christ on the cross." (Birmingham, Alabama, May 1963)
- "A just law is a man-made code that squares with the moral law or the law of God. An unjust law is a code that is out of harmony with the moral law." (April 1963)
- "Nonviolence is not a symbol of weakness or cowardice, but as Jesus demonstrated, nonviolent resistance transforms weakness into strength and breeds courage in the face of danger." (1963)
- "In the midst of outer dangers I have felt an inner calm and known resources of strength that only God could give." (April 1960)

And on and on it goes. If one were to try to compile a book on the wisdom of Dr. Martin Luther King Jr. today and leave out his references to God, Jesus, the Gospel, etc., it would be a mighty short book.

I think one of the aspects of political correctness that is plaguing our times is that the elites think that we must expunge all references to God and Jesus from all public places. But when dealing with historical figures, they are simply projecting their own skepticism onto others—many of whom were not skeptics. Rev. Martin Luther King Jr. said, "We will win our freedom because the sacred heritage of our nation and the eternal will of God are embodied in our echoing demands."

Too bad you would have no clue of the source of his greatness if you only knew about him from the new memorial.

17

LIBERAL TALK HOST SAYS NATIONAL
ANTHEM SHOULD GO

Originally published on June 7, 2012

Liberal talk show host Bill Press is on a mission, what he calls "a major crusade." He says it's time to dump the National Anthem. As in, "O say! Can you see?"[1]

Now, Press doesn't want anyone to label him unpatriotic for his stance. It's just that he finds the song "absolutely monumentally un-singable." He fears, in fact, that for taking such a stance, he'll be accused of not being "a true American." He adds, "I don't think patriotism has anything to do with it."

But he does go on to complain about the content of the song: "Are we the only ones who are brave on the planet? I mean all the brave people live here. I mean it's just stupid, I think. I'm embarrassed. I'm embarrassed every time I hear it." It never even occurred to me until I read Mr. Press's criticism that the song implies we are the only ones on the planet who are brave. (Or for that matter the only ones free.)

When I hear the Anthem sung, I'm often tempted to turn to the person next to me and ask, "Can you name the war?" "Can you name the night?" "Can you name the place?"

To get a better appreciation for the National Anthem, consider its historical backdrop. When America was still basically an infant,

---

1. "Libtalker Bill Press: National Anthem Is 'Stupid And Embarrassing'," *Real Clear Politics*, June 5, 2012, realclearpolitics.com. "The Star-Spangled Banner," Published by G. Schirmer, 1918, loc.gov/item/ihas.100010133.

we entered into our second major war—with the same foe as before. Among other reasons, the war was sparked by British mistreatment of American ships. The Royal Navy would capture American sailors and force those who were British born into service of the British Empire—a practice called "impressment." Thus, not only were they violating the sailors' rights, they were treating the new nation as an upstart.

Numerous pleas to stop this practice and other abuses went unheeded, causing Congress and President James Madison to declare war on England on June 18, 1812. During this war, the British were able to invade Washington, D.C. They even burned down the White House and the Capitol.

Francis Scott Key served as the District Attorney at Georgetown, Washington, D.C. During the War of 1812, President Madison authorized Key to negotiate the release of an American being held captive by the British in a fleet near the mouth of the Potomac River. This was on September 13, 1814.

As Key and his delegation set out for the negotiation, they were taken aboard a British truce ship and held as captives overnight—as the British fleet attempted to decimate Fort McHenry. The fort protected Baltimore's harbor. Through the night of September 13–14, Key watched helplessly as the British mercilessly bombarded the fort.

But when the morning came, at the dawn's early light, Francis Scott Key was overjoyed to see the fort still standing, and the American flag still waving.

This incident inspired him to write a hymn within a month, dedicated to the "Defense of Fort McHenry." The song, "The Star-Spangled Banner," became instantly popular.

In 1931, Congress adopted it as our National Anthem.

Although we're all familiar with the first verse of the anthem, many people don't realize that the fourth verse mentions God:

Blest with vict'ry and peace, may the Heavn'n-rescued land
Praise the Pow'r that hath made and preserved us a nation!
Then conquer we must, when our cause it is just,
And this be our motto, "In God is our trust!"

In 1956, Congress took up Key's suggestion and adopted our national motto: In God We Trust.

Francis Scott Key, a great American, once said, "The patriot who feels himself in the service of God, who acknowledges Him in all his ways, has the promise of Almighty direction....He will therefore seek to establish for his country in the eyes of the world, such a character as shall make her not unworthy of the name of a Christian nation."

I hope Mr. Press fails in his "major crusade." Admittedly, the National Anthem is not an easy piece to sing—maybe that's why it's usually handled by well-trained soloists. I, for one, am not embarrassed by "The Star-Spangled Banner." But I have to admit I'm not sure if I can sing it correctly without shifting keys somewhere along the way.

18

CONTROVERSY SURROUNDING THE NFL AND THE NATIONAL ANTHEM—WHY DOESN'T KAEPERNICK PROTEST FATHERLESSNESS?

Originally published on September 19, 2016

The controversy surrounding San Francisco 49ers quarterback Colin Kaepernick refuses to die. During the National Anthem, the football player chooses not to stand and pay homage to the country that has made him fabulously wealthy. Now, a handful of other football players are also refusing to participate in the National Anthem.

It's a free country, and people are free to express themselves. But it's interesting to note that if it weren't for the soldier, willing to lay down his life for his country, Kaepernick et al would not have that freedom to protest. Kaepernick said he has great respect for such soldiers, but he adds, "People are dying in vain because this country isn't holding their end of the bargain up."

To me, this is a picture of humanity. We have been so blessed by God in so many different ways. But instead of paying homage to Him and showing the gratitude that is the very least He deserves, we show Him our fists and defiance.

If it weren't for the grace of Jesus, by which the hearts of every one of us beat, we would not have the freedom to disbelieve and just live for ourselves. His claim to be our Creator was vindicated when He walked out of His tomb two thousand years ago.

Every once in a while, on the Internet, I'll click on those click-bait lists of alleged unbelievers. When I have seen those lists, I can't help but feel that I'm looking at the Honor Role of the Ungrateful. Everything they have is a gift from God. The apostle Paul asked the Corinthian Christians two thousand years ago, "What do you have that you did not receive?" (1 Corinthians 4:7). The answer is nothing.

As to the protests of Kaepernick and other well-paid football players, their stated concerns are the lack of "social justice" in America. But what is it that is devastating the black community today? Fatherlessness. What has caused the breakdown of the family? Government redistribution of wealth via subsidies, by which liberals buy votes. They have created a permanent underclass of people by subsidizing fatherlessness and unemployment. Prior to the Great Society, the rate of illegitimacy in the black community was relatively low. Today, the rate is about 75 percent— devastating.

I had the privilege to talk recently with Star Parker, an African-American columnist and author of *Blind Conceit*, for our new D. James Kennedy Ministries TV special on the problem of socialism. Star told our viewers: "The problem with government overreach and replacing the church is that they're replacing a real significant part of mankind, a need, a vacuum that we all have, to reach and find God."

Parker is the founder and president of C.U.R.E., the Center for Urban Renewal and Education, a policy institute in Washington, D.C. She knows firsthand what it's like to live off the government dole and to pray in effect, "Our Father, which art in Washington." She added, "I look into my own life and my own testimony and how after believing the lies of the Left for years, that my problems were somebody else's fault, that America was racist—that poor people were poor because wealthy people were wealthy; and buying all of that worldview, I got really lost and ended up in aggressive living, criminal activity, drug activity, sexual activity, in and out of abortion clinic after clinic, in and out of welfare after welfare."

What was it that changed her? She said, "It wasn't until a Christian conversion I was able to change my life. You remove that opportunity for people, and they stay lost. And that's one of the problems when government tries to replace God; people get lost, people don't know what to do, so they look outside to see what everybody else is doing. When you look outside to see what others are doing, you see pop culture, you see secular humanism, you see moral relativism; this is not a good place for people that really want freedom and personal responsibility."

Star notes that freedom and personal responsibility have been the engines for positive change in our nation from the beginning: "As a nation we're built on freedom and personal responsibility. You can't do that outside of heaven's core principles and a rule of law, which are rooted in a worldview; and that biblical worldview is where we were founded and it's where we should stay."

I wish these millionaire football players, many of whom have come up from incredibly challenging backgrounds, would use their energy and their alleged passion for "social justice" to see real, positive, God-centered changes in the country. Then they would express gratitude to the Almighty for the incredible opportunities this nation can offer—opportunities they themselves have profited from.

19

WHAT HATH KAEPERNICK WROUGHT?

Originally published on October 25, 2017

I'm so out of touch with some aspects of contemporary culture that some friends have suggested I'm from a different planet. They've even created a name for it, the "Planet Newton," playing off my last name. I don't even follow football enough to know all the teams' names associated with different cities, and I really don't care. As I recall, just about the only time I sat down to watch a sports game on TV just happened to be in the winter of 1980. I watched some hockey game during the Winter Olympics that year. And everybody said the Russians would smear the Americans, but the Americans surprisingly won. They even made a movie out of it. There, I've spent my time watching sports on TV.

Meanwhile, news about the protests against the National Anthem on the part of some football players has reached even Planet Newton. As noted, only about a year ago Colin Kaepernick, former quarterback with the San Francisco 49ers, started it all. He specifically geared his protest toward reports of alleged racist police violence. And now this protest, spreading to other players, is emptying out the stadiums, as the players kneel rather than stand for the National Anthem.

Note this headline on *Drudge Report*: "NFL Stadiums Nearly Empty As Backlash Continues."[1] The American people are voting with their feet. The article notes: "If the NFL thought Americans would ease the

---

1. Joshua Caplan, "NFL HELL: Several Stadiums Nearly Empty As Anthem Protest Backlash Rolls Into Week 7," *Gateway Pundit*, October 22, 2017, thegatewaypundit.com.

backlash against the league—they were sadly mistaken. Photos of empty stadiums from around the league show how dire a situation kneelers have spurred. Stadiums were nearly empty in Week 6, as well.... The NFL managed to [anger] their core audience by nearly 40 points in the last three weeks. Nearly 60 percent of working class Trump supporters now view the NFL unfavorably."

About a year ago, I produced a television segment on this for D. James Kennedy Ministries' nationally syndicated program, "Truths That Transform." In the piece, we quoted Colin Kaepernick: "I am not looking for approval. I have to stand up for people that are oppressed.... If they take football away, my endorsements from me, I know that I stood up for what is right."

While we might admire Kaepernick's willingness to suffer adversity for his convictions, he also appears to be misguided. He regularly wears t-shirts at press conferences featuring Marxists Fidel Castro and Huey Newton.

David Barton, a man who knows very well America's Christian roots, has noted, "What Colin Kaepernick is doing is absolutely amazing. Here you have a professional athlete who is being paid millions for something you can't get paid for in the rest of the world. He's part of the 1 percent of the American elite, and he's protesting the country that has given him everything he has."

Why all the protest? To Barton, it boils down to years and years of faults in our educational system: "What you see with Colin Kaepernick is: This is typical of what we're teaching in America. We're teaching kids how to hate America." Barton noted that children today are largely not taught even basics of American history.

About the time the protests first began, Roger Goodell, the embattled NFL commissioner, said, "I support our players speaking out on issues that they think need to be changed in society." Barton counters: "But he didn't hold that position when players spoke out on traditional marriage... [or] when the transgender stuff came out.... The NFL is showing itself out of touch with where so many Americans are on some of the other issues."

Another voice of reason in this NFL kerfuffle is Rev. Paul Blair of Fairview Baptist Church, who used to play with the Chicago Bears in the 1980s and with the Vikings in 1990. He speaks at seminars under the banner of "Reclaiming America for Jesus Christ." I attended such a seminar for pastors two months ago. It was most illuminating. On October 10, Blair wrote an open letter to the NFL, protesting the NFL protests of the National Anthem. He notes: "As a vested NFL veteran, whose pension rests on the solvency of the National Football League, I have watched one misguided athlete infect much of the league with the poison of his false narrative, and it has put all of our financial futures at risk."

Blair adds, "America is not perfect, no man-made system ever is, but we are the greatest nation in history because our system is conducive to correcting injustice and providing opportunity. No country has been perfect, but America has always been exceptional when compared to the rest."

Blair concludes, "Alienating America is not a winning strategy. You want a winning strategy? Stand for the flag. Save your kneeling for the cross." Hear, hear.

20

REAGAN AT ONE HUNDRED

Originally published on February 7, 2011

Happy birthday, Ronald Reagan. February 6, 2011, marks the one hundredth anniversary of the Gipper's birth. He was certainly one of the best presidents, if not the best, of the twentieth century.

Did you know that faith played an important role in who Reagan was? In fact, as we'll see in a moment, an obscure novel helped set the direction for his whole life.

Consider some of Reagan's accomplishments:

- In one day, just by getting sworn in, he ended the Iranian hostage crisis, because the Iranians knew enough not to fool around with him at the helm.
- He played a critical role in ending the Cold War.
- He was the key architect of the longest peacetime expansions of the economy in our nation's history, one which lasted about two decades.
- Above all, he inspired hope—especially at a time when we sorely needed it.

What was the source of Reagan's greatness? He managed to successfully pull together various factions. Leaders since his time have not done so well.

Reagan was:

- conservative on defense

- conservative on the economy
- conservative on the social issues

He combined these values in one man—and an articulate man at that. Reagan knew what he believed and why he believed it. Therefore, he was able to inspire members of diverse groups to claim him as their own, thus creating a great coalition.

On the social issues, I remember to this day what Reagan said during a 1980 debate on abortion. A reporter asked him in what I recall was a hostile manner why he wasn't pro-choice. He responded, "Well, first of all, I happen to notice that everyone who's pro-choice has already been born."

One source of Reagan's greatness is often overlooked. Call it the faith factor. I must credit Dr. Paul Kengor, professor at Grove City College who wrote the book *God and Ronald Reagan* (2005), for research on this point. Dr. Kengor once told me, "The great communicator found his first audiences in a church as a young man leading sunrise prayer services at Easter time, emceeing church-related events in northern Illinois, teaching a Sunday school class, learning, as he put it, 'the value of parables'." This was at First Christian Church on 123 South Hennepin Avenue in Dixon, Illinois. Kengor visited the church as he researched his book.

Do you know what Reagan's first experience at leadership was? Teaching Sunday school to boys younger than him at his Dixon church. Kengor told me, "He taught that Sunday school class as a junior and senior in high school and did not miss a single class in almost two and a half years." He taught boys that were a few years younger than him. This is how one of the world's great statesmen first cut his teeth of leadership.

Reagan's father taught him how to tell stories well—a skill he used masterfully. His mother taught him the value of prayer, of dreaming big, and of having faith. Going to church was a lifelong habit for Reagan, except for when he was in office, because of all the security issues—especially after he was shot.

Another thing I learned from Dr. Kengor is that when Reagan was a young man and receiving baptism at the above-mentioned church, his mother gave him a book that helped set the direction of his life. The book was *That Printer of Udell's* by Harold Bell Wright, a heavily religious novel, dated 1903. It's essentially the story of a man who comes to have strong faith and who then sees himself called by the Lord to do something important for the world. So he runs for public office and eventually ends up in Washington, D.C., as a successful statesman—a true public servant, doing much good for the world in his role in politics. This little-known book—at least little-known today—helped set the trajectory for one of our greatest presidents.

So, happy birthday, Ronald Reagan. We're so glad you went to Washington, D.C., as an effective public servant. Reagan always reminded us to remember God, the ultimate source of America's greatness as he saw it. He said, "America needs God more than God needs America. If we ever forget that we are One Nation Under God, then we will be a Nation gone under."

21

RONALD REAGAN AND CONSERVATIVES IN THE POLITICAL WILDERNESS

Originally published on February 27, 2013

It seems like political conservatives are in the wilderness right now. Having been beaten in the November 2012 elections, and fracturing even more since, some are turning on each other.

Reagan has the answers. Recently I reviewed some of his speeches because I was looking for nuggets from him on the subject of prayer. He did not disappoint. Gary Bauer served the Reagan administration in a couple of different capacities, including as an advisor on domestic policy. He told me in a recent interview, "Ronald Reagan was very clear what the winning coalition was if you were a conservative. He referred to it as the three legs of the stool . . . the economic leg . . . the foreign policy leg . . . and the third leg of the stool is the leg of values. . . . He was pro-life. He was pro-family. . . . He spoke out for religious liberty."

I want to focus on that third leg. Consider what Reagan said about prayer: "We can't have it both ways. We can't expect God to protect us in a crisis and just leave Him over there on the shelf in our day-to-day living. I wonder if sometimes He isn't waiting for us to wake up, He isn't maybe running out of patience."[1]

He pointed out why our society is in such a mess today—which is even more true in our day than in his: "Without God, there is no virtue because there's no prompting of the conscience. . . . Without God, there

---

1. From the Alfred M. Landon Lecture Series on Public Issues on September 9, 1982.

is a coarsening of the society. And without God, democracy will not and cannot long endure."[2]

Long before we became a nation, Americans were a praying people. Various colonies, and then later Congress and presidents, called for national days of prayer and fasting and thanksgiving. Ronald Reagan observed, "Throughout our history, Americans have put their faith in God, and no one can doubt that we have been blessed for it." In the same document he proclaimed, "While never willing to bow to a tyrant, our forefathers were always willing to get to their knees before God. When catastrophe threatened, they turned to God for deliverance."[3]

Reagan told the National Religious Broadcasters, certainly a sympathetic audience, "I was pleased last year to proclaim 1983 the Year of the Bible. But, you know, a group called the ACLU severely criticized me for doing that. Well, I wear their indictment like a badge of honor. I believe I stand in pretty good company. Abraham Lincoln called the Bible 'the best gift God has given to man.' 'But for it,' he said, 'we wouldn't know right from wrong.'"

And Reagan added, "Like that image of George Washington kneeling in prayer in the snow at Valley Forge, Lincoln described a people who knew it was not enough to depend on their own courage and goodness. They must also look to God their Father and Preserver. And their faith to walk with Him and trust in His Word brought them the blessings of comfort, power, and peace that they sought."[4]

Somehow if one of our modern politicians—even many conservative ones—started talking like this, the rest of the establishment would start shifting in their seats—feeling embarrassed for the speaker, as if he had somehow lost his marbles. But Reagan had the answers.

Reagan was so opposed to the killing of the unborn that he even wrote a book about it: *Abortion and the Conscience of a Nation.* It's a great book. My copy is dog eared and heavily underlined. He wrote that book in 1984, when he was running for reelection. It's hard to imagine some of our modern "conservative" politicians writing a forthright book against abortion during an election year. But that was Reagan.

---

2. From the Ecumenical Prayer Breakfast in Dallas, Texas, on August 23, 1984.

3. From the National Day of Prayer Proclamation, March 19, 1981.

4. From the Annual Convention of the National Religious Broadcasters in Washington, D.C., on January 30, 1984.

He believed what he believed, and he expressed it well. And he won reelection in a landslide.

In *Abortion and the Conscience of a Nation* (1984), Reagan wrote, "Despite the formidable obstacles before us, we must not lose heart. This is not the first time our country has been divided by a Supreme Court decision that denied the value of certain human lives. The *Dred Scott* decision of 1857 was not overturned in a day, or a year, or even a decade" (p. 19).

In that book, Reagan also wrote, "The question today is not when human life begins, but, *What is the value of human life?* The abortionist who reassembles the arms and legs of a tiny baby to make sure all its parts have been torn from its mother's body can hardly doubt whether it is a human being" (p. 22).

It's hard to picture a politician today being so bold as to write something like that—in an election year no less. Would that more of our leaders took a page from Ronald Reagan's playbook.

As we saw before, Dr. Paul Kengor, political science professor at Grove City College, has written a few books on our fortieth president, including *God and Ronald Reagan* (2005). In 2004 I interviewed Kengor for a TV piece on Reagan's faith. He said, "What the historical record has overlooked is that Ronald Reagan was carried by a set of Christian convictions that goes back to the 1920s, that carried him even longer, and that, in fact, informed those political convictions that came later. And that's the side of Ronald Reagan that we all missed."

22

THE LEFT SHOULD STOP REWRITING THE
HISTORY OF CLARENCE THOMAS'S LEGACY

Originally published on October 4, 2016

There's a battle being waged that does not involve guns or bullets—the battle over history.

A striking example is found in a news story announcing that in a new Smithsonian Museum dedicated to African-American history, Anita Hill is presented as a more important figure than Clarence Thomas.[1] That museum is in a corner of the National Mall in D.C., close to the Washington Monument. In the article, "New Smithsonian hails accuser Anita Hill, barely mentions Clarence Thomas," Raffi Williams writes, "Thomas disputed Hill's allegations and won confirmation, but his side of the story is mostly ignored in the exhibits. Museum officials acknowledged that Thomas has 'very little presence' in any of the exhibitions." He adds, "One of the few mentions of Thomas in the museum reads: 'In 1991 Anita Hill charged Supreme Court nominee Clarence Thomas with sexual harassment.'"

It is astounding that a museum dedicated to black history would essentially snub one of the most important African-Americans of our time, Clarence Thomas—only the second-ever African-American justice to sit on the Supreme Court of the United States.

Now, his accuser from that "high-tech lynching" (as Thomas himself called it) in the battle royal over his confirmation by the Senate a quar-

---

1. Raffi Williams, "New Smithsonian hails accuser Anita Hill, barely mentions Clarence Thomas," *Circa*, October 2, 2016, circa.com.

ter of a century ago gets more attention at the museum than he does. This is the man—Clarence Thomas—who, for sixteen years prior to the election of Barack Obama to the presidency, held the highest office in the land of any black person in America.

He was approved by a close vote in the Senate. And the liberals have continued much of their hysterical disapproval of him ever since. For example, Julianne Malveaux, a liberal black commentator, made this remark on the November 4, 1994, edition of a program on PBS: "You know, I hope his wife feeds him lots of eggs and butter and he dies early like many black men do, of heart disease." When conservative Betsy Hart protested, Malveaux wouldn't back down. "Well, that's how I feel. He is an absolutely reprehensible person."[2]

Why would someone say that, and on a platform paid for by taxpayer dollars, no less? To the Left, it would appear that there is nothing so unforgivable as a black conservative. Those who are pro-life, pro-marriage, pro-conscience, and pro-religious liberty are to be marginalized—no matter how consequential they actually are.

Too often, American museums are increasingly becoming bastions of political correctness. And Clarence Thomas has committed the grave sin of not being sufficiently liberal and P.C. And that's a shame. I consider myself a big fan of museums, but not this new direction.

In this new display at this new museum, one can understand that they would briefly mention the Anita Hill charge, as that was part of the Clarence Thomas story. But it was just a "he said/she said" conflict, and her claims were even disputed by some who knew her. Meanwhile, Clarence Thomas's intriguing and original contributions to the court are completely ignored.

The sad thing is that millions of people will attend this museum and just take these things at face value. And in this way, history gets rewritten. In fact, history gets rewritten by the cultural elites who seem to have all the high places in this culture. I see the same mistreatment of America's founders all the time today, but that's another topic for another day.

My friend Bill Federer is a best-selling author and speaker on history-related themes. He recently wrote a forward for an upcoming book

---

2. PBS Talk Show, "To the Contrary," November 4, 1994, archive.mrc.org.

related to history and Christianity that I've written. In his foreword, Bill commented on the importance of history: "Pulitzer Prize-winning historian Arthur Schlesinger, who was on President John F. Kennedy's staff, wrote, 'History is to the nation as memory is to the individual.'" Bill added, "In America, we have national Alzheimer's. Here we are in America, and we have been the freest, most prosperous country that planet earth has ever seen, but recently we've lost our memory."

He quotes poet Carl Sandburg, who wrote: "When a nation goes down, or a society perishes, one condition may always be found; they forgot where they came from. They lost sight of what had brought them along."

He notes that Karl Marx, the father of communism who advocated the idea of deconstruction—that is, separating people from their historical past so you can then reconstruct society the way you want to—said, "The first battlefield is the rewriting of history," and "Take away the heritage of a people, and they are easily destroyed."

What a tragedy that, unless they correct this error at the museum, millions of visitors will be treated to a deconstructionist, biased, and distorted view of our 106th Justice on the Supreme Court, designed to fulfill a political goal rather than to accurately recount history. Yes, history matters.

23

AU CONTRAIRE, JIM DEMINT DOES KNOW HIS U.S. HISTORY

Originally published on April 23, 2014

Recently I interviewed Jim DeMint for my radio show to discuss his new book, *Falling in Love with America Again.* Some remarks he made on the show, especially about slavery, have burned up the blogosphere. Many of the articles imply or state that Mr. DeMint, former U.S. Senator (R-SC) and now head of The Heritage Foundation,[1] doesn't know his U.S. history.

In the interview, I asked DeMint about the founding fathers, the Civil War, and slavery. He said, "Well, the reason that the slaves were eventually freed was the Constitution. It was like the conscience of the American people. Unfortunately, there were some court decisions like *Dred Scott* and others that defined some people as property, but the Constitution kept calling us back to 'all men are created equal and we have inalienable rights' in the mind of God."

Of course, it is the Declaration of Independence that he was quoting there. But, as he well knows, the Constitution was predicated on the Declaration. The text of the Constitution states that it was signed in the twelfth year of the Declaration (as well as the 1787th "Year of our Lord").

DeMint continued with what became his most controversial remarks in the interview: "But a lot of the move to free the slaves came from the people, it did not come from the federal government. It came from a

---

1. Jim DeMint has now gone on from Heritage to head up Conservative Principles Partnership in Washington, D.C.

growing movement among the people, particularly people of faith, that this was wrong. People like Wilberforce who persisted for years because of his faith and because of his love for people. So no liberal is going to win a debate that big government freed the slaves. In fact, it was Abraham Lincoln, the very first Republican, who took this on as a cause and a lot of it was based on a love in his heart that comes from God."

The DailyKos declared: "Note to Jim DeMint: Ending slavery was a Big Government police action." One blog from MSNBC said of Mr. DeMint: "Don't Know Much About History." But just who doesn't know much about history?

Let's unpack what he said here and look at faith and slavery, proving DeMint's key points. The Bible condones indentured servitude to pay off debts (which has a limited term of service), for which it sometimes uses the word "slavery." But the Bible condemns chattel slavery (owning slaves as property) in strong terms. The Bible condemns the Egyptians for enslaving the Hebrews. And it also prohibits "man stealing" (the premise of U.S. slavery) as a capital crime.

Paul preached the radical doctrine that the slave and the free man are brothers in Christ...and that Philemon would be a better Christian if he freed his slave.

Above all, the great historian Kenneth Scott Latourette (1884–1968) of Yale points out that over the centuries Christianity undermined slavery by dignifying labor.

William Wilberforce was a longtime Member of Parliament in England who engaged in a lifelong Christian crusade against the slave trade and slavery in the British Empire. Even President Obama (not a DeMint fan, I imagine) noted in 2010, "Remember William Wilberforce, whose Christian faith led him to seek slavery's abolition in Britain."

The success of Wilberforce and his evangelical friends who ended slavery in 1833 inspired those in America dealing with the terrible issue here. In the American experience, two-thirds of the members of the abolition society in 1835 were ministers of the Gospel. Leading practitioners of the Underground Railroad were Quakers. The Christian novel *Uncle Tom's Cabin* pricked the conscience of the nation. Abraham Lincoln's love of the Bible is well documented; his writings are filled with quotes from its pages.

One of the articles critiquing Jim DeMint's American history was by Jon Greenberg.[2] In his nevertheless-thoughtful piece, Greenberg notes: "The majority of the leaders of the American Anti-Slavery Society, a powerful voice for emancipation in the decades before the war, identified with some branch of faith. They drew their inspiration from the Bible." He goes on to quote Christian abolitionist Jonathan Blanchard. (On a personal note, Blanchard was the founder/first president of evangelical Wheaton College, where I met my wife and earned my M.A.) Said Mr. Blanchard, "Abolitionists take their stand upon the New Testament doctrine of the natural equity of man." Blanchard then cites Acts 17:26, which says that all men came from one man—thus, undermining racism (not that Christians have always lived up to that ideal, sadly).

It's true that some in the South misused the Bible to justify American chattel slavery. But, most importantly, the death knell against slavery came from the Bible. And that's the key, proving DeMint's thesis. As culture precedes politics, so abolitionism (often faith-based) among the people preceded the Civil War.

---

2. Jon Greenburg, "Did people of faith do more to end slavery than the federal government?" *Tampa Bay Times*, April 18, 2014, tampabay.com.

24

THREE KEY LESSONS FOR MODERN AMERICANS
FROM A REFUGEE OF COMMUNISM

Originally published on October 23, 2012

America is at a crossroads. In a couple of weeks we get to vote which path we will choose—toward bigger or more limited government. Lately I've been hearing from different people who fled communist backgrounds, warning about what they see happening in modern America at the hands of politicians on both sides of the aisle.

A woman from church says of recent presidents (of both parties), "These politicians write executive orders as if they were kings or a Communist Party politburo. I am from Communist Poland (which has recently become communist again), and here in the U.S. I see socialism (and other isms) coming every year—more and more since I got here, except under Reagan."[1]

Another man tells me via email, "No matter what words I use to describe it, people who never lived under communism will never truly understand the social cancer that communism is. In the Romanian church I pastor...we have many members who fled Romania during communism and risked their lives to escape the totalitarian regime; some were caught and brutally beaten....For the communists, people who worked hard and managed to have more than the average were considered to be dangerous and were deported or worked to death in forced labor camps."

Someone might say, "Well, that was then. That was there. This is

---

1. Note: I have corrected grammatical errors and misspellings from these refugees.

now. This is the United States." But my friend continues, "It is scary to see the mentality that resembles that of the communists being more and more openly expressed by the politicians in the USA."

The main voice I want to highlight here is from Carlos, a forty-two-year-old Cuban refugee who escaped to America in 1995. His plea: we should not go down the same path as Cuba. He fears that we could "lose our beloved America" if we don't heed the lessons from communism, such as:

1. NO GOD MEANS NO RIGHTS

Carlos notes, "I grew up in government schools a complete atheist, and the system indoctrinates you all the way to the bones. There is no private school."

In contrast, our founders said that our rights come from the Creator. God-given rights are not up for vote. John F. Kennedy declared, "The rights of man come not from the generosity of the state but from the hand of God." As noted, Ronald Reagan observed, "If we ever forget that we are One Nation Under God, then we will be a Nation gone under."

2. COLLECTIVISM MEANS NO FREEDOM

Carlos says, "Absolutely everything belongs to the government.... For example, you own a cow, and you're starving to death, but cannot eat it.... You can only sell the milk from your own cow to the government, and the government tells you how much it is worth.... The communists try to keep you very poor and try to make you believe that there is only one way you can survive, and it because of government's help."

What's the net effect of over-bloated government? It often saps the strength and will of the people. As Carlos puts it, "It is very important for the government to take all the incentives, aspirations, and ambitions away from you. Government wants to make you a dependent parasite. That way they can control you very easily."

3. YOU HAVE NO FREEDOM TO DISAGREE

Carlos says, "The communists control the media 100 percent.... I remember my mother being taken to jail because there is a law that if you are considered a dangerous person, the government has to isolate you 'for the better of the community.' They took my mother to jail for two years when I was in fifth grade."

Although his mother has now lived in the U.S. for at least ten years, Carlos notes that she still fears being overheard saying the wrong thing. She whispered to Carlos recently, "Don't say that. Somebody is going to hear you."

Carlos continues, "I remember very well that you are afraid of talking about politics with your friends or any family member because you don't know if they work for the government, and any comment can take you to jail for many years—real jail, not the hotel that we have in America! I have many friends that went to jail for just having an opinion against the system."

Carlos escaped (on his fourth attempt to flee) when he and five other males rowed a twelve-foot boat from Cuba to "a rock" in the Bahamas. He wept when an American soldier said, "Welcome to freedom, gentlemen!" Eventually, the U.S. granted him "political refugee asylum."

He looks back at how risky it was to row a twelve-foot boat in the middle of the ocean, but he adds, "Nothing is more precious than freedom.... You would do it for freedom too." He laments that "millions of Americans take this freedom and system for granted. How sad, very sad!"

Carlos warns. "I see the government getting bigger and bigger and controlling more and more, and I am afraid for my child to live what I lived. Well, I try to tell people my opinion every day and thank the Lord that I can do it without hiding. I will try, as long as the Lord wants me to be here, to try to keep this country the way it was founded."

There's a song that says, "You don't know what you got 'til it's gone." May that never be our future lament.

25

HAPPY BIRTHDAY, AMERICA

Originally published on July 2, 2013

Here's a trivia question for you. The Statue of Liberty holds a torch in one hand. What is she holding in the other? It looks like a book, in tablet form.

The answer is the Declaration of Independence, since the tablet is engraved with July 4, 1776, in Roman numerals.

The great British writer G. K. Chesterton once said, "America is the only nation in the world that is founded on a creed. That creed is set forth with dogmatic and even theological lucidity in the Declaration of Independence."

Two hundred thirty-seven years ago, fifty-six men, representing some three million British colonists, voted to approve that revolutionary document. If they failed, these men voted for their own death. In June 1776, the Continental Congress voted to approve declaring independence from Great Britain, and formed a committee to write the document. Thomas Jefferson served on that committee and became the chief author. The committee accepted the bulk of what he wrote.

On July 2, 1776, Congress voted to accept independence from Great Britain. That's why John Adams said about that date: "I am apt to believe that it will be celebrated, by succeeding Generations, as the great anniversary Festival. It ought to be commemorated, as the Day of Deliverance by solemn Acts of Devotion to God Almighty. It ought to be solemnized with Pomp and Parade, with Shews, Games, Sports, Guns, Bells, Bonfires and Illuminations from one End of this Continent to the other from this Time forward forever more." He was off by two days. On July 4, Congress voted to accept the modified Declaration of Independence.

What makes the Declaration so revolutionary? Above all, it says that our rights come from God. John F. Kennedy expressed it so well in his Inaugural Address in 1961: "The same revolutionary beliefs for which our forebears fought are still at issue around the globe—the belief that the rights of man come not from the generosity of the state, but from the hand of God."

God-given rights are non-negotiable. God-given rights supersede rights granted by man.

As Chesterton put it, "The Declaration of Independence dogmatically bases all rights on the fact that God created all men equal; and it is right; for if they were not created equal, they were certainly evolved unequal. There is no basis for democracy except in a dogma about the divine origin of man." In that sense, America is and always will be one nation under God—unless we were somehow cut off from the Declaration, in which case we would no longer be America.

The essence of Americanism is God-given rights to "We the people." For all our flaws, for all the ugly chapters in our history, for all the mistreatment of the Indians and of blacks as slaves and then as second-class citizens, God-given rights are the foundation for our past, present, and future, and Jesus Christ makes it all possible. As we've seen, Dr. Martin Luther King Jr. said the problem with America is not our creed (as seen in the Declaration) but in our failure to live up to that creed. I'm reminded of that musical prayer in the hymn, "America the Beautiful": "America! America! God, mend thine every flaw, Confirm thy soul in self-control, Thy liberty in law!"

In August, a month after the vote on July 4, 1776, to adopt the Declaration of Independence, the fifty-six men of the Continental Congress began the process of signing the revolutionary document. Delegates had to make their way back to Philadelphia—during war time—in order to sign the Declaration. The final signature was not affixed until January 1777.

For the first several months, the only printed copies of the Declaration of Independence contained just two names—one of which was that of John Hancock, the president of that assembly. When he signed the document in August, he deliberately put his "John Hancock" on the form in a way that was so large that King George III could read it without his spectacles.

The other name on the first few printed copies of the Declaration was that of Charles Thomson, the secretary of that Continental Congress. Later he would get involved in Bible translation.

When Ben Franklin signed it, he declared, "We must all hang together or most assuredly we shall hang separately." They were signing their death warrants, defying the strongest nation on earth. We forget sometimes just how impossible the situation must have looked, except by faith. A betting man at that time could easily have felt that the odds were with the British squashing the rebellion in their American colonies. In little time.

No wonder, during and after the war, George Washington said repeatedly how grateful he was to God for our incredible victory. For instance, in 1778, when Benedict Arnold's treason was discovered before it could damage the American cause, Washington said, "The Hand of providence has been so conspicuous in all this, that he must be worse than an infidel that lacks faith, and more than wicked, that has not gratitude enough to acknowledge his obligations."

In his First Inaugural Address, our first president said, "No people can be bound to acknowledge and adore the Invisible Hand which conducts the affairs of men more than those of the United States. Every step by which they have advanced to the character of an independent nation seems to have been distinguished by some token of providential agency."

So as we approach the 237th birthday of America, we should give thanks to the Lord for our God-given rights. May we not squander such freedom, nor let it sift through our fingers.

26

THE POLITICALLY INCORRECT REV. DR. KING

Originally published on August 28, 2013

Surely the fiftieth anniversary of the "I Have a Dream" speech of Rev. Dr. Martin Luther King Jr. (August 28, 1963) is a major milestone in our history. But in our highly secular age, the politically correct Dr. Martin Luther King Jr. has been yanked from his Biblical context— deeply rooted in the Judeo-Christian tradition. That doesn't mean he wasn't a flawed man. However, no one but Jesus is without sin.

Jesus was the driving force behind King's non-violence. King said, "Nonviolence is not a symbol of weakness or cowardice, but as Jesus demonstrated, nonviolent resistance transforms weakness into strength and breeds courage in the face of danger." Gandhi too had influence on him, but Gandhi himself admits that his nonviolence strategy came from Jesus's Sermon on the Mount.[1]

Rev. King said, "Religion endows us with the conviction that we are not alone in this vast, uncertain universe."

In April 1963, four months before the "I Have a Dream" speech, Dr. King wrote, "I would agree with Saint Augustine that 'An unjust law is no law at all.' . . . A just law is a man-made code that squares with the moral law or the law of God. An unjust law is a code that is out of harmony with the moral law."[2] And he added later, "Law and order exist

---

1. Jeremy Holtom, "Gandhi's Interpretation of the Sermon on the Mount," *Oxford Handbooks Online*, May, 2011, oxfordhandbooks.com, and Dr. P.T. Subrahmanyan, "Mahatma Gandhi and the Sermon on the Mount," April–June, 2017, mkgandhi.org/main.htm.

2. "Letter from Birmingham Jail," August 1963, kinginstitute.stanford.edu.

for the purpose of establishing justice."

In 1962, King asked his followers, "Must we, by concluding that segregation is within the will of God, resign ourselves to the will of God, resign ourselves to oppression? Of course not, for this blasphemously attributes to God that which is of the devil."[3]

King even addressed the common notion that you can't legislate morality. He said, "Even though morality cannot be legislated, behavior can be regulated. While the law cannot change the heart, it can certainly restrain the heartless." That reminds me of a common remark of my longtime pastor, Dr. D. James Kennedy: "All legislation reflects someone's morality. The question is, *Whose* morality will prevail?"

Dr. King also said, "The chief purpose for the Christian Church is the salvation of individuals."

King's niece is Dr. Alveda King, who is a strong pro-life advocate and serves Priests for Life. She laments that her uncle's dream can never be fulfilled with such rampant abortion rates. I've interviewed her a few times. She told me, "Statistics today prove that African-American women and their babies, and their wombs, are the most targeted wombs and families in America."

She noted that even to this day, "a majority of the abortion clinics are in urban areas, near highly populated African-American communities; so we have more abortions, with us being about 13 percent of the population and having roughly one-third of the abortions."

Alveda added, "Dr. Martin Luther King Jr. said the Negro cannot win if he's willing to sacrifice the future of his children for immediate personal comfort and safety." And her uncle, she said, also warned us "not to be like the Romans who committed infanticide."

Alveda herself notes: "It's unjust to kill a little person because they're little. A woman has a right to choose what she does with her body, but where is a lawyer for the baby? How can the dream survive, if we murder the children?"

What about homosexuality? A lot of gay rights advocates imply that their movement is the next logical extension of Dr. King's movement. Rev. Bill Owens disagrees. He's the founder and president of the Coalition of African-American Pastors. He once told me, "I marched with

---

3. Martin Luther King Jr., *Strength to Love* (Philadelphia: Fortress Press, 1963), 92.

Dr. King. I marched for civil rights....And they're trying to hijack and take over the civil rights movement and make it their movement. And they didn't pay the price, nor do they suffer the things that blacks suffered."

Similarly, black pastor Dr. Ken Hutcherson noted: "I'm appalled at that comparison....I remember two water fountains in my day. This is me growing up. This isn't something I heard about; this is something I lived—where there [were] colored water fountains, white water fountains. I have never seen a homosexual water fountain, have you?"

In his last sermon (Atlanta, February 1968), Rev. Dr. Martin Luther King Jr. said:

> If I can help somebody as I pass along,
> If I can cheer somebody with a word or song,
> If I can show somebody he's traveling wrong,
> Then my living will not be in vain.
> If I can do my duty as a Christian ought,
> If I can bring salvation to a world once wrought,
> If I can spread the message as the master taught,
> Then my living will not be in vain.

Dr. King's living was surely not in vain.

27

THE MANTLE OF DR. KING

Originally published on August 27, 2010

Who carries the mantle of Dr. Martin Luther King Jr.—Al Sharpton or
Dr. King's niece? On the forty-seventh anniversary (to the day) of Dr.
King's "I Have a Dream" speech, Glenn Beck has organized a gigantic "Restoring Honor" rally, featuring Sarah Palin, Michele Bachmann,
and Dr. Alveda King, the niece of Dr. King. Alveda is pro-life and serves
as a spokesperson for Priests for Life, although she is neither Catholic
nor a priest. But she is one with them on this all-important issue of life.

To counterprotest Glenn Beck's rally, civil rights leader Al Sharpton
will bring out many to oppose Beck. It's a free country, and that's great.
As long as things don't get violent.

As to nonviolence, we know that would sit well with Rev. Dr. Martin Luther King Jr., the long-time minister at Dexter Avenue Baptist
Church in Montgomery, Alabama, the closest church in proximity to
the state capitol. The civil rights movement was born in the basement
of that church in the 1950s, when Dr. King and others decided on a
strategy in which blacks would nonviolently boycott the buses to protest the unfair Jim Crow laws. The catalyst for the boycott, of course,
was an incident involving church member Rosa Parks, who, after a
long, hard day at work, refused to give up her seat on the bus to a white
man. She was arrested for this, and the rest is history. This boycott
led by the senior pastor, Rev. Martin Luther King Jr., propelled King
to national prominence in the fight for justice. He felt that America
needed to live up to its creed that all men are created equal. There was

79

nothing wrong with the creed. It's just that the nation wasn't living up to it.

I could be wrong, but it seems to me that Dr. King's message to America that it live up to its creed and that we become a color-blind society is trumpeted more clearly by today's consistent conservatives, including Dr. King's niece, than by the likes of Al Sharpton. If race problems in America went away, Sharpton would be out of a job. If we strove toward being truly color blind, then it seems to me that the types of raced-based quotas he promotes would be no more. But there's another issue that Sharpton and King disagree on—perhaps far more basic.

I've had the privilege of interviewing Dr. Alveda King a few times for Christian TV and radio programs. She decries the way many black leaders promote abortion today, even though they would claim the mantle of Dr. King. In contrast to such leaders, she says of Uncle Martin, "I began to read my uncle's statements again, and I would begin to hear: injustice anywhere is a threat to justice everywhere. I said, 'It's unjust to kill a little person because they're little. A woman has a right to choose what she does with her body, but where is a lawyer for the baby? How can the dream survive, if we murder the children?'" Fair enough. The leading cause of black deaths in America is abortion, far and away more than any other cause.

But Al Sharpton says, "My religion says that abortion is wrong. And while I may believe that life begins when the sperm meets the egg, and that only God should decide whether to take a life, I will not stand in the way of a woman's right to choose. If women do not have a right to choose, then it's a civil rights violation."

The younger Dr. King doesn't agree with Al, and according to her, neither would Uncle Martin. She notes, "If you read Dr. King's statements or if you knew him as I did, Dr. King said, 'The negro cannot win if he's willing to sacrifice the futures of his children for immediate personal comfort and safety.'... Throughout his lifetime, Dr. King supported the rights of the most oppressed. Dr. King supported the least of these.... Dr. King was a pro-life, gentle person."

On August 28, we can expect to hear Dr. Alveda King give her pro-life message at the very spot where her uncle spoke forty-seven years ago to the day. We can also expect Al Sharpton, who is in favor of abortion rights, to counterprotest.

Alveda notes of Al Sharpton and company, "Other groups are planning rallies and demonstrations in Washington that day, and freedom of speech gives them the right to do so—and to criticize me for not jumping on their bandwagon. But Uncle Martin's legacy is big enough to go around."

28

"THE OTHER SIDE OF THE VIETNAM STORY"

Originally published on May 25, 2016

Another Memorial Day is upon us. Interestingly, President Obama just visited Vietnam to help solidify our formerly strained relations.

The Vietnam War still brings up many painful memories for those who served. No doubt it all turned out tragically, but there is a side of that war we rarely hear about—that is, the gratitude that some feel, that we even tried to keep that nation free from the scourge of communism.

When Vietnam veterans came home, people vilified them. People spat on them. People called them "baby killers." They were shunned. People did not thank them, but treated them badly. And all they did was go and serve when their country called them.

About twenty years ago, I interviewed a Christian journalist and counselor, Uwe Siemon-Netto, who was originally from Germany. He told me, "Our soldiers fought valiantly, despite severe criticism—58,000 Americans were killed, 500,000 were wounded, and more than seven hundred were taken in as prisoners of war. And they were fighting an enemy whose policy included inhumane tactics, an enemy that devalued human life. Although there were some American atrocities during Vietnam, they were *contrary* to U.S. policy."

How did the enemy devalue life? He said, "The North Vietnamese, the Viet Cong—Viet Cong means Vietnamese Communist troops—went into hamlets and villages and slaughtered people, civilians, including children, on a daily basis."

Siemon-Netto not only covered the war as a journalist, he also counseled Vietnam veterans in Minnesota. About two decades after the war, he wrote a book, *The Acquittal of God* (2008), to help Vietnam veterans know that God did not forsake them in Vietnam.

He also said, "Most of the GIs who returned from Vietnam came into a very hostile society. . . . This was the 1960s. It was miniskirts and free love and great fun. And these guys came in, and they were a bother." He said that through the years, thousands of returning Vietnam veterans ended up killing themselves. And he added, "I think America owes them an enormous debt to this day."

One man who recognizes that debt grew up in Vietnam. He spoke at a recent Memorial Day celebration in Fort Lauderdale, where I had the privilege to open and close in prayer. His name is Dr. Du Hua.

Hua was born in Vietnam. He wrote a book called *The Escapes and My Journey to Freedom* (2012). It chronicles his repeated attempts to escape after the Viet Cong took over and turned Vietnam into a living hell. On his eleventh try, he succeeded. Providentially, a German ship intercepted his. After some time in a refugee camp, Hua could eventually come to our country and experience "the life of freedom and dignity in America [away] from the hell of the evil Communists."

Hua then went on to serve in the U.S. Navy—as a way of saying thanks to America for her attempt (albeit a failed one) to free his country of origin from the curse of communism and for the new life he experienced here. An injury cut short his naval career, and he became a pharmaceutical doctor.

When Hua spoke at the 2013 Ft. Lauderdale Memorial Day service, there was a hardly a dry eye. Wayne Ferrell, a friend of mine from church, was there, "crying the whole time." Ferrell wrote of Hua's speech, "This fellow's story was the other side of the Vietnam story that no one tells."

Ferrell continued, "He called the American military his people's angels. He saw freedom right in front of him in those soldiers. He saw evil in socialism and communism all around him. . . . [He became] one of those Vietnamese boat people we read about so long ago that made it to the US."

Ferrell added, "[Hua] said there was no possible way for him to pay back the 58,000 Americans and 300,000 South Vietnamese soldiers that died for people like him, but once he got here to the US, he did his best to try."

Ferrell also said, "The more [Hua] spoke, the more he raised his voice until he was emotionally yelling his speech, shouting, 'you are my angels,' and 'freedom is not free,' and 'welcome home' to his fellow vets that had just returned. Everyone was on their feet as he finished, cheering him."

The organizer of the Memorial Day service emailed me afterwards: "The response from the Vietnam veterans [to Hua's speech] has been overwhelming to say the least, of how they have finally been appreciated."

When America pulled out of Vietnam, the enemy fulfilled virtually every dire prediction about the encroaching evils of communism. This Memorial Day, be grateful for those Americans who served their country when called upon—including those who served in the unpopular Vietnam War.

29

GOD AND THE INAUGURAL ADDRESSES

Originally published on January 18, 2017

With the inauguration of Donald Trump as our forty-fifth president upon us, all the usual suspects from the militant-atheist crowd have been trying to block the Bible from being used—a tradition that began with President Washington. Each president has mentioned God in his inaugural address, even if speaking of the Lord in his own way, fitting with the times. With thanks to Bill Federer in *America's God and Country*, consider this sample:

- George Washington said, "It would be peculiarly improper to omit, in this first official act, my fervent supplications to that Almighty Being who rules over the universe."
- John Adams spoke of "a decent respect for Christianity among the best recommendations for the public service."
- Thomas Jefferson prayed to "that Infinite Power which rules the destinies of the universe."
- James Madison invoked the "guidance of that Almighty Being."
- James Monroe noted, "We can not fail, under the favor of a gracious Providence."
- John Quincy Adams quoted Scripture: "Except the Lord keep the city, the watchman waketh but in vain."
- Andrew Jackson referred to "the goodness of that Power whose providence mercifully protected our national infancy."

- Martin Van Buren looked to "the gracious protection of that Divine Being."
- William Henry Harrison warned of "the false Christs whose coming was foretold by the Savior."
- John Tyler invoked, "the protecting care of an everwatchful and overruling Providence."
- James K. Polk prayed, "I fervently invoke the aid of that Almighty Ruler of the Universe."
- Zachary Taylor gave thanks for "the goodness of Divine Providence."
- Millard Fillmore mentioned "Almighty God" when he announced the death of his predecessor.
- Franklin Pierce mentioned "the nation's humble, acknowledged dependence upon God."
- James Buchanan declared, "I must humbly invoke the God of our fathers."
- Abraham Lincoln stated, "Intelligence, patriotism, Christianity, and a firm reliance on Him who has never yet forsaken this favored land, are still competent to adjust in the best way all our present difficulty."
- Andrew Johnson noted, "Duties have been mine; consequences are God's."
- Ulysses S. Grant told us, "I ask the prayers of the nation to Almighty God."
- Rutherford B. Hayes said he was looking "for the guidance of that Divine Hand."
- James Garfield stated, "I reverently invoke the support and blessings of Almighty God."
- Chester Arthur spoke of "relying for aid on Divine Guidance."
- Grover Cleveland (in 1885) noted, "And let us not trust to human effort alone, but humbly acknowledge the power and goodness of Almighty God who presides over the destiny of nations."
- Benjamin Harrison said, "We may reverently invoke and confidently extend the favor and help of Almighty God."
- William McKinley declared, "Our faith teaches that there is no safer reliance than upon the God of our fathers."

- Theodore Roosevelt thanked "the Giver of Good who has blessed us."
- William Howard Taft mentioned our need for "the aid of the Almighty God."
- Woodrow Wilson spoke of "God helping me."
- Warren G. Harding referred to "God's intent in the making of this new-world Republic."
- John Calvin Coolidge (Reagan's model president) stated that "America seeks no empires built on blood and force.... The legions which she sends forth are armed, not with the sword, but with the Cross."
- Herbert Hoover asked for "the help of Almighty God."
- Franklin D. Roosevelt "humbly" asked "blessing of God" and His guidance.
- Harry S. Truman referenced "that all men are created equal because they are created in the image of God."
- Dwight Eisenhower opened in prayer: "Almighty God, as we stand here at this moment ... "
- John F. Kennedy stated, "Here on earth, God's work truly must be our own."
- Lyndon B. Johnson referred to "the oath I have taken before you and God."
- Richard Nixon spoke of being "sustained by our confidence in the will of God."
- Gerald Ford said, "Let us restore the Golden Rule to our political process, and let brotherly love purge our hearts of suspicion and of hate." It is Jesus who gave us the Golden Rule (Matthew 7:12).
- Jimmy Carter said, "Here before me is the Bible used in the inauguration of our first President in 1789."
- Ronald Reagan noted, "We are a nation under God, and I believe God intended for us to be free."
- George H. W. Bush stated, "And my first act as President is a prayer. I ask you to bow your heads: Heavenly Father... "
- Bill Clinton quoted Scripture: "And let us not be weary in well-doing, for in due season, we shall reap, if we faint not."

- George W. Bush said, "God bless you, and God bless America."
- Barack Obama declared, "This is the source of our confidence—the knowledge that God calls on us to shape an uncertain destiny."

The atheists are the Johnny-come-latelies. Demands to ban God and the Bible from the inauguration should be denied.

30

DOES AMERICA HAVE A PRAYER?

Originally published on May 1, 2013

Thursday, May 2, 2013, is the National Day of Prayer. Yet things are not right in the land. We pray, "May God bless America." But perhaps instead we should pray, "May God have mercy on America."

As we survey the modern American landscape, we see many examples that things are not right—more than 55 million abortions in America since 1973 . . . rampant pornography . . . mass shootings . . . promotion of gay marriage . . . dissolution of marriage in general . . . runaway debt that will enslave our children and grandchildren . . . threats to our religious liberty like never before.

And yet our national motto remains "In God We Trust." I always remember the sign in the ice cream shop (by the cash register) that said: "In God We Trust. All others pay cash."

Prayer is rooted deep in the American tradition—even national prayer. We can see multiple examples of this in Bill Federer's great book, *America's God & Country.* During the days of the American War for Independence, the Continental Congress often put out the word for all the citizens to pray and fast, such as May 17, 1776—a National Day of Humiliation, Fasting, and Prayer.

On that day, the Congress prayed "that we may with united hearts confess and bewail our manifold sins and transgressions, and by a sincere repentance and amendment of life appease God's righteous displeasure, and through the merits and mediation of Jesus Christ obtain His pardon and forgiveness."

At Valley Forge, General George Washington gave this order on April 12, 1778, (speaking of himself in the third person): "The General directs that the day [April 22, 1778] shall be most religiously observed in the Army; that no work shall be done thereon, and that the several chaplains do prepare discourses suitable to the occasion."

Even some of the less religious founding fathers, like Ben Franklin, saw the importance of prayer. He made an impassioned plea during the Constitutional Convention that they pray, and a variation of his request was adopted. He once said, "Work as if you were to live 100 years; pray as if you were to die tomorrow."

Samuel Adams, the lightning rod for American independence, later became the governor of Massachusetts. On October 14, 1795, he declared a day of fasting and prayer, with this petition: "That God would be pleased to guide and direct the administration of the Federal government, and those of the several states, in union, so that the whole people may continue to be safe and happy in the constitutional enjoyment of their rights, liberties and privileges, and our governments be greatly respected at home and abroad."

John Adams, signer of the Declaration of Independence and second president of the United States, in proclaiming a national day of prayer, asked that God "would smile on our colleges, academies, schools, and seminaries of learning, and make them nurseries of sound science, morals, and religion" (National Day of Humiliation, Fasting, and Prayer, March 6, 1799).

John Jay, coauthor of the *Federalist Papers* and first Supreme Court Chief Justice, said, "The most effectual means of securing the continuance of our civil and religious liberties is, always to remember with reverence and gratitude the Source from which they flow" (June 29, 1826).

James Madison, another coauthor of the *Federalist Papers*, a major player at the Constitutional Convention, and fourth president of the United States, issued a national day of prayer (July 9, 1812) during our second war with Great Britain (the War of 1812). Madison proclaimed that a day "be set apart for the devout purpose of rendering the Sovereign of the Universe and the Benefactor of mankind the public homage due to His holy attributes; of acknowledging the transgressions which might justly provoke the manifestations of His divine displeasure; of seeking His merciful forgiveness, and His assistance in the great duties of repentance and amendment."

Various presidents have often declared national days of prayer and of thanksgiving to God. Abraham Lincoln said of prayer, "I have been driven many times to my knees by the overwhelming conviction that I had nowhere else to go."

Since the Truman administration, we have held an annual National Day of Prayer. Ronald Reagan made it the first Thursday of each May. President Reagan once said about our nation and prayer, "We can't have it both ways. We can't expect God to protect us in a crisis and just leave Him over there on the shelf in our day-to-day living."[1]

Of course, there are many today who scoff at the notion of prayer, corporate or individual. Some view it as accomplishing absolutely nothing. Liberal activist Saul Alinsky said as much.

But prayer can be very hard work. Besides, prayer is not nor should ever be an excuse for doing nothing. It's not an either/or. It's a both/and.

Many times in many municipalities we find that at noon on the National Day of Prayer, right outside of City Hall, various people of God will gather to pray. Sometimes the mayor will even join the participants. All are welcome.

Of course, we should pray without ceasing—not just on one day of the year. But it's nice to have an annual reminder on the National Day of Prayer of our great need for God's help, all year round.

My wife has hung in our front hall a needlepoint that she made. It sums it all up: "Life is fragile. Handle with prayer."

1. Ronald Reagan, *Public Papers of the Presidents of the United States: Ronald Reagan, July 3 to December 31, 1982*, 1122, books.google.com.

31

RIOTS IN THE STREETS—THE NEW NORMAL?

Originally published on February 8, 2017

One of the greatest milestones in world history was March 4, 1797. Why? What happened then? America, under the guidance of the Constitution, transitioned from our first president to our second. George Washington stepped down, and the recently elected John Adams stepped in.

No bloodshed. No rioting in the streets. No town-hall meetings cancelled for fear of the speaker being torn limb from limb.

Even the acrimonious battle over who would be the third president did not prevent a peaceful transition. This contest was in Congress in 1801 and ultimately stretched out day after day (involving thirty-six ballots) to see who would win: Thomas Jefferson or Aaron Burr, who had tied him in the electoral college.

While the people who oppose President Trump or his policies are free to peacefully express their opinions, they are not free to hurt people and destroy property. As the saying goes, "Your right to swing your arm ends at the tip of my nose"—even if they claim the mantle of "tolerance."

The Left likes to compare Trump to Hitler and the Nazis. Yet it was Goebbels, Hitler's propaganda minister, who said, "History is made in the streets." Get enough brown-shirts to beat up and silence the opposition, and you seize power. Might makes right.

That's not the American way.

An example can be found in the *Daily Caller* (January 30, 2017), where Justin Caruso noted, "During an anti-Trump protest in Seattle this weekend, an activist associated with the Black Lives Matter (BLM) movement took to the megaphone to voice her support for, among other things, 'killing people,' and 'killing the White House'."[1]

What happened last week at the University of California, Berkeley, was a horrible bellwether. In a place famous for standing for "free speech," free speech died last week when the sponsoring organization disinvited a controversial "gay conservative," *Breitbart News* editor Milo Yiannopoulos—a Trump-supporter, from speaking after violent protests broke out over his appearance that caused more than $100,000 in damage and several injuries. The cancellation of his talk was not by the college, and not by the organizers of the talk, but by mob rule.[2]

The *San Francisco Chronicle* quoted one of the student protesters (February 1, 2017): "The whole reason we're here is for free speech.... Milo's hate speech is not allowed here. When it's hate speech, our free speech is to shut him down." The *Chronicle* added, "The protest turned violent around 6 p.m. when dozens of masked anarchists, dressed in black and wearing backpacks, emerged from the otherwise peaceful crowd."[3]

Tucker Carlson interviewed Yiannopoulos that night, and the *Fox News* broadcaster commented, "This looks like political violence designed to squelch opinions the perpetrators of that violence disagree with."

Some Hollywood people spoke out in favor of the protests:

- Director Judd Apatow said of the Berkeley riots: "This is just the beginning."
- Sarah Silverman, with whom I once appeared on an episode of Bill Maher's *Politically Incorrect* (2002), has called for a violent overthrow of the duly elected president. She tweeted: "WAKE UP & JOIN THE RESISTANCE. ONCE THE MILITARY IS W US FASCISTS GET OVERTHROWN. MAD KING & HIS HANDLERS GO BYE BYE." (emphasis hers)

1. Justin Caruso, "BLM Anti-Trump Protest In Seattle: 'We Need To Start Killing People,'" *The Daily Caller,* January 30, 2017, dailycaller.com.

2. Max Greenwood, "Milo Yiannopoulos disinvited from CPAC," *The Hill,* February 20, 2017, thehill.com.

3. Bob Egelko, "Milo Yiannopulius' Speech Unwelcome in Berkeley, but Protected by Constitution," *San Francisco Chronicle,* February 2, 2017, sfchronicle.com.

- Filmmaker Lexi Alexander, according to *FoxNews Entertainment* (February 2, 2017), defended the Berkeley riot on Twitter, "telling her followers to 'punch Nazis,' 'riot when your college invites a Nazi,' and 'set it all on fire'." And she tweeted, "Hate speech is not free speech. It's called incitement. It's a crime."

The next night, protesters at New York University attempted to shut down another conservative speaker, but the event happened anyway and the police arrested eleven protesters.

So many of these recent protesters are, as my brother put it, "real fascists in the name of pretend anti-fascism."

And *who* is to define "hate speech"? I have a friend who is a former lesbian. She was converted to Christ and is grateful to be free from her former lifestyle. Back when "hate crime" laws (aren't all crimes hateful?) were being proposed, she expressed concern that some politically correct folks would absurdly interpret her Christian testimony as so-called "hate speech."

Yiannopoulos made a little YouTube video responding to the Berkeley protests, saying, "The progressive Left in America has been engaged in this project of conflating ideas with action." And he added, "America, of all places, now is seeing political violence in response to ideas."

Is this the new normal? Riots in the streets to wear us down?

The Left didn't win at the ballot box, in a surprising upset, and now do they want to invalidate the election results by causing violence in the streets? We should not permit thuggery to undo the genius of what the founding fathers gave us in the Constitution and all the blessings that flow from our God-given liberty.

32

TEN REASONS I'M GRATEFUL
TO BE AN AMERICAN

Originally published on October 3, 2017

I'm not proud to be an American—I'm grateful. I didn't do anything to become a citizen of this country. I was just born. But in appreciating America today, I feel like I'm a freak or something.

So many Americans hate America. Why? There's so much to love. Some would-be immigrants risk their lives to get here, so they might have a chance to enjoy the freedom we take for granted every single day.

Our schools and our media foster hatred against America. It's cool to bash America. You can see it in the now-regular pushback against the National Anthem and the flag at some of the football games.

But here are ten reasons I am thankful to live here:

1) America is more of an idea than a nationality, and it's a good idea. We are the proverbial melting pot of all sorts of nationalities.

Dr. Richard Land, president of Southern Evangelical Seminary, once told me in a television interview, "We're the only nation in the world that is a creedal nation. Every other nation in the world is tied to ethnicity. We're not; we're tied to ideas." We're a people that was not a people (1 Peter 2:10).

2) We are endowed by our Creator with certain unalienable rights.

Land went on to say that the ideas that animate this country "are embodied in the Declaration of Independence,... that all men are created equal and that they are endowed by their Creator with certain unalienable rights." Land continues, "So anybody can become an American in a way that you can't become a Frenchman or become a German. . . . That makes us unique in the world, and that creed is formed and shaped by the Puritans, by those who came here seeking religious freedom. As Martin Marty once said, 'We are a nation with the soul of a church.'"

3) Even when America doesn't live up to its creed stating that all men are created equal, we can correct those mistakes.

Knowing that man is sinful, the founding fathers built in mechanisms to correct our errors. Slavery was a terrible evil that our nation was able to constitutionally correct, after its most brutal and bloody war.

4) In America, we are all free to worship according to the dictates of our conscience (or to not worship at all). Religious freedom, though at risk in our day, is part of the very foundation of the nation.

Dr. Richard Land also said, "If you want to understand America, you have to go back to Massachusetts Bay, and you have to go back to Governor Winthrop. . . . We came here to be a shining city on a hill, the New Jerusalem, to light the way for the old world."

5) Although religious freedom is at risk today in America, it still exists for the most part. As Rev. Winthrop once said in a letter to his wife, after listing one challenge after another, "Here we worship Jesus Christ, and is that not enough?" Though tattered and torn, the First Amendment is still in place.

6) We have no fear of things like secret police coming knocking in the night to see if we have Bibles in our homes—Bibles that we plan to give away.

This actually happened to Harry Mihet, an attorney who grew up in communist Romania, who is working for Christ today in America. His family almost got in trouble for having Bibles for distribution, but they managed to outwit the secret police. Later, when he was about twelve and his family came to America, Harry was so excited that he kissed the ground of his newly adopted country.[1]

7) We have the right to provide a quality education for our children.

In many cases, we have to work harder to provide an alternative to the politically correct indoctrination of the government schools. But

---

1. "Vocal Point—Harry Mihet," *Jerry Newcombe*, May 21, 2015, jerrynewcombe.com.

those alternatives exist. For example, in America, we can legally home-school our children—in all fifty states.

8) We can make of our lives what we wish. We have the freedom to pursue our God-given dreams. Often we can find the means to fulfill them.

9) We have the freedom to choose the Congressmen and Senators we wish to represent us in this republic. If we don't like the current crop, we can vote in new ones. I see some people protesting Trump, holding signs saying, "He's not my president." Ironically, some of those protesters did not even vote.

10) We have the freedom to disagree with our government and voice our disagreement. We have the freedom to work and pray for positive change.

America is far from perfect. That's why the prayer in the hymn "America the Beautiful" is so appropriate: "America, America, God, mend thine every flaw." Praying for that and working together for the common good is far better than America-loathing and working to destroy the nation from within.

33

MEMORIAL DAY 2017:
"FREEDOM IS NOT BOUGHT CHEAPLY"

Originally published on May 24, 2017

Freedom, of course, is not free. It has been bought and paid for. The freedoms we enjoy in America are ours because of those who laid down their lives in service to our country. With another Memorial Day upon us, it's good to be reminded of the debt we owe to their sacrifice.

On Memorial Day 1982 at Arlington National Cemetery, Ronald Reagan said of those who died in service of our country, "Our first obligation to them and ourselves is plain enough: The United States and the freedom for which it stands, the freedom for which they died, must endure and prosper. Their lives remind us that freedom is not bought cheaply. It has a cost; it imposes a burden. And just as they whom we commemorate were willing to sacrifice, so too must we—in a less final, less heroic way—be willing to give of ourselves."

Frequently, during these Memorial Day services, a bugler performs "taps," often bringing a lump to the throat. There are slight variations on the lyrics associated with taps, but they all tend to end with the phrase, "God is nigh," that is, God is near. Here's a common rendition of the lyrics for taps:

Day is done, Gone the sun,
From the lake, From the hill,
From the sky.

All is well, Safely rest,
God is nigh.

Perhaps as the influence of Christianity has waned in the culture, so has the commitment to patriotism. Consider some remarks from our nation's founding:

One of our country's great founding fathers was Rev. John Witherspoon, the president of Princeton, who was a signer of the Declaration of Independence. Witherspoon said in a sermon entitled "The Dominion of Providence over the Passions of Men" (May 17, 1776), "It is in the man of piety and inward principle, that we may expect to find the uncorrupted patriot, the useful citizen, and the invincible soldier. God, grant that in America true religion and civil liberty may be inseparable and that the unjust attempts to destroy the one, may in the issue tend to the support and establishment of both" (Witherspoon 1778).

General George Washington, then the head of our armed forces, made a similar remark—and this was to his troops during the terrible winter at Valley Forge: "To the distinguished character of Patriot, it should be our highest Glory to laud the more distinguished Character of Christian."

In 1941, when FDR was president, he had a special edition of the New Testament by the Gideons issued to the military. My dad, who served in the Navy, got one. I got to keep it after he died. President Roosevelt wrote these words in the preface to that edition: "To the Armed Forces: As Commander-in-Chief, I take pleasure in commending the reading of the Bible to all who serve in the armed forces of the United States. Throughout the centuries men of many faiths and diverse origins have found in the Sacred Book words of wisdom, counsel and inspiration. It is a fountain of strength and now, as always, an aid in attaining the highest aspirations of the human soul."

It's hard to picture such a practice today. Now, we live in what Dr. Richard Land has called "the Divided States of America." I think that is an apt description. The late Charlton Heston once remarked, "Rank-and-file Americans wake up every morning, increasingly bewildered and confused at why their views make them lesser citizens."

Yet Reagan once told us, "Our Nation's motto—'In God We Trust'—was not chosen lightly. It reflects a basic recognition that there is a divine authority in the universe to which this nation owes homage. Throughout our history, Americans have put their faith in God, and no one can doubt that we have been blessed for it."

This Memorial Day, we should, if nothing else, thank the Lord for those who laid their lives on the line for us. We enjoy the freedom we enjoy because they shed their blood for us—reminiscent of the freedom the Christian enjoys because the Savior shed His blood for us at Calvary.

I like what Colin Powell said about this holiday: "All of us lead busy lives. We have little time to pause and reflect. But I ask of you: Do not hasten through Memorial Day. Take the time to remember the good souls whose memories are a blessing to you and your family. Take your children to our memorial parks and monuments. Teach them the values that lend meaning to our lives and to the life of our nation. Above all, take the time to honor our fellow Americans who have given their last full measure of devotion to our country and for the freedoms we cherish."

34

SAUL ALINSKY WOULD BE PROUD

Originally published on June 25, 2014

The Tenth Amendment says, "The powers not delegated to the United States by the Constitution, nor prohibited by it to the States, are reserved to the States respectively, or to the people." But Barack Obama says, I've got a pen and I've got a phone, and I can do what I want. Not the states, not the people, but Me, Myself, and I.

Every week there seems to be a new scandal du jour for this administration. Although the president famously said there's not a "smidgen of a scandal" involving the IRS (which allegedly targeted conservative and Christian groups), we know now that the critical emails of Lois Lerner are not only apparently lost, but the hard drives were destroyed. Every day of this administration, Richard Nixon looks more and more like a Sunday school teacher.

Congress voted against the Dream Act, but the president is bypassing Congress. This has sent signals to thousands south of the border, who are uprooting themselves and their families to try to get a chance at the American dream. No matter the human cost for these families (as hundreds have died attempting perilous crossings). This just means more votes for the Progressive movement.

Then there are advances of the Islamic radicals under this president. The Arab Spring spells out death for Christians and moderate Muslims alike in nations like Egypt, Libya, and Syria. Christians are also on the run in Iraq, where the gains of the past eleven years seem to be lost. And there could be another eventual 9/11 attack in the making on U.S. soil.

Obamacare passed only because of the president's promise to pro-life Democrats not to fund abortions, but now, through the HHS mandate, businesses and organizations must cover abortion services or the government could fine them out of business (e.g., Hobby Lobby), conscience be darned.

Then there's the V.A. scandal, where former soldiers have died while waiting for care after allegedly being placed on phony waiting lists, and meanwhile those responsible have received huge bonuses. The captives in Gitmo (the ones left) get better medical care than the approximately twenty million veterans through the V.A. system. Just another scandal in the Obama administration.

Not to sound conspiratorial, but one has to wonder if some of these scandals aren't by design.

I think it's helpful to look at one of Barack Obama's indirect mentors. I say indirect because Saul Alinsky (1909–1972) died long before the future president arrived in Chicago, Alinsky's home. Saul Alinsky was a community organizer and the father of the modern community-organizer movement. In fact, he wrote the book for community organizers: *Rules for Radicals* (1971).

In his 2010 book for Truth in Action Ministries, *Radical Rulers: The White House Elites Who Are Pushing America Toward Socialism,* journalist Robert Knight writes, "A 'community organizer' since at least the 1920s, Alinsky had schooled countless young idealistic reformers in the arts of obtaining political power in order to promote various left-wing causes." (Knight 2010, 44).

Here is what Alinsky wrote in the dedication page of his book: "Lest we forget at least an over-the-shoulder acknowledgement to the very first radical; from all our legends, mythology, and history (and who is to know where mythology leaves off and history begins—or which is which). The first radical known to man who rebelled against the establishment and did it so effectively that he at least won his own kingdom—Lucifer." After pointing out that "Alinsky saluted Satan as his inspiration," Knight notes: "And a devilish business it is since Alinsky's primer is all about using deception, manipulation and raw power to bring about a communistic future." (Knight 2010, 44).

A committed Marxist, Alinsky grew up in a rough part of Chicago and worked hard to implement social justice—as he understood it. He believed that the ends justified the means. He said the community organizer is "a political relativist." (Alinsky 1971, 11) Author Bill Federer said, "This idea that Saul Alinsky adopted is: You're convinced your agenda is so good, any means necessary to get there is okay—lying, voter fraud, intimidation, bribery, threats, anything."

Obama studied Alinsky and is reported to have taught Alinsky's views. David Alinsky, Saul's son, has spoken of "Barack Obama's training in Chicago by the great community organizers." Saul Alinsky's influence helped create ACORN—ostensibly dedicated to mobilizing more minority votes. Successful lawsuits against ACORN have found it to be guilty of subverting the electoral process.

While many people want to resolve conflict and controversy, Saul Alinksy relished it as a way to achieve power. He stated, "First rule of change is controversy. Change means movement, and movement means friction and friction means heat and heat means controversy."

Saul Alinsky also believed that you could achieve your radical goals by demonizing the opposition. He states: "Pick the target, freeze it, personalize it, and polarize it. The real action is in the enemy's reaction. The enemy properly goaded and guided in his reaction will be your major strength. Tactics, like life, require that you move with the action."

While seemingly caring about the poor, critics note that what Saul Alinsky and his followers really want is political power, and they will use any means necessary to seize it. Tragically, reading *Rules for Radicals* is like reading the playbook for the Obama administration, as the president is engaged in "fundamentally transforming" the United States.

35

OUR LAWLESS PRESIDENT OPENS THE BORDERS

Originally published on July 16, 2014

Our founders based our nation on the rule of law. But now lawlessness is becoming the rule. One of the Bible's definitions for sin fits here: "Sin is lawlessness" (1 John 3:4).

The border crisis is a strong case in point. Congress said no to the DREAM Act, but the president has a phone and a pen, and he says yes. So now tens of thousands of young people are pouring in through our porous southern borders in hopes of having a chance at the American dream—a dream eluding many already here.

During this administration, there has been a decrease in border enforcement. Therefore, people from south of the border have been encouraged to take advantage of the opportunity. Writing for *The Daily Caller* (July 14, 2014), Neil Munro points out: "If you came illegally to the U.S. seeking asylum in 2013, you had better than a four-in-five chance of successfully filing an asylum claim." The title of Munro's column says it all: "Leaked Data Shows 10-Fold Increase In Obama's Asylum Approvals."

Meanwhile, CBSDC (July 14, 2014) quotes Homeland Security Secretary Jeh Johnson as saying, "Our border is not open to illegal immigration." But actions speak louder than words. The news source adds that Jeh Johnson "said staff told him that some of the immigrants [at a holding center] told them they were surprised to be detained." Some sources are even noting that many of the "children" are fourteen- to seventeen-year-old males, some with ties to the notorious MS-13 gang.

Central American families are being separated and uprooted. Diseases are running rampant. It's a humanitarian crisis. What is this current border meltdown all about? It seems to me:

- For the Democrats, it's all about more voters. It's all about their political base. To paraphrase George Bernard Shaw, if you rob Peter to pay Paul, you will have always have Paul's vote.
- For the Republicans (the country-club type, not the values voters), it's all about cheap labor. Some big corporations and mega-wealthy businessmen clamor for the same thing.

This is a nation built on immigration, and the Bible tells us to be kind to the stranger and foreigner amongst us. Lest you dismiss me as a xenophobic bigot, please note that I have nothing—zero, zip, nada—against legal immigrants. In fact, I'm married to one. She played by all the right rules. It was not an easy process, but it was doable. When we got married in 1980 in her home country (Norway), we were both grad students about to finish our course work in the states.

When we tried to return to the U.S., she was not allowed to go with me until I could prove I had a source of income. I postponed my studies, got a job and proof of income, and she was able to join me about a month later. She eventually became an American citizen.

Fast-forward to 2014 and our current border crisis. The president has sent repeated signals to illegal immigrants that we have all kinds of free stuff available here. For example, one source reported that the Obama administration reached an agreement with the Mexican government to run radio ads promoting American food stamps.

But there's no such thing as a free lunch. Someone has to pay for it. Many of us have to hold down two jobs to keep up with our expenses. Will we now have to take on a third job to pay for the social services for all the illegals? Open borders and our growing welfare state seem to be on a collision course. How can we afford to have open borders without true welfare reform?

As a Christian, I have deep compassion for those seeking a better life. Writing for *The Gospel Coalition* (July 11, 2014), Felix Cabrera captures the dilemma well: "Crossing the border between Mexico and the

United States without the proper permission certainly violates the law, and we must not ignore this fact. We are not encouraging parents to send their children to the United States. It is not only illegal, it is also dangerous, putting their children's lives at risk."

He adds, "However, we need to ask, 'Why do these parents feel the need to send their children to the [U.S.]?' . . . We must understand that in many Latin American countries violence is rampant and governments are corrupt. Too often, parents cannot find sufficient work, and there is not enough food to feed their children. . . . Parents are desperate for a better future for their children."

Any of us can understand that. And this humanitarian crisis gives a great opportunity for the church to help these people caught in the middle, and many churches are helping.

But that doesn't mean that encouraging dangerous illegal immigration is morally the right thing for the president to do—encouraging all this suffering and upheaval—just to achieve a political goal.

As a friend of mine put it, "Lawlessness is the issue here, and it's negatively affecting both the immigrants and the border states—and ultimately all of us."

36

THE ESSENCE OF LIBERALISM

Originally published on June 10, 2014

As the fallout from the swap of Bowe Bergdahl for five Taliban prisoners of war continues to reverberate, one MSNBC host made a fascinating statement on the subject. On "Now with Alexander Wagner" (June 4, 2014), the MSNBC host said she hoped the swap leads to "broader negotiations" with the Taliban. (Hat tip to newsbusters.org).

"Broader negotiations" with the terroristic Taliban? Reasoning with those who have proven themselves incapable of humane reasoning?

This got me to thinking: What is the essence of liberalism? Is it elitism—the notion that big government can take better care of you and yours than you can? Is the essence of liberalism the abolition of private property? Is it that people should have the freedom to do whatever they want to, to define their own right and wrong?

I think all these things are corollaries, no doubt. But in my view, the essence of liberalism begins with a flawed premise—a flawed anthropology—that says that man is basically good. In the liberal view, we can negotiate with the Taliban—even though they want to kill us unless we convert to their brand of Islam—because deep down they're good.

In 1938, British Prime Minister Neville Chamberlain could proudly declare that there would be "peace in our time," because he had the signature of "Herr Hitler" to prove it. Subsequent events in World War II proved him stupendously wrong.

The problem of liberalism is that it doesn't recognize the Biblical truth, proven repeatedly in history, that man is sinful and that the best form of government recognizes that and therefore separates power so that no individual or oligarchy can amass too much of it. Why has America historically succeeded in granting us freedom? It's because the founding fathers recognized this fact. They did everything in their power to limit how much power any one man or group of people might have.

James Madison played an important role in the writing of our Constitution. He noted that since men are not angels, government is necessary. But—again—men are not angels, and since government is run by men, we also need protection *from* the government (*Federalist* #51). Belief in the sinfulness of man can be seen in the Constitution with its strict separation of powers.

The Bible is very clear. It does not teach that we are perfect, but rather that we are sinful. Jesus said, "If you then, though you are evil..." (Matthew 7:11). Paul said, "There is no one who does good, not even one" (Romans 3:11). Jeremiah noted, "The heart is deceitful above all things and beyond cure. Who can understand it?" (Jeremiah 17:9).

Mankind tends toward evil. Therefore, power must be separated. I am not aware of a single example among the founders of America who believed that man is basically good. This is not cynical. It's just the reality and has led to the most prosperous forms of government—and of economics too.

Like the other founders, Thomas Jefferson said that power should be divided for everybody's sake: "The way to have good and safe government is not to trust it all to one, but to divide it among the many." No oligarch using his phone and pen there.

James Madison said, "All men having power ought not to be trusted."

Ben Franklin said, "There is scarce a king in a hundred who would not, if he could, follow the example of Pharaoh, get first all the peoples' money, then all their lands and then make them and their children servants forever."

Alexander Hamilton wrote, "'Til the millennium [Jesus's reign on earth] comes, in spite of all our boasted light and purification, hypocrisy and treachery will continue to be the most successful commodities in the political market."

In the early twentieth century, Christian apologist G. K. Chesterton once wrote a letter to his newspaper on "What's Wrong with the World?" His essay contained only two words: "I am."

There's a link between correct anthropology and good government. Those governments like that of the U.S. (as the founders envisioned it), have given freedom because the founders acknowledged man's corrupt nature.

As an opposite example, the former Soviet Union built their system of government on an atheistic, Marxist base—on the notion that man is basically good, but corrupted by capitalism and religion. Marx thought that when the workers seized the means of production and the reins of government and imposed the worker state, then government would become unnecessary and wither away. So the new Soviet man or woman was to be free from religious superstitions and from the curse of selfishness as found in capitalism with its emphasis on private property. Who created a better system? The communists or America's founders? The answer is obvious.

Note what Roger Baldwin, the founder and long-time head of the ACLU, once said in his official biography: "I believe, generally speaking, that the human race is fundamentally good in the sense that people want to get along with each other. And if you think that people are good and can live by the Golden Rule, and you have faith in them as I do, then you believe that social relations are perfectible. Therefore, you can have a government that works without conflict and a society that is not bent on self-destruction. Now when you cast it on a world scale—you believe in the same thing—the capacity of people of all nations and colors and races to get along with each other and to create a world order."[1] Baldwin's sympathies were not hidden. He once said, "Communism is the goal." Many have shared Baldwin's utopian vision—and it has been a nightmare.

Historian Paul Johnson said that the twentieth-century state, in large part because of communism (which asserted the basic goodness of humanity), has proven to be the greatest killer of all time.

No wonder God sent a Savior to save us from our sins. Meanwhile, we should take into consideration man's nature as it really is, and not as it should be according to someone's flawed playbook.

---

1. Peggy Lamson, *Roger Baldwin: Founder of the American Civil Liberties Union* (Boston, MA: Houghton Mifflin Company, 1976), 64.

37

GEORGE WASHINGTON'S WARNING TO AMERICA

Originally published on June 2, 2014

Washington envisioned an America where people of all faiths could enjoy peace. He wrote to the synagogue in Newport (August 14, 1790): "May the children of the Stock of Abraham, who dwell in this land, continue to merit and enjoy the good will of the other inhabitants, while every one shall sit in safety under his own vine and fig-tree, and there shall be none to make him afraid."

And he also spoke of the need as a nation to ultimately imitate the Savior. For example, after the British surrender at Yorktown in 1781, George Washington, the Commander-in-Chief of the Continental Army, wrote a famous letter to the governors of the thirteen states. This was in June 1783, and it is called the Circular to the States. At the end of that letter, he offered a prayer—a prayer that today is politically incorrect in part because of its reference to Jesus. He said that we can't be a happy nation unless we imitate Him. This is exactly how he worded it:

> I now make it my earnest prayer, that God would have you, and the State over which you preside, in his holy protection, that he would incline the hearts of the Citizens to cultivate a spirit of subordination and obedience to Government, to entertain a brotherly affection and love for one another, for their fellow Citizens of the United States at large, and particularly for their brethren who have served in the Field.

Washington went on in his "earnest prayer" to mention Jesus (whom he calls "the Divine Author of our blessed Religion"), in this way:

And finally, that he would most graciously be pleased to dispose us all, to do Justice, to love mercy, and to demean ourselves with that Charity, humility and pacific temper of mind, which were the Characteristics of the Divine Author of our blessed Religion, and without an humble imitation of whose example in these things, we can never hope to be a happy Nation. (Rhodehamel 1997, 526)

Let's break this down into modern English.

He is praying that God would be pleased to protect each state and that He would allow citizens to obey the state and to love one another and to especially care for those fellow Americans who "served in the Field," i.e., the soldiers who have made our freedom possible.

Then he echoes the words of Micah 6:8 (from the Old Testament): "He hath shewed thee, O man, what is good; and what doth the Lord require of thee, but to *do justly*, and to *love mercy*, and to walk *humbly* with thy God?" (KJV, emphasis mine). Washington prays that our citizens will: *do justice, love mercy*, show the love, *humility*, and peacefulness of Christ. If we do not humbly imitate Jesus's example, says Washington, "we can never hope to be a happy Nation."

Thus, one of the great things we can learn from the father of our nation is that the more the nation imitates Jesus, the happier we will be.

This is not the only place where George Washington spoke of the importance of imitating Christ. For example, one time a delegation of Delaware Indian Chiefs came to ask him how their young men could learn from the ways of the British settlers. This was in 1779. Washington told them, as we've seen, "You do well to wish to learn our arts and ways of life, and above all, the religion of Jesus Christ." He added an interesting post-script to his message: "Congress will do everything they can to assist you in this wise intention."

But surely this flies in the face of the "separation of church and state," someone may object.

The idea of the separation of church and state (especially the separation of God and state) was not the prevailing view during the founding era. It is more of a recent invention. The founders did not want any one Christian denomination "by law established" to be our national state-church. They certainly didn't want atheism (essentially unknown to the vast majority of them) to be our national "religion."

It's well known that today you can hold up Christians—evangelicals, fundamentalists, or Catholics—to ridicule, but virtually no other subgroup. In fact, it's now my opinion that liberals who oppose prejudice, racism, and bigotry of any kind actually believe that it is bigoted to *not* treat conservative Christians with bigotry.

In other words, their understanding of tolerance demands that they be intolerant of Christians. In short, they abhor bigotry of any kind, except when it applies to conservative Christians, who, they believe, somehow deserve to be discriminated against.

Question: Are we imitating Jesus as a nation, as the father of our country recommended? No. Next question: Are we a happy nation? No. Any questions?

38

THE GOD FACTOR—AMERICA'S KEY TO SUCCESS

Originally published on July 2, 2014

Two hundred thirty-eight years ago, on July 4, 1776, our founding fathers voted to affirm a revolutionary document—the Declaration of Independence. Since that time, there have been numerous other political revolutions. Most have failed miserably and ended in bloodshed and chaos, with conditions worse than before.

The French Revolution, the Bolshevik Revolution, Hitler's National Socialistic takeover of Germany, Mao's communist uprising in China, Ho Chi Minh's victory in Vietnam, Castro's Cuba, and Pol Pot's revolution in Cambodia all produced incredible bloodshed. Why have all these experiments in forced socialism failed? The great historian Paul Johnson notes in his book *The Quest for God* that all the failed totalitarian regimes of the twentieth century were "godless constructs."

So why was the American Revolution different than normal revolutions, which usually end in bloodbaths? The founders had a revolution, but it was very different than secular revolutions, such as the Marxist takeovers with their unending bloodshed.

When there is no God to whom we must give an account, then the state can become god. That was certainly true in the minds of many a totalitarian dictator. For example, Hitler was dismayed when one of his generals surrendered rather than face certain slaughter for himself and his army. Hitler would have seen the man commit suicide and the army destroyed rather than surrender. He said, "What is Life? Life is the Nation. The individual must die anyway.... What hurts me most, personally, is that I . . . promoted him to field marshal." (Antony Beevor, *Stalingrad*, 1998, 392).

"What is Life?" Life is a privilege given to us by a loving Creator. The founding fathers, even the few who may not have personally known the Creator through a relationship with Christ, had a Christian worldview and life view. As Donald S. Lutz, author of *The Origins of American Constitutionalism* (1988), once told me, the founders knew the Bible "down to their fingertips." From the founders' perspective, the God who gave us life gave us liberty at the same time, to paraphrase Jefferson. The purpose of government is to protect and secure those God-given rights, not to trample on them—as the King of England ("the Royal Brute") had so often done.

So why did the founders' revolution succeed? The answer is because they saw God as a major, irreplaceable part of the whole process. Men must answer to God for their action. The God factor is the key to America's success.

Michael Novak of American Enterprise Institute writes, "The dogmatic atheism of the continental Enlightenment and of German historicism left their proponents stranded on the shoals of tyrannical fanaticism—from Robespierre to Pol Pot."

The Declaration of Independence, our nation's birth certificate, mentions God four times:

- "The Laws of Nature and Nature's God"
- "All men are created equal, that they are endowed by their Creator with certain unalienable rights"
- "Appealing to the Supreme Judge of the World for the Rectitude of our Intentions"
- "With a firm Reliance on the Protection of Divine Providence"

Some want to say that the founders were not necessarily talking about the Christian God. Historian Rod Gragg, author of *Forged in Faith* and *By the Hand of Providence,* disagrees. He once told me, "I think when you look at the founding fathers, it's not really a question of how many of them are Christians. . . . The evidence on that is very clear. You can look at church membership and you can look at their writings and see that. The bigger question is, whom did they represent? And they represented the American people in the colonial era, and American culture in the colonial era was overwhelmingly Judeo-Christian in its worldview."

Because of the Christian roots in America, people of all faiths or no faith are welcome here. Thus, the God-factor is the key to America's success.

But someone might say, what about the God-factor in an Islamic state, like Iran or Saudi Arabia? When Muslims control a government, they actively seek to implement strict sharia law, which leads to a lack of freedom, especially for non-Muslims. Christians, on the other hand, strongly believe in freedom of conscience in religious matters within a basic moral framework shaped by the Ten Commandments. And indeed, that's the system the founding fathers gave to us.

As noted before, President Eisenhower said in 1955, "Without God, there could be no American form of Government, nor an American way of life. Recognition of the Supreme Being is the first—the most basic—expression of Americanism."

When you see the skies light up on the Fourth of July, remember that God has been a key part of America's history.

39

AMERICA'S 225TH BIRTHDAY—APRIL 30

Originally published on April 30, 2014

Two hundred twenty-five years ago, on April 30, 1789, George Washington, the first president under the Constitution, was sworn in with his hand on a gigantic open Bible. He leaned over and kissed the book. Many today say he was not really a Christian. But what does the evidence show? And why does it matter?

Let me answer the second question first. To paraphrase Woodrow Wilson, a nation that doesn't remember where it came from doesn't know where it is or where it is going. In that same speech, Wilson said we were born as a Christian nation. I would add, because of that fact, people of all faiths or no faith are welcome here. But we should honor the faith that helped shape the country.

The rest of this column deals with the first question. In the book on the faith of George Washington that I cowrote with Dr. Peter Lillback, we document that Washington was a devout eighteenth-century Anglican and not a deist, as some revisionists say.

Recently, I visited Mount Vernon, the home of our nation's famous first president. I was thrilled to see that the bookstore carried many copies of our book. George and Martha Washington's red-roofed estate sits on a hill overlooking the Potomac River and is perhaps the most famous and visited home in America. If you know where to look and what to look for, you can see many reminders of Washington's devout faith.

At Mount Vernon, they have a re-creation of George's pew from Pohick Church, which is in Lorton, Virginia. Washington not only at-

tended weekly services earlier in his life at this box-shaped, red-brick
Anglican church, he also served there as a Vestryman—an Anglican version of an elder and a deacon rolled into one. Other replicas from Pohick Church at Mount Vernon include miniatures of the cross and two
sections of the *reredos*. The reredos (pronounced RARE-uh-doss) was a
large plaque bearing the words of the Lord's Prayer, the Ten Commandments, and the Apostles' Creed, with its affirmation of the Trinity, often
placed behind the altar in colonial Anglican churches. The congregation
would rise and recite these things together. There were reredoses not
only in the churches regularly attended by Washington, but also in those
attended by Patrick Henry, James Madison, and even Thomas Jefferson.

I personally have seen reredoses in churches in Williamsburg, Alexandria, Philadelphia, New York City (at St. Paul's Chapel), and Providence, Rhode Island. There are many churches in the East where it can
be truly claimed, "George Washington worshiped here."

At Mount Vernon, you can see Washington's "chariot," the red horse-
drawn carriage with which he would routinely travel several miles (on
muddy roads) to Christ Church in Alexandria in the last several years
of his life. This was the church where his funeral was eventually held.

Washington is buried on the grounds of Mount Vernon. Behind
the sarcophagi of Martha and George are the words of Jesus from John
11:25–26, written in stone. It says, "I am the resurrection, and the life:
he that believeth in me, though he were dead, yet shall he live: And
whosoever liveth and believeth in me shall never die" (KJV).

As to his faith, Nellie, the granddaughter whom he and Martha
reared, said that to question his Christianity, you might as well question his patriotism.

Washington said that only by the hand of God was he able to ac-
complish what he did. He referred to God as "God" some one hundred times in speeches and letters. In addition, he used many respectful
terms for God, such as the great governor of the universe, the invisible
hand, etc., in baroque (i.e., decorated) language, similar to many other
Christians of his day. Dr. Lillback notes that he also referred to Providence (a fancy name for God) some 270 times.

After George Washington was sworn in 225 years ago in the then-cap-
ital, New York City, he led everyone to nearby St. Paul's Chapel (where

they also have a reredos) for a two-hour worship service, including Holy Communion, to implore God's help. Witnesses say he himself participated in the Lord's Supper.

I could go on and on, but our 1,200-page book documents the case thoroughly (Lillback and Newcombe, *George Washington's Sacred Fire*, 2006).

Even though April 30, 1789, marks the beginning of our nation, with Washington serving as the first president under the Constitution, we actually had another first president, not well known to most of us. In 1781, the first president was sworn in under the Articles of Confederation. His name was John Hanson, and I've seen a memorial to him in a Lutheran church in Philadelphia, honoring him as our first president. As was often done, there was "A Proclamation for a Day of Thanksgiving" issued by John Hanson, president of the Continental Congress, on October 11, 1782.

The Articles of Confederation was our nation's first Constitution, but it was so unworkable that the founders met in the summer of 1787 to amend it. They ended up deciding to start all over. Hence, the Constitution.

I believe that America has been blessed by God. But as Washington warned us in his First Inaugural Address, how can we expect His continued blessings if we disregard the rules of right and wrong that heaven itself has ordained? Rules such as the Ten Commandments seen on the reredoses.

40

WHO DIED AND MADE THE
SUPREME COURT GOD?

Originally published on July 3, 2018

To hear some on the Left tell it, you would think that with the retirement of Supreme Court Justice Anthony Kennedy, America is finished as a nation. One such person tweeted, "Literally in tears. Haven't felt this hopeless in a long time. With Justice Kennedy leaving, we now have two options as Americans: get fitted for your Nazi uniform or report directly to your death camp. How do you fight the darkness without light? My spark is going out."[1]

California Senator Kamala Harris said that Trump's replacement for Kennedy (whoever that will be—unknown as of this writing) means the "destruction of the Constitution of the United States."

These sentiments are terribly wrong on so many fronts. The founders created an experiment where "we the people" would govern ourselves. But in recent decades the high court has taken upon itself more power than King George III could possibly have lusted after. In fact, the swing voter on the Supreme Court, the now-retiring Anthony Kennedy, often experienced such power.

But the founders clearly felt that both a monarchy and an oligarchy (the rule by a few) were tyrannical. James Madison, a key architect of the Constitution, put it this way: "The accumulation of all powers, legislative, executive, and judiciary, in the same hands, whether of one,

---

1. Dean Garrison, "Thousands #WalkAway From Democrat Party," *Freedom Outpost*, June 28, 2018, freedomoutpost.com.

a few, or many, and whether hereditary, self-appointed, or elective, may justly be pronounced the very definition of tyranny." However, through the years, we have experienced the Supreme Court virtually governing our lives, and we assume that's the way it is supposed to be.

Consider what the courts, especially the Supreme Court, have ushered in during the last several decades by legislating (not adjudicating) from the bench:

- Pornography on demand, *Roth v. United States* (1957) and *Miller v. California* (1973).
- No school prayer allowed, *Engel v. Vitale* (1962) and *Murray v. Curlette* (1963).
- No official Bible reading of a devotional nature in schools, *Abbington v. Schempp* (1963).
- Abortion on demand, through *Roe v. Wade* (1973), which dissenting Justice Byron White called an act of "raw judicial power." Justices based *Roe* on a series of lies. Before she died, the "Roe" in this case, Norma McCorvey, became a pro-life activist and tried in vain to get the case overturned.
- No Ten Commandments to be posted in the schools, *Stone v. Graham* (1980). They actually said in that decision: "If the posted copies of the Ten Commandments are to have any effect at all, it will be to induce the schoolchildren to read, meditate upon, perhaps to venerate and obey, the Commandments. However desirable this might be as a matter of private devotion, it is not a permissible state objective under the Establishment Clause."
- No equal time for creation science in the classroom, *Edwards v. Aguilard* (1987).
- States are not free (as in the case of Colorado) to prohibit the granting of special legal rights to homosexuals, *Romer v. Evans* (1996).
- States are not free (as in the case of Texas) to outlaw sodomy, *Lawrence v. Texas* (2003). The Massachusetts Supreme Court cited this decision when it took the next logical step and granted the right to same-sex marriage.
- Same-sex marriage is supposedly the law of the land, *Oberge-*

fell v. Hodges (2015). In their hubris, the Supreme Court actually thought they could redefine what marriage is, thus overturning millennia of marriage traditions all over the world in virtually every culture. Anthony Kennedy wrote that decision, as he did the *Lawrence* decision, which was a precursor to it.

- Colleges (or law schools, as in this case) are free to oust a Christian group from campus if it will not allow for homosexuals to be among their leaders, *Martinez v. Hastings* (2010).

And on it goes....

Yet, the Supreme Court is supposed to interpret the Constitution and evaluate whether a certain law being challenged does or does not pass Constitutional muster. The justices are not supposed to just dream about what they think the Constitution should say. In the history of the world, America has enjoyed the stability of the Constitution, which was predicated on our God-given rights, as seen in the Declaration of Independence.

Ronald Reagan put it this way: "In this country of ours took place the greatest revolution that has ever taken place in world's history.... Every other revolution simply exchanged one set of rulers for another. But here for the first time in all the thousands of years of man's relation to man, a little group of the men, the founding fathers—for the first time—established the idea that you and I had within ourselves the God-given right and ability to determine our own destiny."

Instead, activist courts, taking on more power than they ought to have under the Constitution, have helped turn America into a moral swamp.

41

A CHRISTIAN RESPONSE TO FERGUSON

Originally published on August 20, 2014

When will the rioting in Ferguson, Missouri, end? There has been much mayhem—including the use of tear gas by police—and much looting in the St. Louis suburb. The media covers this story heavily. Some estimate there may be as many media members on the scene as there are protesters.

All of this follows the shooting death of a black teenager, Michael Brown, allegedly by a white police officer, the previous Saturday (August 9, 2014). Though the facts are sketchy, many are convinced that an injustice has been done.

The reaction has created an additional crisis. Reports indicate that thugs from all over have descended on Ferguson to take advantage of the chaos, to get "justice" "by any means necessary." How? By looting small-shop owners out of business? By changing Ferguson into a war zone? Said C. S. Lewis, "The devil is always trying to trick us to extremes."

Here we are at fifty-one years to the month (August 28, 1963) after Rev. Martin Luther King Jr. articulated his vision for a color-blind society, and some things seem to be worse. "I have a dream..."

Surely, America has made great progress in its race problem since the night in 1955 when Rev. King hosted a meeting in the basement of his Dexter Avenue Baptist Church in Montgomery, Alabama, to deal with the crisis of Rosa Parks's arrest for not giving up her seat to a white man. That meeting led to a successful nonviolent bus boycott and launched the civil rights movement.

Dr. King said in 1955, "If you will protest courageously, and yet with dignity and Christian love, when the history books are written in future generations, the historians will have to pause and say, 'There lived a great people—a black people—who injected new meaning and dignity into the veins of civilization.' This is our challenge and our overwhelming responsibility."[1]

He also quoted Booker T. Washington, a premier leader of African-Americans after the Civil War, who said, "Let no man pull you so low as to make you hate him."

King sought to lead the civil rights movement in a nonviolent way. As noted before, he said in 1963, "We must meet hate with creative love.... Let us hope there will be no more violence. But if the streets must flow with blood let it flow with our blood in the spirit of Jesus Christ on the cross."[2]

Fast forward to today. How are we doing overall on the racism front? America elected and reelected the first African-American president, something virtually unimaginable in Dr. King's time. Yet the incident in Ferguson shows that deep divides remain.

Many of us strive to live up to the Biblical ideal expressed in Acts 17:26: "From one man he made every nation of men, that they should inhabit the whole earth." Biblically, there is no basis for racism. Obviously, Christians have not always lived up to that ideal.

On the other hand, committed Christians have been among the most ardent opponents of racism. Consider William Wilberforce of England, the longtime Member of Parliament, whose lifelong crusade ended slavery in the British Empire.

Watch raw tape of civil-rights marches and activities in the 1950s and 1960s some time. It was a religious movement, with leaders from all sorts of Christian denominations. King himself was president of the Southern Christian Leadership Conference.

In reference to the present crisis in Ferguson, Martin Luther King's niece, Dr. Alveda King, has called for calm and prayer. In a press release sent out by *Christian Newswire* (August 12, 2014), she says, "To burn down gas stations, loot and steal and rampage local business es-

1. Montgomery, Alabama, December, 1955.
2. Birmingham, Alabama, May 1963.

tablishments won't bring Michael back, to his family or to our hurting world."

She adds, "This painful incident brings to mind my father Rev. A. D. King in Birmingham, Alabama in 1963 when our home was fire bombed by rabid racists. The people were angry and wanted to riot. Daddy stood on the hood of a car with a megaphone and calmed the people. This is not the time to riot. This is the time to pray. Please, protest, stand up for our rights, but do this with nonviolence!"

And she said, "In memory of my father and in honor to God, I urge nonviolence in the demand for justice of Michael's death. This is not the time to burn, this is the time to turn our prayers towards heaven and seek nonviolent and just solutions to what has happened to Michael."

Alveda King once told me that the real issue is spiritual: "We were founded as a nation under God. And today, we have become lawless, and we're running away from God, and we're letting the government and other institutions replace the Creator by the created, and that's the problem."

As long as we continue to forget God as a nation and evildoers take advantage of the ensuing chaos, it is hard to see how we can move closer to Dr. King's vision of a color-blind society.

42

ROBERT E. LEE AND GOD'S JUDGMENT ON A NATION GONE ASTRAY

Originally published on April 22, 2015

April 2015 marks the 150th anniversary of Robert E. Lee's surrender to Ulysses S. Grant, effectively ending the U.S. Civil War, the bloodiest conflict our nation ever witnessed.

A new book on Lee is a great read. It's called *The Man Who Would Not Be Washington: Robert E. Lee's Civil War and His Decision that Changed American History* (2015). The book is by Jonathan Horn, a former presidential speechwriter for George W. Bush.

Although I thought I knew many things about Lee, I learned much more through the book. It's the kind of book that keeps you up at night. Interestingly, Robert E. Lee has been described as "the marble man," noble and unyielding like a statue. This book certainly shows the marble man had feet of clay.

I enjoyed having Horn on my radio show recently.[1] He clarified the point that the "civil war" referred to in the subtitle was Lee's own conflict—his personal civil war if you will—over which side to serve.

While Lee viewed secession with horror and the union with honor, he ultimately asked, "How can I draw my sword upon Virginia, my native state?" He could not. Once Virginia chose to secede from the Union in 1861, with it went Robert E. Lee.

Lee is interesting because he was seemingly a man of contradictions. Because of legal obligations, before the Emancipation Proclamation he

---

1. "Vocal Point—Jonathan Horn," *Jerry Newcombe*, April 5, 2015, jerrynewcombe.com.

freed the slaves he and his wife inherited from her father. As a Christian, he hated slavery, yet he ended up fighting essentially for its continuance. He favored the Union, yet he chose to apply his incredible military skill to the side that was dissolving the Union.

If he had been born just a few miles north, we could possibly have had President Robert E. Lee. But he wasn't, and we didn't. Ironically, as Horn points out, President Grant once hosted his former nemesis to a short social meeting in the White House several years after the war.

One friend of mine said years ago that Robert E. Lee had more character in his little pinky than most men have in their whole bodies. How then could he have chosen to serve the South?

If God led him—and I think this book amply shows that once Lee was converted he tried to deny himself and to do what he understood the Lord wanted him to do—how then could he have been the ultimate leader of the armies of the Confederacy? My personal answer to this spiritual question comes from President Lincoln, who greatly and rightly feared Robert E. Lee. He stated that it was possible that the war was God's judgment on a nation that had neglected Him and knowingly engaged in disobedience.

The month before Lee's surrender, Lincoln delivered his Second Inaugural Address, which Professor Daniel Dreisbach noted has forty-five Biblical allusions, references, or quotes. It's a terrific speech and only about seven hundred words.

Said Lincoln, "Fondly do we hope—fervently do we pray—that this mighty scourge of war may speedily pass away. Yet, if God wills that it continue until all the wealth piled by the bondsman's two hundred and fifty years of unrequited toil shall be sunk, and until every drop of blood drawn by the lash shall be paid by another drawn with the sword, as was said three thousand years ago, so still it must be said, 'The judgments of the Lord are true and righteous altogether.'"

Gary Bauer summarizes Lincoln's point: "Slavery was a violation of America's promise that all are created equal. Lincoln worried that the Civil War would last until God had extracted as much blood from the North and the South as had the slave master's lash."[2]

---

2. Gary Bauer, "End of Day Report," *American Values*, April 16, 2015, ouramericanvalues.org.

If Lincoln's speculation is correct, what does that say about our nation today? One shudders. Just take one notable example: abortion. We have killed more than 55 million unborn babies in the name of "choice." What choice did those babies have—or in many cases, even the mothers (or fathers) themselves? Jefferson once said, "I tremble for my country when I reflect that God is just; that his justice cannot sleep forever."

History has some sobering lessons for a wayward nation. Perhaps Robert E. Lee was essentially a sword in the hands of the Lord to punish a country that should have known better. Quoting Lincoln again, "With malice toward none, with charity for all, with firmness in the right as God gives us to see the right," may God help us today to get back on the right track.

43

COMMENTING ON THE TRAGEDY
IN CHARLOTTESVILLE

Originally published on August 16, 2017

On a sunny morning in the summer of 2012, I visited Charlottesville, Virginia, Thomas Jefferson's hometown. My host was a local pastor, Dr. Mark Beliles. He and I were working on a book entitled *Doubting Thomas* on the faith (and sometimes lack thereof) of our third president. Beliles took me to two parks downtown on that peaceful day and showed me two statues that he said were shrouded in controversy, although they have stood for a hundred years. They were of Robert E. Lee and Stonewall Jackson.

Fast-forward to this past weekend, and the scene was anything but peaceful. The protests centered around the Robert E. Lee statue, apparently slated for dismantling. Protesters for and against the statue clashed in ugly violence. A twenty-year-old reportedly Hitler-loving racist from Ohio allegedly drove his car into a crowd of counterprotesters and killed a thirty-two-year-old woman and maimed others. Our thoughts and prayers are with the victims and families.

After this awful melee, President Trump said (August 14, 2017): "We condemn in strongest possible terms this egregious display of hatred, bigotry, and violence. It has no place in America. And as I have said many times before, no matter the color of our skin, we all live under the same laws. We all salute the same great flag. And we are all made by the same almighty God."

And he added, "Racism is evil. And those who cause violence in its name are criminals and thugs, including the KKK, neo-Nazis, white supremacists, and other hate groups that are repugnant to everything we hold dear as Americans."

Whether Confederate statues should remain in the parks (as opposed to museums) is one issue. But the irony of all the fuss over Robert E. Lee is that the man himself would have been among the first to eschew racism. The real Robert E. Lee is an ironic lightning rod for such violence.

In research for this piece, I came across an article from *National Geographic News* from 2001. Edward C. Smith wrote an opinion piece, "U.S. Racists Dishonor Robert E. Lee by Association." Hear. Hear. He writes: "Lee, the epitome of the image of the noble, chivalric cavalier, accepted the loss of the quest for Southern independence with extraordinary grace."

General Lee didn't fight to preserve slavery. He freed slaves, at great personal cost, that he had inherited by marriage. He hated the "peculiar institution." He also was in favor of the preservation of the union and was opposed to secession. But when asked by President Lincoln to lead the troops to squash the burgeoning rebellion, he asked, "How can I draw my sword upon Virginia, my native state?"

States' rights were the ostensible reason men like Lee and Jackson fought for the Confederacy, but clearly, the catalyst cause was slavery. This reality is clearly a mark against Lee, Jackson, and others who fought for the South. But we should also remember them for who they actually were, rather than as two-dimensional cutouts in a simplistic morality play of obvious good versus obvious evil.

If we start to tear down all statues of Lee and Stonewall Jackson and Jefferson Davis, the president of the Confederacy, why stop there? What about the nine presidents of the United States who owned slaves? Washington was the only one of those who freed his slaves.

And why stop with just slavery? Didn't the Union General Sheridan go on to fight Native Americans in the West? He reportedly declared (although he denied it), "The only good Indian I ever saw was dead"? Too many statues. Too little time.

We should be honest about our history, and not try to revise it with a giant eraser, like the "unpersons" in George Orwell's *1984*. America needs a great revival, where we can honor the past, yet not let it hold us captive.

In one particular incident after the war, Robert E. Lee himself provides a great example of the kind of change we need in this country going forward. Smith writes: "One Sunday at St. Paul's Episcopal Church in Richmond, a well-dressed, lone black man, whom no one in the community—white or black—had ever seen before, had attended the service, sitting unnoticed in the last pew. Just before communion was to be distributed, he rose and proudly walked down the center aisle through the middle of the church where all could see him and approached the communion rail, where he knelt. The priest and the congregation were completely aghast and in total shock. No one knew what to do…except General Lee. He went to the communion rail and knelt beside the black man and they received communion together— and then a steady flow of other church members followed the example he had set."

44

SOME GOOD NEWS OUT OF CHARLOTTESVILLE

Originally published on December 13, 2017

Bad news gets press. "If it bleeds, it leads." Good news tends not to spread as well and as far. We all know about the horrible events of August 12, 2017, in Charlottesville, where protests and counter-protests over the city's plan to tear down a statue of Robert E. Lee ended in violence and a woman's death. It was a low spot in the year. It was a low spot in recent American history.

But what most of us don't know about was a recent event in Charlottesville, on the first weekend of December 2017. I didn't even know about it until I was talking with Dr. Mark Beliles, who pastors a church in Charlottesville. I wrote a book with him once on the faith of Jefferson, *Doubting Thomas* (2014).

After the tragic riot there, Mark Beliles, as a white minister in Charlottesville, teamed up with a black minister, Dr. Alvin Edwards (a former Charlottesville mayor), to organize the December 1 and 2 event they called "Healing4Charlottesville." By admission, their politics and backgrounds are quite different. Nonetheless, there is too much at stake for them not to join forces.

A. Larry Ross Communications wrote, "National leaders joined the city's Christian community Saturday for Healing4Charlottesville, a day of prayer to encourage peace, healing and reconciliation after the tragic racial violence of last summer."

Beliles, who is also the founder and president of America Transformation Company, said, "We believe that [healing] starts not by continuing to blame others but by humbling ourselves and finding out what we can do different and what we can do better."

Edwards, pastor of Mt. Zion First African Baptist Church, declared, "I believe healing the city begins with prayer. But after prayer, not only becoming hearers of the word, but doers of the word.... It's not just about today. It's about what's going to happen afterward. Scripture teaches us if we come together in unity, we can make a difference wherever we go."

Beliles and Edwards wrote a joint op-ed for a local paper in Charlottesville (*Daily Progress,* December 3, 2017), saying, "And so, we want to state emphatically, that we both love our city, and even more, we love our Lord and Savior Jesus Christ, and are loyal to His Kingdom even more than to any earthly political party. We are also friends who respect each other and believe that we can find common ground and work together for [the] good of our Lord."

They continued, "We acknowledge that our City is very divided, as well as churches.... We respect and celebrate differences and diversity, but we believe that these are serious times in our city and nation, and that we need to find some common ground for the good of our city."

Beliles told my radio audience recently about his relationship with Dr. Edwards, both of whom settled in Charlottesville in 1981: "We've been friends and we've done things together, even though we're very different.... But he and I both believe that Jesus Christ can transcend the politics and the divisions in our country. So we worked together to organize something in response" to the August tragedy.[1]

I asked Beliles about the makeup of the August Charlottesville riot as compared with the December Charlottesville prayer rally. He estimated that there were about 1,300 people at the August melee—about 1,200 of whom came from *out of town*. In contrast, the prayer rally in December was only about two hundred people. However, the vast majority of these were Charlottesville residents. Hence, more people from Charlottesville attended the peaceful prayer rally than attended the August riot.

The prominent African-American bishop Harry Jackson, who is the chairman of the High Impact Leadership Coalition and the pastor of

---

1. "Vocal Point—Dr. Mark Beliles," *Jerry Newcombe,* December 11, 2017, jerrynewcombe.com.

Hope Christian Church in Beltsville, Maryland, spoke at the prayer rally.

I asked Bishop Jackson why he chose to participate. He told me he was glad to see the churches of "different denominational stripes" working together to bring about real interracial healing and to meet the needs of the community. "It was a great investment of time and energy."

Jackson was pleased that the church leaders came up with a seven-point strategy² for positive changes, using the churches as a key for transformation of the community.

Jackson told the rally: "Many of us have been looking to politics to fix our problems. The reality is the government cannot fix these problems....The church has been, in some ways, complicit with the problem, because we never said, 'On this day, on our watch, the madness stops.'"

Jesus Christ is ultimately the solution to the racial divide in America. As Isaiah the prophet foretold: "For to us a child is born, to us a son is given, and the government will be on his shoulders. And he will be called Wonderful Counselor, Mighty God, Everlasting Father, *Prince of Peace*.'" (emphasis mine)

---

2. "Respect Charlottesville," respectcharlottesville.com/index.html.

45

"FAKE NEWS" AND
"OUR DEMOCRACY"

Originally published on April 11, 2018

One of the most interesting videos I have seen lately shows broadcast-ers from the Sinclair network all reading the same script about the threat of "false news," and how fake news threatens "our democracy."[1] My favorite part is the last section where anchor after anchor (fifteen of them by my count) declares with great conviction—as if they just thought of this profound statement, "This is extremely dangerous to our democracy."

My purpose here is to address two issues: first, the issue of so-called "fake news." I think it's a given that in a country where our Constitu-tion forbids the government from abridging the freedom of the press, some might abuse that freedom and declare what is false. There are legal and societal remedies for that. Besides, who gets to define what is "fake news"? Sometimes "fake news" seems like it's the other guy's story or the other network's report. *WorldNetDaily.com* has a great slogan along these lines: "A free press for a free people."

Thehill.com reports (April 4, 2018) that Senator Dick Durbin (D-IL) is calling Sinclair Broadcast Group on the carpet because this "un-dercuts the journalistic integrity of local news anchors who are required to deliver corporate-scripted messages." Mark Levin (April 5, 2018) called Durbin a "tyrant" over this on his radio show.

---

1. Timothy Burke, "How America's Largest Local TV Owner Turned Its News Anchors Into Soldiers In Trump's War On The Media," *Deadspin: The Concourse*, March 31, 2018, theconcourse.deadspin.com.

Jarrett Stepman of the Heritage Foundation, whom I've had the privilege to interview several times on my radio show, wrote an article for dailysignal.com about this.[2] He writes: "A vast right-wing conspiracy is taking over America's newsrooms. That's the narrative that has taken off with the release of a video by the popular news site *Deadspin*, which shows news anchors on multiple local stations reciting the exact same lines. Those local stations are all owned by Sinclair Broadcast Group, a media group that is generally considered conservative or right-leaning. According to the *Washington Examiner*, Sinclair owns '193 TV stations spanning over 614 channels in 89 U.S. markets.'"

Stepman concludes, "It is that desire to shut down alternative media, not the editorial slant of private media companies, that would put our institutions and liberty at risk."

Writing about this recent controversy, veteran broadcast news journalist Sharyl Attkisson notes what she thinks is the real danger: "The more worrisome trends (to me) are when national news personnel censor entire themes or viewpoints, shape stories in ways that aren't reflective of the facts, bend to the will corporate advertisers, layer news stories with reporters' opinions and biases, uncritically use talking points *du jour* from political and corporate interests, report unsubstantiated and sometimes false information, and use 'consultants' without disclosing their conflicts of interest. I've written extensively about how I believe these conflicts have woven their way into many national newsrooms."[3]

Second, what is a republic and what is a democracy? And does it matter? It certainly doesn't matter when newsmen or politicians or teachers refer to "our democracy," in that they mean "we the people" are to be in power. But technically it does matter in the sense of *how* we the people have our power.

A republic is more stable, whereas democracy is subject to the whims of a bare majority. Witness nations like Greece, that seem to change direction and leadership on a dime. A republic does better at giving voice to all, including marginalized groups, who are drowned out in a pure democracy. A constitutionally limited representative republic is

2. Jarrett Stepman, "Sinclair Controversy Is About the Legacy Media's Fear of Losing Control," *The Daily Signal*, April 05, 2018, dailysignal.com.

3. Sharyl Attkisson, "You've Been Hoodwinked," *Sharyl Attkisson*, April 4, 2018, sharylattkisson.com.

essentially relational. A democracy is essentially the exercise of collected power and force.

A republic is governed by elected representatives. That's how "we the people" are supposed to rule—through our representatives empowered by the "consent of the governed."

Pure democracy is essentially rule by the mob. But mobs don't rule well. Think of the French Revolution. Pure democracy leads to anarchy. Anarchy leads to tyranny. The blood spilled in the anti-Christian French Revolution paved the way for the rise of Napoleon, who tried to take over the world.

John Adams once said, in arguing for the superiority of a republic over a democracy, "There is no good government, but what is republican; for a republic is an empire of laws, and not of men; and, to constitute the best of republics, we enforced the necessity of separating the executive, legislative, and judicial powers."

In an email to me, best-selling author and speaker Bill Federer wrote, "The United States is a hybrid [of a democracy and a republic], where representatives of the people are democratically elected. Additionally, they are not free to do whatever they want. They are limited by the Constitution. Pure democracy, as a political structure, is unpredictable, as it is subject to those who control what information the people receive. The danger in a democracy is that people can be swept up into an irrational mob frenzy, where rights are insecure."

Our democratic republic is truly at risk when only a few self-selected people get to decide what is true and what is "fake news."

46

CONFESSIONS OF A "CHRISTIAN CONSTITUTIONALIST"

Originally published on April 17, 2018

After a recent column on "fake news," someone sent me an email accusing me of propagating fake news by saying the Bible had anything to do with the founding of America. The email made the common charge that the Constitution was the product of men of the Enlightenment, with Masonic influence as well.

Unfortunately, that reader, like so many others, fails to understand the historical truth that the Bible played a unique role in helping to create the U.S. Constitution.

The Biblical concept of covenants gave rise to the Puritan-type covenants. The Pilgrims began the process with the Mayflower Compact of 1620, which formed their community "in the name of God." In it, the Pilgrims declared that their purpose was "for the glory of God and the advancement of the Christian faith," as they formed "a civil body politic." After this Compact, there came about a hundred or so Bible-inspired covenants, frames of government, and articles in America, leading all the way to the U.S. Constitution in 1787.

One of these Puritan documents was the Fundamental Orders of Connecticut of 1639, which says they started their colony for the "liberty and purity of the gospel of our Lord Jesus." The Fundamental Orders was the first complete constitution written on American soil. Historians believe the Fundamental Orders impacted the U.S. Constitution. This is why Connecticut calls itself "the Constitution State."

The U.S. Constitution itself says that it was done "in the year of our Lord"—meaning Jesus. But also, it was done in the twelfth year of independence. The Constitution is predicated on the Declaration of Independence—our national birth certificate, which mentions God four times.

Was all this the product of men of the Enlightenment?

The late Michael Novak of the American Enterprise Institute made a great point about the Enlightenment. It was not monolithic, and there were really two types of Enlightenment thinkers: those that were solidly within the Judeo-Christian tradition (e.g., Montesquieu, John Locke, Sir William Blackstone) and those not (e.g., David Hume, Voltaire, Diderot).

America's founders quoted heavily from the Bible, Montesquieu, Blackstone, and Locke—in that order.

- In his *The Spirit of Laws,* Baron Montesquieu wrote: "We shall see that we owe to Christianity, in government, a certain political law, and in war a certain law of nations—benefits which human nature can never sufficiently acknowledge.

- Sir William Blackstone, often quoted by the Supreme Court, said that the laws of nature were written by God and were supplemented by the Holy Scriptures. He wrote, "This law of nature being...dictated by God Himself, is of course superior in obligation to any other. It is binding over all the globe, in all countries, and at all times. No human laws are of any validity if contrary to this."

- John Locke penned, "The Bible is one of the greatest blessings bestowed by God on the children of men." I used to have a Sunday school teacher, Dr. Greg Forster, who earned his Ph.D. at Yale studying Locke and became a Christian because of Locke's classic book, *The Reasonableness of Christianity.*

Although not all framers of the Declaration and Constitution were orthodox Christians, about 95 percent of the founding fathers were active members of Trinitarian Christian churches. To many of them, the Christian faith was central in their lives:

- In his Circular to the States (1783), George Washington said that America could never hope to be a happy nation unless we learned to imitate Jesus, "the divine author of our blessed religion."
- In his Inaugural Address (1797), John Adams called "a decent respect for Christianity among the best recommendations for the public service."
- Thomas Jefferson said that Jesus is the reason we can have religious freedom. To force people to believe in religious views they don't share is a departure from Him, "the holy author of our religion." Jefferson wrote this in his Virginia Statute for Religious Freedom (1777, adopted 1786).
- James Madison, a key leader in the creation of the Constitution, wrote that our obligations to God come before those to the state: "Before any man can be considered as a member of Civil Society, he must be considered as a subject of the Governor of the Universe."

As to the Masonic charge, I view it as an anachronistic charge. The Masons in America did not become anti-Christian until the 1830s and thereafter, long after the time of the framing of our founding documents.

God and the Bible are greater than any one person or any country. But I think we do a disservice to our history to discount the incredibly positive role the Scriptures played in helping to shape this nation.

In the email that prompted this column, I was accused of being a "Christian constitutionalist." Guilty as charged.

PART II

RENEWING OUR ROLE AS ACTIVE CITIZENS

47

TEN REASONS WHY THE CHURCH SHOULD NOT ABANDON POLITICS

Originally published on January 7, 2015

Recent events have raised the issue, Should the pulpit always avoid politics? It depends on what we mean by "politics." It demeans the pulpit to use it for partisan politics. But here are ten reasons I don't think politics and religion should (or even can) be completely separate:

1) The Word of God has something to say about all of life, beyond just the spiritual.

My long-time pastor Dr. D. James Kennedy once noted that the Church of Jesus Christ has always opposed abortion—from the very beginning. It still does. In the last generation, abortion has become a "political" issue. Does that mean, asked Dr. Kennedy, we should now ignore it in the pulpit? No, because the Bible is pro-life.

2) The Bible itself addresses the issue of governing in different texts.

There are Biblical books dealing with political rulers—1 and 2 Samuel, 1 and 2 Kings, and Judges. In Genesis and in Daniel, we see godly men serving well in pagan courts, for the good of all. In Romans 13 and 1 Peter 2, we hear that God has established the civil magistrate and we are to obey the government. In Exodus, we see Moses rebuking Pharaoh for mistreating the Hebrews.

3) The Scriptures also teach that, on occasion, there may be a need for civil disobedience.

When the apostles were commanded to stop preaching the Gospel, Peter said that we must obey God rather than man. If there is an either/

or, then civil disobedience can be the right path. Many early Christians died for Christ rather than worship the emperor, clearly a false god.

4) Jesus said, "Give to Caesar what is Caesar's, and to God what is God's" (Matthew 22:21).

Nature abhors a vacuum. Someone will be involved in politics. Why should we abandon our role as citizens? According to Jesus, we have a positive duty to render certain obligation to the state. Justice will reign when the righteous rule, not the wicked, as we read in Proverbs: "When the righteous thrive, the people rejoice; when the wicked rule, the people groan" (Proverbs 29:2).

5) When the Church does not speak out, evil can fill that void.

Silence in the face of evil can signal assent. We hold up those Christians who went against Hitler and the Nazis as heroes—not the millions who acquiesced to them. The December 23, 1940, *Time* magazine article called "Religion: German Martyrs," opens, "Not you, Herr Hitler, but God is my Führer. These defiant words of Pastor Martin Niemoller were echoed by millions of Germans. And Hitler raged, 'It is Niemoller or I.'"

6) The Church is called to be salt and light. Salt preserves and prevents decay.

Christians in society should help prevent corruption. As goes the pulpit, so goes the nation.

7) We pray, "Your kingdom come, your will be done on earth as it is in heaven" (Matthew 6:10).

That doesn't mean we should try and force the kingdom of God by use of the sword. We are still apologizing for the times that Christians did that in the past, as in the Crusades, and the Inquisition. But it does mean that Christians can apply Biblical principles to government that result in good for all of us. And to be sure, someone is always legislating their morality. It is not a question of "if," but of "what" and of "whose."

8) Christians bless everybody when we properly apply our faith to politics.

Our Constitution grew out of the Biblical concept of covenant. University of Houston Professor Dr. Donald S. Lutz, author of *The Origins of American Constitutionalism* (1988), said that Americans "invented modern Constitutionalism and bequeathed it to the world." And where did *we* get it? Says Lutz: "The American constitutional tradition derives in much of its form and content from the Judeo-Christian tradition as interpreted by the radical Protestant sects to which belonged so many of the original European settlers in British North America."

9) Politics may be the calling of some in the congregation. Therefore, ministers should encourage political involvement that is motivated by the desire to serve.

When the Member of Parliament William Wilberforce converted to Christ in the 1780s, he sought counsel from Rev. John Newton, a former slave trader. Should he leave politics and pursue the ministry? Newton advised him to stay in politics because maybe God could use him where he was. Wilberforce's crusade to free the slaves in the British Empire took him fifty years and was a direct outgrowth of his faith in Christ. I shudder to think if one of today's "no politics" ministers had counseled the young reborn Wilberforce. We might still have legal slavery in the Western world.

10) Religion and morality are "indispensable supports to our political prosperity."

So said Washington in his Farewell Address. John Adams said, "Our Constitution was made only for a moral and religious people. It is wholly inadequate to the government of any other." This was in a day when about 99 percent of the Americans were professing Christians. And on it goes.

I remember when I once interviewed former Secretary of Education William Bennett. He said, "Does anybody really have a worry that the United States is becoming overly pious? That our young people have dedicated too much of their lives to prayer, that teenagers in this country are preoccupied with thoughts of eternity?" In short, our problem today is not too much Christian influence on society, but not enough.

48

VALUES VOTERS MADE THE DIFFERENCE IN THE MIDTERM ELECTIONS

Originally published on November 12, 2010

This story points out a timeless truth: when Christians show up at the polls and vote our values, we often win.

The 2010 midterm election is significant in many ways. One of those ways is that it showed that the value voters still matter. Those who care about abortion. Those who favor traditional marriage. Those who believe in fiscal responsibility.

By his own admission, Obama got a "shellacking" in the vote. And I might add, it was well deserved. There's too much of an elitist attitude in Washington, D.C., these days.

Evangelicals and conservative Catholics swung this election. They showed up. In fact, they showed up in record numbers. According to a survey by the Faith and Freedom Coalition, the "largest single constituency" going to the polls last week was "self-identified evangelicals." They represented 29 percent of those who voted. How did they vote? Seventy-eight percent voted Republican.

In addition to evangelical voters, 12 percent of those who voted in the mid-term were Catholics who frequently attend church. They voted 58 percent Republican versus 40 percent for Democratic candidates. As for Catholics overall (church-goers and non-church-goers mixed together), they voted this time 53 percent for the Republican candidates and 45 percent for the Democratic ones. What's fascinating about the Catholic vote is the change from just two years ago. Between 2008 and last week's election, voters made an astounding eighteen point shift, from liberal to conservative.

Ralph Reed, who was the president of the Christian Coalition in its heyday (in the 1990s), founded and leads the Faith and Freedom Coalition. He said of last week's balloting, "People of faith turned out in the highest numbers in a midterm election we have ever seen, and they made an invaluable contribution to the historic results."

Issues like abortion, traditional marriage, and fiscal responsibility were key. Steven Ertelt, who runs the *Life News* website, a clearinghouse on the abortion issue from a pro-life perspective, said on the day after the election, "Look no further than the health-care reform bill that allows for taxpayer funding of abortions as the reason why so many pro-life candidates won elections to federal and state offices on Tuesday."

One study on the issue of abortion found that abortion was important to 30 percent of those who voted. This is according to results from the conservative group, the polling company, inc. Pro-life candidates enjoyed a three-to-one advantage over their pro-choice counterparts, all things being equal. Here's the breakdown: 22 percent of all voters voted pro-life. 8 percent of all voters voted pro-choice.

Traditional marriage also fared well in Tuesday's election. For example, three of the supreme court justices of Iowa were voted out. Why? Because several months ago they supposedly found "the right" for same-sex couples to marry in the Iowa constitution. These three justices were specifically, explicitly targeted by the voters for trying to force same-sex marriage by judicial fiat. Now, thankfully, they're out of a job.

Writer Jim Jewel summed up the values voters' contribution to last Tuesday this way: "Exit polling showed that not only did the Republican wildfire spread throughout the country but that the coalition of white evangelicals and Catholics that powered prior conservative success (before the youthful senator from Illinois split the alliance) fueled the 2010 inferno."

Obviously, the Tea Party movement played an important role in the 2010 election. Just two years ago, the only reference to a "Tea Party" rally was in the history books, referring to the classic episode in December 1773, when colonists dressed up like Indians and cast tea into the Boston Harbor to oppose an unfair tax hike. It's interesting to note that Dr. Martin Luther King Jr. mentioned that rebellious act in his 1963 "Letter from a Birmingham Jail." "Of course, there is nothing new about this kind of civil disobedience.... In our own nation, the Boston Tea Party represented a massive act of civil disobedience."

Jump ahead to 2009 and 2010, where we see a new Tea Party movement impacting the outcome of the national election. Election-wise, the Tea Party movement won some and lost some. The pundits sneer at it as if it's a net negative. Yet the amazing thing is that such a new movement, not even two years old, would have such results as to propel a few candidates into prominent national office. To wit, Senator-elect Rand Paul of Kentucky. Fifty-two percent of members of the modern Tea Party movement self-identify as evangelicals.

Thus, the values voters made a huge difference in last week's election. Ralph Reed said there's a lesson for all politicians from the 2010 midterm election: "Those who ignore or disregard social conservative voters and their issues do so at their own peril."

49

HAVE THE PEOPLE "CEASED TO
BE THEIR OWN RULERS"?

Originally published on August 20, 2010

When I read the headlines, I find a repeated theme in our time. Politicians repeatedly do what they want, regardless of the will of the people. In a different context, Abraham Lincoln spoke about how the people "have ceased to be their own rulers." This phrase comes from his First Inaugural Address, where he was talking about the problem of the Supreme Court trumping the will of the American people. Sound familiar? Meanwhile, it isn't just the high court that is causing the people to cease to be their own rulers.

Last year, Obama and the Democrats said, "Let's take over the health-care system." The American people said, "No!" The Democrats even stopped having town-hall meetings because the opposition to Obamacare grew so great. But the politicians gave it to us anyway.

The Politicians: 1. The People: 0.

The voters of Arizona passed a common-sense law essentially providing that the government should enforce current federal laws regarding illegal aliens pouring over the borders of that state. Since the federal government isn't doing it, Arizona will. This law is supported by a margin of 70 percent, including many Hispanics, though not the majority of them. Rather than yield to the will of the people, our rulers sued Arizona, and put the law on hold for who knows how long.

The Politicians: 2. The People: 0.

An Islamic group wants to build a mosque at Ground Zero, even

149

though plenty of mosques already exist throughout New York City, including in Manhattan. Religious liberty in America certainly allows for Muslims to build mosques throughout the country. There are about 1,200 mosques throughout the U.S., which is about 1,200 more than the number of legal churches in Saudi Arabia. The problem with the Ground Zero Mosque is that it is a monument to alleged Islamic supremacy. Critics note that even the original name of the new proposed mosque (Cordoba) refers back to a "victory mosque" in Spain. Does the Islamic group intend for this site to honor a supposed victory that took place on 9/11? Virtually all the territories where the crescent reigns supreme were gained at the point of the sword.

The funding source for the hundred million dollars to build the mosque is not yet known, but surely much of it would come from enemies of America. In hearing after hearing, many New Yorkers, including the surviving relatives of 9/11 victims, pled that the mosque not go up or that it be built elsewhere, but not near such hallowed ground. But the mayor supported it (as well as the president). Meanwhile, the NYC Commission voted for it, even though the people passionately opposed it (and still do).

The Politicians: 3. The People: 0.

In California, one judge silenced the voice of seven million voters when he ruled against Proposition 8 on the issue of same-sex marriage. It was a major struggle even to place the proposal on the ballot. Special interests contested the proposition in the courts in an attempt to wrest the power away from the will of the people. But the people prevailed, and in 2008 the measure passed. This happened despite vandalism to churches and despite intimidation tactics like revealing the names, addresses, and phone numbers of donors, even those who gave as little as $35 for the Prop 8 campaign—so much for the right to privacy. The judge who ruled against Prop 8 was himself a homosexual. You would think that common decency would have caused him to recuse himself from the case. But noooo.

The Politicians: 4. The People: 0.

President Lincoln was right. It seems that the people have ceased to be their own rulers. I think his comment about the courts also applies today to many politicians in general.

At least this November we will have the opportunity to show the politicians who works for whom. If we don't take advantage of that opportunity and vote intelligently, then the people will have indeed ceased to be their own rulers.

50

IMMIGRANTS: TURN BACK— AMERICA STINKS ACCORDING TO THE LEFT

Originally published on August 1, 2018

Those poor people at the southern border. So many of them are risking their lives to get what they think is a better life here in America. They don't realize how bad things are here. They haven't been exposed to the constant America-bashing message coming from the liberal institutions that dominate our schools, our culture, our entertainment, and even our museums.

I love museums. Recently, I visited the Smithsonian Museum of American History in Washington, D.C. I must admit I was very disappointed. The overall impression it can easily leave is that America, for the most part, stinks.

For example, in the display on World War II, the big headline-grabbing focus is on the terrible, ugly chapter when the U.S. interned Japanese-Americans during the war. The liberal icon FDR oversaw that chapter. Years later, the Supreme Court ruled that those prison camps for Japanese-Americans were unconstitutional and regrettable.

But was that the sum total of America's experience in World War II? What about all those millions of young Americans who served in both the Pacific and Atlantic sides of the war? My dad was one of those (Pacific, to be specific). A few hundred thousand Americans died in faraway places like Normandy, Iwo Jima, Luzon, and Okinawa.

The overall impression the museum display on American democracy and voting leaves is that, for too long, America denied voting rights to certain segments of the population. Our founding fathers pledged their "lives, their fortunes, their sacred honor," while relying on God, so that "we the people" shall govern. In America, we govern by the consent of the governed. Obviously, the nation was slow in getting that privilege extended to African-Americans and women. But we did ultimately get it right.

This is the same museum system that has a separate building dedicated to exhibiting African-American history, and they slighted one of the most prominent blacks in American history—Supreme Court Justice Clarence Thomas. Why? One can only surmise that it is because they don't like his politics. He doesn't march in lockstep with the predominant liberal ethos—that America stinks. America always stinks. America has no hope for improvement.

Dinesh D'Souza disagrees with this ethos. He came from India and has managed to thrive in this country, writing books and making powerful and successful documentaries. In one of those movies, he said that he loved America because in this country you can write your own script. To paraphrase Dr. D. James Kennedy, the freedoms we enjoy in America "did not spring full blown like Athena from the head of Zeus. Rather, it took some time and experimentation and trial and error to work out the flaws and perfect the system that was developing."

What is the net result of the constant drumbeat clamoring about how America has always gotten it wrong, and often still does get it wrong? Writing for Gallup Polls (July 2, 2018), Jeffrey M. Jones observes, "For the first time in Gallup's 18-year history asking U.S. adults how proud they are to be Americans, fewer than a majority say they are 'extremely proud.' Currently, 47 percent describe themselves this way, down from 51 percent in 2017 and well below the peak of 70% in 2003."[1]

I met a lady recently who grew up in Alabama. When she was in high school about thirty years ago, she spent a few months in Soviet Russia as an exchange student. Whatever starry-eyed notions she may have had about the resplendent glory of the communist state were quickly and completely shattered. She was struck by how depressed and hopeless the

---

1. Jeffrey M. Jones, "In U.S., Record-Low 47% Extremely Proud to Be Americans," July 2, 2018, *Gallup*, news.gallup.com.

average citizen was. When she returned to the States, she got down on her knees at the tarmac and kissed the American ground.

America is not perfect. It never has been. As Dr. Martin Luther King Jr. reminded us, America has a good creed—all men are created equal. Our problem is that we haven't lived up to the creed.

I once asked Rabbi Daniel Lapin about the impact of the life of Jesus, including Judeo-Christian influence in the creation of America. He told me, "The easiest way to answer the question of whether life on planet earth is better because Jesus walked Jerusalem or not is very simple, and that is: Just watch the way people vote with their feet. Watch where the net flow of immigration is in the world today. Is it from Christian countries to non-Christian countries or the other way around? It is so obvious."

But I thought of all those people risking their lives to make it into this country. If only they knew how much America stinks—always has and perhaps always will, according to the Left—they wouldn't bother.

51

OBAMACARE THREATENS
CHARITABLE HOSPITALS

Originally published on August 14, 2013

It's a good thing our current administration wasn't around in the fourth century when St. Basil of Caesarea invented what writer George Grant calls "the first non-ambulatory hospital" in history, i.e., a medical facility with beds.

Pouring forth the love of Jesus Christ, history credits the good saint who lived in the Mediterranean port city northwest of Jerusalem with this humanitarian development of the institution of the hospital. Roberto Margotta, author of *The Story of Medicine*, says of Basil's hospital that the "rule of love" prevailed with the "care and comfort of the sick."

The longest-lasting hospital still operating (no pun intended) is Hotel Dieu (i.e., God Hospital) in Paris, founded in the year of our Lord 600. It borders Notre Dame Cathedral. In the New World, the oldest still-operating medical facility is Jesus of Nazareth Hospital in Mexico City, founded in 1524.

In many other places and times, Christians of various stripes started all sorts of hospitals and health clinics. That's true across the globe. Even to this day, many hospitals show their Christian origin in their very name. Good Samaritan. Holy Cross. Christ. Baptist. Bethesda. St. Mary's.

Some hospitals are named after St. Luke (e.g., St. Luke Presbyterian, Rush St. Luke) because the author of the third Gospel and Acts was a doctor. He was even Paul's doctor.

Many people of good will, regardless of their religious convictions (or the lack thereof), work at the healing of the sick. Christian charity—voluntary love for the Lord and for others—historically motivated many of the great developments in organized healthcare in the first place. That remains true to some degree today.

It's disturbing, then, to learn that the government's takeover of the health-care system will likely punish charity hospitals in the future. In short, Obamacare could be bad for our health.

A headline in *The Daily Caller* notes, "Obamacare installs new scrutiny, fines for charitable hospitals that treat uninsured people" (August 8, 2013). Patrick Howley reports, "Charitable hospitals that treat uninsured Americans will be subjected to new levels of scrutiny of their nonprofit status and could face sizable new fines under Obamacare." Howley adds, "A new provision in Section 501 of the Internal Revenue Code, which takes effect under Obamacare, sets new standards of review and installs new financial penalties for tax-exempt charitable hospitals, which devote a minimum amount of their expenses to treat uninsured poor people. Approximately 60 percent of American hospitals are currently nonprofit." The fines could be as stiff as $50,000 "if they fail to meet bureaucrats' standards," he writes.

I thought Obamacare was supposedly about providing healthcare for the poor and uninsured. It seems to me this is more about government control than it is about helping people.

Dr. David Stevens is the president of the Christian Medical and Dental Associations, located in Bristol, Tennessee. They represent about 16,500 members and are in contact regularly with over 30,000 physicians and dentists. I've interviewed him a few times for radio and TV. He once told me, "All three of my children work with a health-care ministry in inner-city Memphis. They're motivated by their faith, and they sacrifice every day, not only at their workplace; but they live [there], right with the people that they serve, because of their faith."

But enter Obamacare with its stifling regulations in the health-care field, and such good works could be ultimately discouraged to satisfy the bureaucracy.

Dr. Stevens observes: "If ever we needed Christians in healthcare, it's now; but unfortunately, we're putting a system into place that ultimately could drive them out of healthcare." For example, if laws forced them to violate their conscience. He laments, "That's scary, especially as we look at the bioethical issues we're facing on physician-assisted suicide, embryonic stem cell research, abortion, and the list just goes on and on—where having a doctor that shares your Christian worldview is going to become more and more important in beginning-of-life care and in end-of-life care."

Stevens adds, "We need health-care reform, but we need to attack the real problem—out-of-control costs—not open the doors for millions and millions of more people at this point to enter the system and increase costs even more. We need to deal with access, but if we can get costs under control, it's going to be cheaper for everyone, the insured now and those that can be insured when the cost is lower."

Driving conscientious Christians out of healthcare is the worst thing that could happen to that field, yet it seems that Obamacare regulations could end up doing just that. Ironically, at the same time, many are losing their jobs because of Obamacare and may need charity healthcare.

I remember from the early 1960s the comedy phonograph record *The First Family*, where comedian Vaughn Meader did a masterful job imitating JFK. At a mock press conference, a reporter asked "JFK" what his solution would be to the coming social-security crisis. Meader's reply as JFK was, "Try to stay young." Applying the same humorous logic to today: What would be the solution to the health-care crisis, should Obamacare go fully into effect? "Don't get sick."

Sadly, more government bureaucracy in the health-care field may ultimately drive out that spirit which gave birth to much of healthcare in the first place.

52

OBAMACARE AND *ANIMAL FARM*

Originally published on October 23, 2013

Now that we've had just a few weeks of the mess that is Obamacare, it brings home how grossly unfair it is that the political class imposes it on the rest of us and yet needn't abide by it themselves—for as long as it lasts. It may yet collapse under its own weight.

I feel sorry for the younger generation, just out of college. They have less of a chance to get a good job with benefits. Many companies continue to downsize because of Obamacare. So these young people get less work. But they'll have to pay more for healthcare, which supposed care they may never see. Assuming they can register for it, which we now know is a huge assumption.

Last week, one liberal blogger described how he had been all for Obamacare. He was one of the relative few who managed to get through the computer system and register online. Lo and behold, his insurance costs promised to go through the roof, as well as the deductible. So he said, forget it. He even said he wouldn't pay the fine either. Well, good luck with that.

On pjmedia.com (October 20, 2013), Roger Simon wrote, "Over fifteen hundred a year for a sixty-three hundred plus deductible? What healthy thirty year old would waste his or her money?"

Obamacare seems simple to understand in a sentence: You pay more, but you get less. Not to mention the loss of freedoms, the institution of a massive governmental bureaucracy, and the potential annihilation of healthcare as we know it.

At the very least, fairness would demand that all the politicians live under it. It's grossly unfair to force the rest of us into a system that doesn't seem to work, while the elite class exempts itself from it. For now, they're even exempting the big companies from it (for a year).

All of this reminds me of the classic anti-communist novel *Animal Farm* by the great British writer George Orwell (1903–1950). The short book is a parable of the Soviet Union. And no, I'm not calling anyone a communist. On the other hand, Dr. Paul Kengor, Grove City College professor, documents in his book *The Communist* (2012) that Frank Marshall Davis, a member of the Communist Party USA (#47544), mentored Obama. This is part of the public record.

Here's a spoiler alert. In Orwell's novel, you will recall, the animals revolt against the tyrannical farmer (Mr. Jones, a human), who represents the czar. But then as the animals look forward to sharing everything equally, the pigs in charge ultimately live high off the hog, so to speak. After killing the farmer, the animals declare, "Remove Man from the scene, and the root cause of hunger and overwork is abolished forever."

The animals post "Seven Commandments"—the final one stating, "All animals are equal."

But as the plot develops, it becomes clear that the pigs (representing Josef Stalin, Leon Trotsky, and other Soviet leaders) have become an elite class.

At the end of the book, the other animals—who do all the work and do not get enough to eat—look into the farmhouse, where they see the pigs enjoying a great meal. They can barely distinguish the pigs from the humans, whose regime they had rebelled against. The Seven Commandments now appear as just two: *"All animals are equal, but some animals are more equal than others."*

Today, we seem to have an elitists' class and the hoi polloi—the rest of us. As long as Obamacare operates as the law of the land, it ought to apply to the president, his family, his staff, the Senators, the Members of the House of Representatives, and their staff. The law (and tax) should be good enough for the Supreme Court and their staff. This is a fundamental of America's rule of law.

I've heard some Congressmen complain that their staff members can't afford it. Well, what about the rest of us? In an earlier draft, I wrote that only the Amish should be exempt, since they don't take part in the medical system. But on second thought, we all should be exempt!

Meanwhile, the Bible says differing standards are unfair and unjust: "Differing weights and differing measures—the Lord detests them both" (Proverbs 20:10). Psalm 94:20 criticizes those "who frame mischief by statute" (RSV). Paul strongly criticizes Peter in Galatians 2:14 for forcing a standard on the Gentiles that he himself was not living by.

Our nation's birth certificate declares that "all men are created equal." Are we to assume that under Obamacare, some are created more equal than others?

53

WHO WILL CONTROL YOUR HEALTHCARE CHOICES?

Originally published on October 29, 2012

Because of the 2010 passage of the Patient Protection and Affordable Care Act, more popularly known as Obamacare, our healthcare in the future could potentially change quite dramatically. Many opponents had hoped that the Supreme Court would rule it unconstitutional, but that ship sailed in late June.

One of the key features of the Affordable Care Act (ACA) is the Independent Payment Advisory Board. Critics feel that this board will basically decide who gets what treatment, and who doesn't. Some critics have called the Independent Payment Advisory Board a "death panel." Is that a fair criticism?

Amy Ridenour, president of the National Center for Public Policy Research, thinks it is. She says that it "basically says, if a piece of medical technology, a drug, a procedure is more expensive than the government thinks is worth saving your life, or your mom's life, or your six-year-old son's life, then you're not going to get it or they're not going to get it: that is a death panel."

Dr. David Stevens, president of the Christian Medical and Dental Associations, decries the political (as opposed to medical) nature of the board: "That panel doesn't have one physician on it. It's going to be government bureaucrats in Washington making the decision who's going to get care and who's not. That scares me, and it should scare you." Dr. Stevens adds, "We're going to see in funding decisions this whole quality of life ethic; is this person worth saving? Are they going to have a good enough quality of life to pay for this?"

The quality of life ethic is a utilitarian approach to human life. In contrast to that is the sanctity of human life view—based on the Judeo-Christian concept that every human being is made in the image of God and therefore has intrinsic value. Dr. Stevens sums up the medical implications of a sanctity of life ethic: "Life is sacred. From the moment of conception to the point of natural death; therefore, we must treasure it and preserve it where we can."

Grace-Marie Turner of the Galen Institute, a think-tank in the Washington, D.C., area that focuses on medical issues, asks: "How much is your life worth, to the government, not you and your family?" Unless something changes, the Independent Payment Advisory Board will make those decisions and not you and your family.

Back in the 1990s, I spoke with columnist Cal Thomas about Hillary Clinton's push for nationalized healthcare. He was concerned about medical decisions based on the quality of life ethic. He observed, "This means that the government, based on a formula it will come up with, will decide basically who shall live and who shall die."

He homed in on the potential implications of this. "Now they'll begin as they usually do in these sorts of cases with the extreme cases: a ninety-eight-year-old Alzheimer's and cancer sufferer with multiple kidney dysfunctions. And then, everybody will agree that maybe we shouldn't spend several millions of dollars to extend that kind of life. But it will be a very short move from that, as we've seen with abortion, and increasingly with infanticide, to the government deciding your life is no longer valuable; therefore, we are not going to pay to sustain it."

Many critics of the health-care overhaul bill see it moving us closer to complete nationalized healthcare, as we see, for example, in the United Kingdom or Canada. Grace-Marie Turner says, "Well, in the United States we don't have rationing of care yet, but in the UK they absolutely do. . . . Survival for breast cancer in the United States is about 50 percent higher than it is in the UK; it's dramatically higher for prostate cancer. In the United States 92 percent of men diagnosed with prostate cancer are alive five years later; in Great Britain only 50 percent are."

Amy Ridenour coauthored a book, *Shattered Lives*, which documents the horrors that can result from a nationalized health-care system. The book contains one hundred individual stories, such as people from Great Britain (Amy says it's 6 percent) who have resorted to pulling their own teeth because of the long waiting list to see the dentist. She says, "In any given year the British government estimates that seven hundred and fifty thousand people are on a waiting list for surgery. Now, some of those people die" (2009).

The sad thing about the ACA is how it may well drive out of medicine some of the most caring and conscientious doctors and nurses—those of conscience. Dr. Stevens comments, "Many Christian doctors are very concerned about what this is going to mean to them personally. They're already being pressured—discriminated against because of their unwillingness to do abortions or provide certain forms of birth control or other aspects of healthcare where they have religious reasons—they do not want to participate."

A study by the Doctor Patient Medical Association found that 83 percent of American physicians have considered leaving the field because of Obamacare (dailycaller.com, July 9, 2012).

In the future, who will control our choices in this realm? On November 6, we will find out who will control our healthcare. Your vote can help determine that outcome. A medical free market based in the ethics of Christian care—trusting God, not men—would be a superior system in every way.

54

OBAMANOMICS ISN'T WORKING
AND NEVER WILL WORK

Originally published on October 14, 2010

Less than three weeks away from a major midterm election, a new poll reveals that 85 percent of Americans are angry at or dissatisfied with the economy. ABC and *Yahoo! News* released the poll. Independents are angry as well as most Republicans, and they blame the Democrats and Obama for it.

The man in charge says just give him some more time, and it'll all work out—for the most part. At least, President Obama has finally admitted that the so-called "shovel-ready jobs" to fix our infrastructure weren't quite ready after all. The nearly trillion-dollar stimulus bill didn't stimulate anything but the national debt.

Under Obama, the federal government has taken over many private companies. Obamacare saddles our children and grandchildren with unsustainable debts. Already, people are receiving *less* medical coverage not more coverage—because of Obamacare, not despite it. Obama opposes reinstating the Bush tax cuts, even though letting those cuts lapse will make a bad economy worse.

What's the problem here?

It's very simple. Obamanomics doesn't work, and it never will work.

At a very vulnerable time in Obama's life, card-carrying member of the Communist Party Frank Marshall Davis mentored him. This was when he was in Hawaii as a young man. (Documentation of Davis's affiliation with the communists can be seen in Dr. Paul Kengor's incredible new book *Dupes* [2010] which shows how liberals and progressives in the twentieth century allowed themselves to be duped by Stalin and his minions.) Others beside Davis helped mentor the young Obama. He also surrounded himself with fellow travelers while he was in Chicago, imbibing Marxist ideas from the likes of Saul Alinksy, who was, if you will, "Marxism in shoe leather."

Even in church, Obama repeatedly received exposure to Marxist ideas from his longtime pastor, Jeremiah Wright. Wright was always condemning America, no matter what. At least we can rest assured the future president wasn't listening on *those* days.

Obama thinks in Marxist terms. His opposition to the tax cuts is a prime example. He opposes tax cuts clear across the board because then rich people will get tax cuts too. In one sense, he has declared war against the rich, not realizing that the rich can take their money elsewhere—to other countries even. When you overtax the rich (and I'm beginning to wonder if Obama would think that's impossible), then they just cut back on their entrepreneurial ventures and thus do not hire people, including many non-rich. This stuff seems so elementary, but because Obama has imbibed socialist ideas, he'll have none of it.

"The problem with socialism," said Margaret Thatcher famously, "is that sooner or later you run out of other people's money."

Contrary to Obama's campaign pledge, the middle class in America (those earning considerably less than $200,000) are feeling the pinch. If they feel the pinch now, how much worse will it likely be come January 1, 2011, unless Congress somehow acts to continue the Bush tax cuts, which are scheduled to expire at the end of this year.

My question is: Mr. Obama, why don't you just call the Bush tax cuts the "John F. Kennedy Memorial Tax Cuts" and then pass them into law?

Tax cuts worked for Kennedy. They worked for Ronald Reagan, who created some 17 million jobs just from 1981–1989. They worked for George W. Bush. And they'd work for Obama if he'd let them. But I don't think he has it in him. He doesn't realize the wisdom of John F. Kennedy on the results of tax cuts—a rising tide lifts all boats.

Mr. Obama, if you really cared about the poor, then you would work more toward creating the one thing that eliminates poverty more than anything else: jobs. Government doesn't create jobs—except government jobs, which, of course, are funded by taxpayers, a net cost overall. Government can certainly kill jobs—with over-regulation, with forced mandates, with higher taxes. In short, government at its best essentially gets out of the way for the private sector to create jobs.

A few weeks ago, James Tarranto in his "Best of the Web" column jokingly applied to Barack Obama something Abraham Lincoln once said. Lincoln had said about the Lord, "It's a good thing God loves poor people. He made so many of them." After the number of poor in America under this president increased to the point that one out of seven Americans lives under the poverty line, Tarranto quipped, "It's a good thing Obama loves poor people. He made so many of them."

55

OBAMACARE DECISION PROVES
ELECTIONS MATTER

Originally published on June 28, 2012

My first reaction to the Obamacare decision was, Well, it was a great country while it lasted.

My second reaction to the Obamacare decision was to re-remember just how important elections are. Elections have far-reaching consequences. Obviously, the president nominates the judges, who generally serve for life, and the Senate confirms (or rejects them).

The Supreme Court virtually governs our lives today, although that should not be the case.

The affable Chief Justice John Roberts was the swing vote upholding Obamacare, despite its assault on the sanctity of life (at both ends of the spectrum). The liberal press will surely embrace Chief Roberts as having "grown" while in the office.[1]

Though Roberts nixed the so-called "individual mandate" requiring all Americans to buy insurance as unconstitutional under the commerce clause, he "helpfully" reclassified the mandate as a "tax," thus putting it under Congress's constitutional powers—even though Congress vehemently denied that it was a tax while passing the law since it would never have passed as such. As Mitch McConnell said, "This bill was sold to the American people on deception."

A friend dredged up a blog he had written on his concerns about

---

1. Author's note: Thankfully, in the big picture of things, it would seem that Chief Justice Roberts has tried to be faithful to the Constitution for the most part, the Obamacare decision notwithstanding.

the unknown John Roberts at the time of his nomination. He wrote: "The Amen Corner is saying that Roberts is just an excellent, excellent choice. Now, he's no ideologue, they caution. He's not going to 'slash and burn his way through an opinion' like Scalia does. But he's conservative nonetheless."

My friend went on to say, "But what does this mean, exactly? Are Thomas and Scalia considered 'ideologues' even by people on the right because they believe the meaning of the text of the Constitution ought to be what governs decisions? And if Roberts isn't one of them, then what meaning does he think should govern decisions? It's kinda like being pregnant: either you are or you aren't. You cannot be a semi-originalist. Either the text governs, or the opinion of the judge does. If it's not the text, it's not originalism. If that is 'ideological,' so be it."

Pro-life author Wesley J. Smith once said this to me on the subject of judges moving from originalism to activism (but not visa versa): "I used to wonder why it is that a supposedly liberal judge will very rarely if ever move to the conservative side, but conservative judges often move to the liberal side. And it occurred to me that perhaps the reason for that is: If you're a conservative judge, a so-called strict constructionist, you are pushing away power. You are saying, 'It's not up to me to judge, but it's up to a legislature.' But if you become a more liberal judge, what you may be saying is, 'Hey, I have the power to make that decision.' And that can be a very heady seduction, to be able to say, 'The law says what I say it says.'"

Robert Bork, who was "borked" from serving on the Court because of a massive smear campaign against him, once said, "The fact is that the public is far more conservative than the court is, but that's because the court is part of the intellectual class and it responds to the intellectual class. You know, they may not even be conscious of it, or some of them may not be conscious of it. But if, when you go one way, you get praised by all of *New York Times* and the *Washington Post* and NBC and CBS and ABC, that's kind of seductive. But if you go the other way, you get criticized, and over time that, I think, has some effect on some justices, not all."

If anybody takes a half hour or so to actually read the Constitution, he will see that the founders said much more about the legislative and executive branches than they did about the judicial branch. The founders never envisioned the day—nor would they have countenanced it—when our robed masters essentially rule us.

Third President Thomas Jefferson warned what can happen with runaway courts that legislate from the bench, instead of simply adjudicating: "The germ of dissolution of our federal government is in . . . the federal judiciary."

Name the issue today—abortion, pornography, loss of religious liberty, same-sex marriage—and we find that it's generally the courts, many times the Supreme Court, that have legalized something contrary to God's will, and often contrary to the will of the people.

Writing in *Federalist* #49, James Madison said, "The members of the executive and judiciary departments are few in number, and can be personally known to a small part only of the people." And he added, "The members of the legislative department, on the other hand, are numerous. They are distributed and dwell among the people at large." Regarding the members of the executive branch, this is no longer true, though one could wish it were so.

In *Federalist* #78, Alexander Hamilton said—in a footnote, no less— "The celebrated Montesquieu, speaking of them [the branches of government], says: 'Of the three powers above mentioned, the judiciary is next to nothing.'" In the same essay, Hamilton said, "It is not otherwise to be supposed, that the Constitution could intend to enable the representatives of the people to substitute their will to that of their constituents. . . . It is far more rational to suppose, that the courts were designed to be an intermediate body between the people and the legislature, in order, among other things, to keep the latter within the limits assigned to their authority."

In short, the founders viewed the courts as interpreting laws, not writing them. They envisioned the justices adjudicating from the bench, not legislating from it.

If freedom and the right-to-life issues mean anything to you, remember how important your vote is in November and tell your friends who share your values. As my friend author and speaker Bill Federer always reminds me, in America, we get the country we deserve.

56

A BIG LIE OR JUST A PRONOUN MIX-UP?

Originally published on February 5, 2014

A majority of Americans now oppose Obamacare (which has the euphemistic title of the "Affordable Care Act")—even those who supported it earlier. Once the program began, sticker shock set in.

Long before any of us had heard of Obamacare, P. J. O'Rourke famously said: "If you think healthcare is expensive now, wait until it's free." Particularly painful to watch was a recent video showing the candid reactions of a handful of employees of a small business in Pennsylvania.[1] A TV crew captures their initial responses, to find out what Obamacare means to them personally. For most of them, the monthly premium increased dramatically. So did the deductible. How can people afford this thing? Many full-time employees are becoming part-timers because of the law.

Jackie Bodnar writes, "The 'cheapest' insurance policy option on Healthcare.gov for a single twenty-six-year-old making $35,000 annually is $1,863." Bodnar is the Director of Communications for Freedomworks. She notes that it is millennials (of which she is one, as a twenty-six-year-old) who are tapped to pay for it. "At the most basic level, Obamacare is a cross-generational wealth transfer designed to coerce young Americans into subsidizing those older and richer, all in the name of 'spreading the pain around'."

Another hidden problem is the deductible rates, which have also in-

---

1. "Observe Small Business Employees' Reaction to Changes in Healthcare Plan under Obamacare 01292014," YouTube, January 30, 2014, youtube.com/watch?v=Vl8JsycbHR8.

creased under Obamacare. I've heard of many middle-class Americans facing deductibles of about $6,000 a year.

Of course, the president sold the plan on a promise repeated so often that maybe he even believed it: "If you like your insurance plan, you can keep your plan." And, "If you like your doctor, you can keep your doctor." We all know now that these statements were blatantly untrue. Was this a big lie or just a pronoun mix-up? In effect, Obamacare says, "If WE like your insurance plan, you can keep your plan." And "If WE like your doctor, you can keep your doctor." In other words, it's the government that decides what is approved and what is not, who is eligible and who is not. Of course, that's not what he said. Yet in effect, isn't that what he meant? If we the government approve, then you can have it. But if we don't, forget it.

Obamacare is simply another manifestation of the nanny state. The government knows better than you do how to take care of you—including your healthcare.

In an incredible understatement, one of the president's former speechwriters said that the "keep your health-care plan" statement "didn't turn out to be as accurate as the administration planned."

The writer, Jon Lovett, spoke at a function in Washington, D.C., and said that they intended well, even if the results didn't work out that way: "It was never, ever something that was viewed as not being true but something that should be said anyway. It was viewed as something that largely described the underlying structure of this bill and that is absolutely true."

The problem with Obamacare isn't just the pronouns or the website. It's the premise. Where is it written that the government is responsible for our healthcare? Certainly not in the Constitution. Certainly not in the Bible—although it is a historical fact that Christianity (without government help) gave birth to the phenomenon of the hospital and that missionaries have provided healthcare virtually all over the world to those who never had it before. Even to this day, despite our society's secularization, many hospitals retain their names pointing to their Christian origins.

In Obamacare, as a nation, we are reaping what we have sown. Too many of us wanted something "free" (although that was by the sweat of our neighbor's brow), such that we were willing to be duped. Government freebies don't grow on trees—they are plundered from other Americans.

Hopefully, the fiasco that is Obamacare will help us rethink our relationship with our government. Former South Carolina Senator Jim DeMint, now the president of the Heritage Foundation think tank, once told me in a television interview, "We have to repeal Obamacare. It is going to destroy healthcare in America, and it's going to bankrupt our country."

He also said, "It's another government-centric approach that believes that government can make decisions about things that are very personal in our lives, of the patient/doctor relationship or how we care for the medical needs of our family."

Mr. DeMint added, "But the federal government cannot run our health-care system. We've seen that with Medicaid, that has created more unhealthy people by the way it is set up, instead of encouraging people to take better care of themselves and to learn more about health insurance and how to be personally responsible for yourself."

Is Obamacare really about making healthcare more affordable and more accessible to more Americans? If so, how come one of the law's provisions in the approximately 2,600-page act includes hiring 16,000 more IRS workers to implement the law?

As the reality of Obamacare continues to shock more and more Americans, I am reminded of Ronald Reagan's classic line: "The nine most terrifying words in the English language are, 'I'm from the government and I'm here to help.'"

57

SO, IT'S ALL JESUS'S FAULT?

Originally published on February 10, 2012

How well is President Obama doing on fixing the nation's financial crisis? Not very, say most Americans. A Rasmussen poll notes that only 36 percent of Americans feel the president is doing a good job on the economy.

But now we know who's really to blame for all this: *Jesus.*

The president spoke about his faith, as a professing Christian, at the National Prayer Breakfast last week, and said that it was Jesus Christ who inspired him to pursue all the big policies that conservatives would argue are hurting our economy. For example, Obamacare—his center-piece legislation. President Obama said, "When I talk about making sure insurance companies aren't discriminating against those who are already sick...or making sure that unscrupulous lenders aren't taking advantage of the most vulnerable among us, I do so because I genuinely believe it will make the economy stronger for everybody. But I also do it because I know that far too many neighbors in our country have been hurt and treated unfairly over the last few years, and I believe in God's command to 'love thy neighbor as thyself.'"

The president went on to qualify the notion that the Golden Rule is found in other religions too. He added, "But for me as a Christian, it also coincides with Jesus's teaching that 'unto whom much is given, much shall be required.'"

However, before he became too non-inclusive for his progressive base, he added that Jews and Muslims essentially teach the same as well.

Islam does? Tell that to the Christians being murdered in Muslim lands, as described in *Newsweek*'s cover story.

I won't argue about the Jewish teaching on that point. After all, "love thy neighbor as thyself," which is emphasized in the New Testament, is quoted from Moses in Leviticus in the Old Testament. The president is certainly correct that Jesus cared for the downtrodden and the poor and told us to do likewise. But things go astray when the government tries to do it.

The president goes on to say that the notion of caring for the least of these informs all of his policies, including foreign aid. He bases this on what Jesus said in His parable of the sheep and the goats in Matthew 25—that when people care for the least of these, they care for Him. Of course, Obama doesn't see the unborn as among the least of these. But that's a discussion for another day.

Backing up for a moment, let's consider the wider question of letting the Bible have a say in our government. Not too long ago, a politician derisively said that the Bible can't be used to fashion any meaningful politics. He noted, "Which passages of Scripture should guide our public policies? Should we go with Leviticus, which suggests slavery's ok? Or we could go with Deuteronomy, which suggests stoning your child if he strays from the faith? Or should we just stick to the Sermon on the Mount, a passage that is so radical that it's doubtful that our own Defense Department would survive its applications? [Laughter] Folks haven't been reading their Bibles."

Who said these things?

That was Senator Barack Obama, June 28, 2006.

I disagree with his interpretations and his examples. But based on his recent revelations, I guess the moral of the story is that if one uses the Bible to promote a liberal agenda, then that's fine. Not so a conservative one.

As I see it, the president basically hides behind Jesus to promote a form of big government dependency. Socialism light, if you will. The problem with socialism, according to Maggie Thatcher, is that sooner or later you run out of other people's money.

Did Jesus teach socialism? No. Jesus taught the sinfulness of man. Socialism is predicated on the alleged innate goodness of man. Socialism has never worked and never will work because man is not basically good. Capitalism works because it conforms to our nature as it is. Hard work and enlightened self-interest, with individual generosity, help the poor far more than big government can do. Let big government get out of the way, so more people can get back to work.

Also, Jesus put His seal of approval on the law, that is, the Old Testament. Of course, the Ten Commandments tell us that it's wrong to steal. Implied in that commandment is private property. The Decalogue also states, "Thou shalt not covet." Socialism builds on the twin pillars of state envy and theft.

In addition to these considerations, nowhere does the Bible say that the state—which is ultimately brute force—is responsible for taking care of the needy. That's the family's job, the church's role, and individuals' duty—all on a voluntary basis.

The Bible also condemns illegitimacy. Yet the welfare state, in the name of helping the poor, has subsidized illegitimacy—thus plunging tens of millions of Americans into perpetual poverty. The family is the key to upward mobility, but welfare has destroyed the urban family. Many people, gifted by God with all sorts of abilities, essentially waste their lives just barely getting by on government handouts. We have decades of proven experience that welfare as we know it keeps the recipients down. Using the force of government to take from one citizen the fruit of his labor in order to give to another citizen constitutes a form of theft and promotes laziness.

While a young man in Hawaii, a man he called Frank mentored Obama. Research has uncovered that it was Frank Marshall Davis. History professor Dr. Paul Kengor, author of the book *Dupes*, documents that Davis was a card-carrying member of the Communist Party, USA. May the president unlearn those heresies.

However well intentioned, all government redistribution of wealth ends up with virtually everyone losing. No, it's not Jesus's fault if men misrepresent Him.

58

REPEAL THE BILL

Originally published on October 28, 2010

The government rammed Obamacare down our throats despite the will of we the people. Congress, to represent us, should repeal it.

Every poll I'm aware of shows the Republicans regaining the House. It doesn't seem likely, but it is also possible that they could regain the Senate. Regardless of how this comes down on Tuesday, I think they should make every effort to repeal Obamacare. The only reason it passed was all sorts of backroom deals, such as "the Louisiana Purchase" to acquire Mary Landrieu's vote, or the Nebraska deal to get Ben Nelson's vote.[1]

Since the Democrats are beholden to the trial lawyers, Obama's version of health-care "reform" did not include tort reform. Genuine health-care reform would have seriously dealt with runaway lawsuit abuse, which is certainly one factor in driving up health-care costs.

Meanwhile, the real cost of Obamacare will pass onto the shoulders of our children and grandchildren. It's as if the eighth commandment has been rewritten as, "Thou shalt not steal—unless thou art the government."

One of the provisions in the 2,000-page bill of Obamacare—that nobody seems to have read, perhaps not even Obama—is the hiring of some 16,000 new IRS agents. When I first heard that, I thought of the phrase in the Declaration of Independence describing how King George III has done such and such "to harass our people."

---

1. Neither Mary Landrieu nor Ben Nelson was reelected to the Senate after their votes in favor of Obamacare.

The saddest aspect of the whole Obamacare deal was Congressman Bart Stupak falling for the president's pledge not to pay for abortions through the federal takeover of our health-care system. Stupak represented a handful of other House members' votes. Those votes were enough that if they had held the line for the pro-life cause, Obamacare would not have passed. When the president promised on paper, through an executive order, to do that which was contrary to the written piece of legislation, Stupak fell for it. I once interviewed Rep. Stupak on the subject of partial-birth abortion. He was appalled at that barbaric form of infanticide by any other name. Tragically, if we do not repeal Obamacare, perhaps partial-birth abortions will be performed—at taxpayers' expense, no less. I think Bart Stupak spared himself a lot of grief by deciding not to run again. This is a sad ending to an overall noble career of public service.

Meanwhile, the effect of his caving in to the president's pressure and that of Nancy Pelosi is beginning to hit the rest of us. Already, many doctors of conscience (the very men and women I would prefer as my doctors—the kind that would agree with the Hippocratic Oath) speak of leaving medicine. What a tragedy. Reportedly, 46 percent of doctors have said they will leave the profession because of Obamacare.

Even those Americans who are pro-abortion rights might have qualms about their taxpayer dollars going to fund abortions. Obamacare is not only bad news for the unborn and those who care about the unborn, it's also bad news at the other end of the life spectrum. When the government takes over the healthcare system, eventually they decide to ration care. There are not unlimited dollars. So Sarah Palin wasn't far off when she said "death panels" would decide who should live and who should die.

The problem with Obamacare is the premise itself. Who says it's the government's responsibility to provide healthcare? By definition, to do so, they forcibly take money from Taxpayer A to redistribute to Taxpayer B. The only people who enrich themselves through such a socialistic scheme are the bureaucrats. That's why some bedroom communities in Maryland and in Virginia (suburban Washington, D.C.) are among the wealthiest in the country.

We have not really begun to feel the full damage of Obamacare—

although, already some people are losing their insurance—something we were told would not happen. During the debate, one conservative noted the lopsided unfairness for government to assume power over private health-insurance providers. It was akin to an alligator facing off with a duck. The duck doesn't stand a chance.

Rather than make healthcare more affordable and more available in America, Obamacare will jack up the price for everyone and limit our choices. It will prematurely kill more people—all in the name of helping the poor, the very ones who can't afford some life-saving operation by flying to Costa Rica or elsewhere.

Tuesday's election will be in part a referendum on Obamacare. I hope the voters will speak loudly and clearly against it, and the victors will work to defund it and ultimately repeal it before it's too late.

59

DETROIT: THE TRAGEDY OF BIG GOVERNMENT RUN AMOK

Originally published on October 10, 2012

We can see what America could become if we went down a path toward more big government, and it's not a pretty picture. Detroit, Michigan, formerly one of our finest cities, is a stark reminder of what can happen when big government programs grow to the nth degree. The nanny state has made life dangerous. The police in that city now warn that visitors enter there at their own risk. On Saturday, officers held an "Enter at Your Own Risk" rally to make it clear to outsiders that the police cannot protect everybody.

Donato Iorio serves as an attorney for the Detroit Police Officer Association. He told a reporter with the CBS affiliate: "Detroit is America's most violent city. Its homicide rate is the highest in the country, and yet the Detroit Police Department is grossly understaffed" (Source: Kathryn Larson, WWJ, October 6, 2012). He also added, "The DPOA believes that there is a war in Detroit, but there should be a war on crime, not a war on its officers." And he noted that out of a force of two thousand officers, hundreds have left the department since June.

And he pointed out that the situation has grown desperate: "These are the men and women [to whom] we look to protect us... and police officers can't protect you if they're not there. Officers are leaving simply because they can't afford to stay in Detroit and work twelve-hour shifts for what they are getting paid.... These police officers are beyond demoralized. These officers are leaving hand over fist because

they can no longer afford to stay on [at] the department and protect
the public."

So what does this have to do with the rest of us? Detroit is a picture
of big government run amok. It's a picture of what America could look
like if some politicians get their way and we change from a network of
free-enterprise zones, with personal and family responsibility and private sharing into a planned command economy.

Of all the video shoots I've been on (and I've been on many, all
over the country, and even a few overseas), our visit to Detroit a couple years ago was among the most memorable. As you drive around
Detroit, for miles and miles you see ruined houses everywhere. Often
there are blocks where most of the houses are completely abandoned
and in shambles. But then there's also one or two families living in one
of the houses.

A local black pastor, Levon Yuille, acted as our guide. He also got a
"lookout" for us, to watch our backs during the taping of our program.
Pastor Yuille said, "We are not in a Third World nation. This is Detroit,
Michigan."

Yuille noted, "In the fifties, Detroit was the number one industrial
city of America. It was the gem of middle-class prosperity....Detroit
used to be one of our most vibrant cities, but now it's lost half of its population and has a skyrocketing crime rate....The homicides here in the
city are just out of control, and only about 10 percent of them are solved."

Only about 30 percent of the children of Detroit graduate high
school. About a third of the population is on welfare. About 50 percent
are unemployed. Many factories are closed down.

What happened to a city that was once the eleventh largest city in
the country?

Pastor Yuille says that big government programs played a key role.
He told me, "The design of welfare was to make things better for people.
And I think with good intentions, folks thought if you go in and you
give folks something, rather than motivate them—you know, the old
cliché, 'If you give a person a fish, they'll never learn to fish, but if you
take and teach them how to fish, they learn how to be self-sufficient.'
Welfare didn't teach them how to fish. It taught them how to wait for
somebody to do for them what they could've done for themselves."

Furthermore, the big government programs broke the back of the family. Yuille laments, "When you had a mother that may have seven or eight kids and, you know, no dad in the home and welfare discouraged a dad from being in the home, and so that diminished the quality of life in the community as well as discipline in the home,... [that] contributed so much to the demise of this community." I still believe in a safety net, but this is a complete abuse of the system.

Joseph Farah, founder of *WorldNetDaily*, says, "Americans need to see what that city looks like, because that city is an illustration of what happens when you've got big government in charge. All the big government programs of the sixties, seventies, and eighties all contributed to the blight that we see today in Detroit. And of course, the crumbling auto industry, now taken over in part by big government, once again, doesn't make it any easier."

As we toured ruined neighborhood after neighborhood, Pastor Yuille added, "It breaks my heart to see what's happened in the last forty-two years. There was a time when these neighborhoods were beautiful, the lawns were well maintained, and you had houses in every one of these vacant spots. And to think that this is what's happened to a city when the government said they were going to take care of people, this is the tragic end result."

Yuille sees a warning for the whole country in the "Enter at Your Own Risk" city: "If we continue to do what Detroit did for forty years—give people things they didn't work for, give them social programs—we can expect this to happen all over America."

60

DID THE DEVIL MAKE HIM DO IT?

Originally published on February 23, 2012

GOP presidential candidate Rick Santorum is getting a lot of flack right now for some remarks that he made at a Catholic college in 2008. He said that Satan is out to get America.

Here's a portion of the candidate's quote (not to a general audience, but to fellow believers at Ave Maria College in Florida): "If you were Satan, who would you attack in this day and age? There is no one else to go after, other than the United States. And that's been the case for now almost two hundred years—once America's pre-eminence was sown by our great founding fathers. He didn't have much success in the early days—our foundation was very strong—in fact, *is* very strong. But over time, that great acidic quality of time corrodes away even the strongest foundations. And Satan has done so, by attacking the great institutions of America, using those great vices of pride, vanity, and sensuality."

And the problem is?

Did the devil make him do it, i.e., say foolish things that everyone knows are not true? If there is no devil, if Satan does not exist, then Santorum would be the fool as some portray him. But what if there really is a devil, as described in the Bible—the great angel who asserted himself above God and took a third of the angels with him in a revolt in heaven, which he lost? Now he aims to steal, kill, and destroy.

About three hundred years ago, Puritan writer John Milton wrote *Paradise Lost,* which is a retelling of this Biblical theme. Some scholars have called that book the greatest epic in the English language. To the modern intelligentsia, Santorum may be crazy. Yet his opinions are closer to Milton's than those of Bill Maher. The press is having a field day with this whole controversy, another chance to paint Senator Santorum as out of the mainstream.

What exactly comprises "the mainstream"? If the mainstream refers to the opinions of the majority of Americans, then Rick is in the mainstream. A Gallup poll found that 68 percent of Americans believe the devil exists. Twenty percent do not, and 12 percent aren't sure. Is this not enough to establish Santorum in the mainstream? Or do the liberal media have the sole right to define for politicians what religious opinion is "in the mainstream"?

Are Rev. Jeremiah Wright's opinions "in the mainstream"? He famously said, "Not God bless America, but God d—— America." The mainstream media, for the most part, ignored his diatribes in the 2008 election. And Obama claimed that, even though he attended weekly for twenty years in that church, he basically didn't listen to Wright's sermons.

Mitt Romney is a Mormon. But during this campaign, for the most part, the press has ignored the particular views of Mormons, which are out of the mainstream of historic Christian views—such as the idea that Satan and Jesus are brothers (although some Mormons don't consider that a part of Mormon doctrine). So far, Americans for the most part have chosen not to delve into the details of Mormon doctrine, presumably out of respect.

So why should Santorum's remarks make him seem like a whack job? His statements are clearly in the mainstream of historic Christian theology. That would include the opinions of the vast majority of the founding fathers.

Historian David Barton once told me that of the two hundred fifty men we call the founding fathers, only about a dozen of them, at the most, had theological views that would not fit the mode of conservative theological positions. The vast majority were Trinitarian Christians and would have affirmed the belief that Satan exists.

So Santorum's remarks don't put him out of the mainstream with the founding fathers. Besides, the Constitution prohibits imposing a religious test for those running for national office.

Nowadays, to hear some pundits, you would think that the only people who should run for president are those holding a basically agnostic or atheistic worldview.

C. S. Lewis, probably the greatest Christian writer of the twentieth century, was a professor at Oxford, then Cambridge. In the 1940s, he made the cover of *Time* magazine to feature his innovative book *The Screwtape Letters*. The *Letters* presented a fictional account of an older demon corresponding with a younger one to help produce the most effective spiritual shipwreck of a man who had recently joined the church.

In his foreword to the book, Lewis observed that one of Satan's most clever strategies is to encourage people to deny his existence. I'd say, in light of the firestorm sparked by Santorum's remarks, the devil is doing a remarkable job.

61

IT'S MOURNING IN AMERICA[1]

Originally published on November 7, 2012

After the election results, I'm tempted to say, "Well, it was a great country, while it lasted." Someone quipped they could picture a gravestone: "The United States of America. Born: July 4, 1776. Died: November 6, 2012."

But the election results didn't take God by surprise. He once said, "Put not your trust in princes" (Psalm 146:3 KJV). Meaning, don't put your confidence in politicians. Even the good ones can let you down. The results appear to be very bad for traditional values. Government leaders have upheld abortion rights in virtually every case. For the first time to my knowledge, same-sex marriage won in three state referenda—Maine, Maryland, and Washington. Until now, usually judicial fiat has imposed same-sex marriage on the people, despite their voting against it.

Where were the churches? Where were the values voters? Clearly, we need a great deal of education.

While the economy was such a critical issue in the election, even there the vote seemed to go toward more bloated government. Apparently, 47 percent of the country relies heavily on government subsidies. Some of these, such as Social Security, the people themseleves paid into. In other cases, they have not. I guess the 53 percent who work had better work harder now to help feed their own families and others too.

George Washington once warned the nation against heavy debt. In his Farewell Address, he wrote, "As a very important source of strength

---

1. Written after the election results of 2012.

and security, cherish public credit. One method of preserving it is to use it as sparingly as possible, avoiding occasions of expense by cultivating peace, but remembering also that timely disbursements to prepare for danger frequently prevent much greater disbursements to repel it." In sum, we should have credit available to us when necessary—but go into debt as little and as seldom as possible.

And Washington added that we should be "avoiding likewise the accumulation of debt, not only by shunning occasions of expense, but by vigorous exertion in time of peace to discharge the debts which un-avoidable wars may have occasioned, not ungenerously throwing upon posterity the burden which we ourselves ought to bear."

This is a lesson we need to heed but at present are not heeding. When the president took office, the nation owed nearly $10 trillion. Yet in less than four years that number has shot up to $16 trillion. How can that possibly be paid off? As Washington put it, we are "ungenerously throwing upon posterity [our children and grandchildren] the burden," which we ought to pay ourselves.

I'll never forget how a conservative talk host once contrasted conservatism and liberalism. The difference between a conservative and a liberal is simple: The conservative believes that you are best qualified to take care of you and your family. The liberal believes that the government is best qualified to take care of you and your family.

After the election, a friend wrote: "So, what do we do? Buy as little as you possibly can, pay off all of your debt, save up a healthy emergency fund, put as much of your money as you can into hard assets, and continue buying as little as possible. Many people buying fewer things will hurt the economy. So be it. We can then watch the economy tank, watch the dollar devalue even further than it already has, and watch Obama leave office in disgrace after another failed term."

Meanwhile, as to healthcare? Take care of yourself. Eat right, exercise a lot, die anyway. But seriously, as a friend of mine who got me into running about eight years ago said, "Sure beats the doctors' bills." But even that will only go so far. When Obamacare kicks in, don't be surprised that we'll have fewer health-care options and pay more for them.

My wife (who grew up in Norway) says she thinks a big reason for the voting results were decades and decades of godless education in the public schools. She may be right.

Ann Coulter said this to me in an interview she gave me about five years ago: "What the government schools do—it is the Left's madrassas, and they propagandize to the children, six hours a day, twelve years of the child's life. I would give them [i.e., the Left] the presidency, the House, the Senate, if we could have children for six hours a day to give them our religion. But no, no. That used to be the purpose of school, oddly enough, to teach Biblical truths. No, that is absolutely prohibited. Now, it is baptism—it's six hours a day being brainwashed into the liberal religion."

The biggest losers in Tuesday's election? The unborn. Probably millions of unborn babies will die because of Tuesday's election results. They will be denied the fundamental "right to life" theoretically guaranteed in our nation's birth certificate, the Declaration of Independence.

Tragically, millions of women will be deceived into thinking that abortion is a solution to their unwanted pregnancy. They'll have an abortion, only to regret it for the rest of their lives. (Some of the most ardent pro-life advocates today are women who have had abortions. They often volunteer untold hours in pro-life pregnancy centers.)

Even Thomas Jefferson once observed—and you can see this chiseled in stone at the Jefferson Memorial, "I tremble for my country when I reflect that God is just; that his justice cannot sleep forever."

62

WHAT WOULD GEORGE WASHINGTON
SAY ABOUT THE 2012 ELECTION?

Originally published on November 6, 2012

That seems like a speculative topic—to try and guess what our first president under the Constitution would have to say to modern Americans. But actually, I won't speculate at all. I'll use some of his own writings to make my points (or his points). And they won't be from some of his obscure writings, gleaned from arcane, private letters the way the Supreme Court did in a 1947 decision with a private letter Thomas Jefferson wrote to the Danbury Baptists, that changed the way religion—specifically Christianity—is treated in the public square.

Upon facing retirement after two terms, which he thought enough, George Washington, the father of our country, sent out his Farewell Address in written form (September 19, 1796). In this classic piece of American political writing, he gave some warnings to his fellow Americans (and us), as a "parting friend" might do.

He said in that message, "Of all the dispositions and habits which lead to political prosperity, religion and morality are indispensable supports. In vain would that man claim the tribute of patriotism, who should labor to subvert these great pillars of human happiness." When the founding fathers spoke of "religion," they spoke of Christianity, in a nation that at the time was 99.8 percent Christian.[1]

Like the other founders, Washington believed that for the Constitution to work, the people needed to be virtuous. As he himself put

1. Benjamin Hart, "The Wall that Protestantism Built," *Policy Review,* Fall 1988.

it in the Farewell Address, "Virtue or morality is a necessary spring of popular government."

What was the source of virtue, according to them (even some of the unorthodox amongst them)?

Religion, on a voluntary basis—always with the rights of conscience in place. Thanks to the framers of our nation, we are free to believe (or not believe) whatever we want in this country. Only to God, and not the state, shall we give an account.

Washington elaborated on the importance of "religion and morality" (again from his final public message): "The mere politician, equally with the pious man, ought to respect and to cherish them. A volume could not trace all their connections with private and public felicity. Let it simply be asked: Where is the security for property, for reputation, for life, if the sense of religious obligation desert the oaths which are the instruments of investigation in courts of justice?"

In case anyone doesn't get the point, he basically asked, How can morality continue without faith? It cannot: "And let us with caution indulge the supposition that morality can be maintained without religion. Whatever may be conceded to the influence of refined education on minds of peculiar structure, reason and experience both forbid us to expect that national morality can prevail in exclusion of religious principle."

But so many today think we're so much smarter than that these days. In fact, in 1980, in *Stone v. Graham,* the U.S. Supreme Court struck down the posting of the Ten Commandments in schools. Why? Because Little Johnny might read them and obey them.

They declared: "If the posted copies of the Ten Commandments are to have any effect at all, it will be to induce the schoolchildren to read, meditate upon, perhaps to venerate and obey, the Commandments. However desirable this might be as a matter of private devotion, it is not a permissible state objective under the Establishment Clause."

However the outcome of today's elections, in all the different races, from local dogcatcher to president, we have a lot of ground to make up.

George Washington also said that as a nation we should never expect God's blessings if we continue to defy His Word. In his First Inaugural Address, as we have seen, he said: "The propitious smiles of Heaven can never be expected on a nation that disregards the eternal rules of order and right which Heaven itself has ordained."

The propitious smiles seem to have turned into a frown lately. But why should God be pleased with a nation that slaughters millions of unborn babies, redefines God-ordained marriage, and is awash with immorality?

And, of course, we have also seen how George Washington said we must imitate Christ ("the Divine Author of our blessed Religion") if we "hope to be a happy nation."

How far we have fallen from the vision of the father of our country, who said that we would only be a happy nation if we imitate Christ. So I have two questions:

Are we imitating Christ? No, not at present.

Are we a happy nation? Not at present. May God help us to get back on the right track.

63

OBAMA IS THE "PICK-AND-CHOOSE PRESIDENT"

Originally published on March 2, 2011

The rule of law should count for something in America, but Obama is the pick-and-choose president. "I'll take a little of this; I'll take a little of that. But I don't like this, so I won't deal with it." He decides which laws he'll enforce and which ones he'll ignore. For example, the president has decided that DOMA, the Defense of Marriage Act, passed by a majority in Congress in 1996 and signed into law by President Clinton, is not worth fighting for. So Obama has instructed Attorney General Eric Holder to halt any attempt to fight off challenges to this law.

DOMA, which was passed in opposition to same-sex marriage, is still the law of the land. But apparently not to our "pick-and-choose president," who is presumably trying to throw red meat to his far-left base. Meanwhile, as Obama jettisons any support for DOMA, he ignores court rulings against his crown jewel—Obamacare—which has already been declared unconstitutional.

The founding fathers in their brilliance set up a system of checks and balances. Knowing that we human beings by nature are prone to do wrong—especially if we have too much power—the founders worked hard to make sure that no one group or no one individual would be able to lord it over the others. Article II, Section 3 of the Constitution says of the president, "He shall take Care that the Laws be faithfully executed."

But Obama makes up his own rules, it would seem. I guess the "pick-and-choose president" has overlooked that clause.

If the president doesn't like a law that Congress has duly passed and signed into law, counteracting legal remedies exist. But the president can't just arbitrarily pick and choose which laws to apply and which ones not to apply.

He's the president, not a dictator.

This is America, not a banana republic.

Perhaps we should have listened more carefully when he said in late October 2008, "We're just five days away from *fundamentally transforming* America" (emphasis mine). Fundamentally transforming America? The Constitution be damned. Obama does what he pleases.

Judge Robert Bork is a former Yale professor and a best-selling author. Politics infamously torpedoed his 1987 nomination to the Supreme Court by Ronald Reagan. He was so well qualified that one authority said he was the most qualified candidate to be nominated to that position in half a century. However, because he believed the Constitution should be taken as the founding fathers intended, and not as a "thing of wax" (to borrow a phrase from Thomas Jefferson), the Left pulled out all the stops, lied about him, and did everything to stop him from serving on the Court.

Tragically, they succeeded.

I interviewed him once on the subject of judicial activism. He made this point to me: "I've seen some writings saying that the framers did not intend that we should be bound by their understanding of what they had done. I can think of few more preposterous statements. Why they argued and deliberated and carried on and negotiated and so forth to get the words just right, if they didn't think anybody would be bound by them, is a mystery. It doesn't make any sense at all."

If this were a conservative doing what Obama is doing, I don't think we'd hear the end of it.

Rush Limbaugh made the point recently that should Sarah Palin be president in 2013, what if she said something like this: "I don't like *Roe v. Wade*. So I'm just throwing it out. From now on, abortion is illegal in America. I have spoken." Similarly, Newt Gingrich said that if a conservative did what Obama has done, he or she could be open for impeachment charges.

The ultimate remedy for this is at the ballot box. You would think that with the recent shellacking the president received he would have learned his lesson. But noooooo.

I guess you can take the politician out of Chicago politics. But you can't take Chicago politics out of the politician.

Truly, Barack Obama is the "pick-and-choose president."

64

MADAM SPEAKER, YOU'VE GOT TO BE KIDDING

Originally published on June 8, 2010

Well, now I've heard it all. For the last several months, we have witnessed in America a government that is not of the people, by the people, or for the people, but rather a government where "the people have ceased to be their own rulers," to borrow a phrase from Lincoln's First Inaugural Address.

Nancy Pelosi, who's at the heart of the most arrogant abuse of power we have witnessed—perhaps ever—in American history, blames it on Jesus. She claims that her inspiration for all that she's doing to the American people (she would say, *for* the American people) is that she's simply trying to implement governmental policies that are "in keeping with the values of" the Word made flesh, that is, Jesus Christ.[1]

Wow.

I didn't realize Jesus was pro-abortion. Nancy Pelosi has pushed a pro-abortion agenda in all sorts of legislation, including the new healthcare bill. I didn't realize Jesus was pro big government. Government takeover of healthcare is supposedly in keeping with His values. I didn't realize Jesus was so anti-freedom, as seen in example after example of Nancy Pelosi's legislation.

It's ironic too that when the Left finds religion, no one raises a stink about the so-called "separation of church and state." That principle apparently only applies to people with conservative values.

---

1. Nancy Pelosi at a Catholic Community Conference on Capitol Hill, May 6, 2010, cnsnews.com.

"And that Word," Pelosi said, "is, we have to give voice to what that means in terms of public policy that would be in keeping with the values of the Word. The Word. Isn't it a beautiful word when you think of it? It just covers everything. The Word. Fill it in with anything you want. But, of course, we know it means: 'The Word was made flesh and dwelt amongst us.' And that's the great mystery of our faith. He will come again. He will come again. So, we have to make sure we're prepared to answer in this life, or otherwise, as to how we have measured up."

If we take her remarks at face value, then she is telling us Jesus would sanction abortion—since Mrs. Pelosi certainly does. As a student of Scripture and a follower of Jesus, I don't see how that could be.

In the Word of God, which Christ said He came to uphold (and which Nancy Pelosi claims to want to reflect in public policy), David states in Psalm 139:13–16, "For you created my inmost being; you knit me together in my mother's womb. I praise you because I am fearfully and wonderfully made; your works are wonderful, I know that full well. My frame was not hidden from you when I was made in the secret place. When I was woven together in the depths of the earth, your eyes saw my unformed body. All the days ordained for me were written in your book before one of them came to be."

Or Jeremiah, the weeping prophet, says this in the very opening of his book: "The word of the Lord came to me, saying, 'Before I formed you in the womb I knew you.'" This is God talking: "'Before you were born I set you apart; I appointed you as a prophet to the nations'" (Jeremiah 1:4–5). So, here's this little unborn baby being appointed a prophet of the nations.

Jumping ahead to the New Testament, in Luke 1, we read of two pregnant cousins visiting with each other—Elizabeth, who is pregnant with John the Baptist, and Mary, who is pregnant with Jesus. Elizabeth says, "As soon as the sound of your greeting reached my ears, the baby in my womb leaped for joy" (Luke 1:44). Baby? Not according to Nancy Pelosi, who fights for abortion rights through all nine months of pregnancy. The Greek word in Luke 1 is *brephos*, which is the same for baby, born or unborn.

Mother Teresa once said this: "If we accept that a mother can kill even her own child, how can we tell others not to kill one another?" I think that's a very, very profound question.

I really do wish Nancy Pelosi's policies were *truly* impacted by the Word of God. When I see the legislation she pushes for, including all the pro-abortion laws—just as one example—I just have to wonder, Which translation of the Word is she reading from?

65

GOVERNMENT SHOULD STOP
RUINING THE FAMILY

Originally published on June 15, 2010

In all of the talk about the health-care takeover by the Obama administration, there was a story that was almost completely overlooked: the
potential impact on the family. The family is the key to upward mobility. Any government move that weakens the family hurts all of society.
The old expression sums it up well: As the family goes, so goes society.

Lost in the maze of stories about the government takeover of our
nation's health-care system is this story from Martin Vaughan in *The
Wall Street Journal*: "Couples Pay More Than Unmarried Under Health
Bill" (January 11, 2010). Vaughan writes, "Some married couples would
pay thousands of dollars more for the same health insurance coverage
[than] unmarried people living together.... For scores of low-income
and middle-income couples, it could mean a hike of $2,000 or more in
annual insurance premiums the moment they say 'I do.'"

This is very bad news because if the bill goes into effect (without
being repealed—an uphill struggle to say the least), it will further hurt
the working poor. It will further subsidize illegitimacy and weaken the
marital ties proven over and over to be helpful for society.

A decade ago, Linda J. Waite and Maggie Gallagher wrote a definitive book on how marriage is good for society on virtually every front,
*The Case for Marriage: Why Married People Are Happier, Healthier, and
Better Off Financially* (2000). They pored through all the research and
concluded:

The scientific evidence is now overwhelming: Marriage is not just one of a wide variety of alternate family forms or intimate relations, each of which are equally good at promoting the well-being of children or adults. Marriage is not merely a private taste or a private relation; it is an important public good. As marriage weakens, the costs are borne not only by individual children or families, but also by all of us taxpayers, citizens, and neighbors. We all incur the costs of higher crime, welfare, education and health-care expenditures, and in reduced security for our own marriage investments. Simply as a matter of public health alone, to take just one public consequence of marriage's decline, a new campaign to reduce marriage failure is as important as the campaign to reduce smoking. (Waite and Gallagher, *The Case for Marriage*, 2000, 186)

But we have seen the government interfere with marriage—especially among the poor. In the name of helping the poor, the government has largely broken the back of the urban family. In the welfare state and in the so-called "War on Poverty," government bureaucrats said in effect, "Dad, if you get out of the house, then we'll give mom more money." It legitimized illegitimacy and made it harder for these families to stay afloat while staying together. And a fatherless family is generally a difficult situation for a child to deal with. It's not insurmountable, but it's still very, very difficult. Children need both their dad and their mom.

The government bureaucrats also said, "Mom, if you have more babies, regardless of who the father is, we'll give you more money." People aren't stupid. They'll do whatever the government subsidizes. Government bureaucrats have gained power at the expense of the virtual destruction of poor families.

Walter Fontroy is a civil rights leader and Baptist minister who has spoken out against the devastating impact of the absence of fathers from the African-American family. He notes that such policies have been particularly terrible for the black family, where the number of children born in broken families skyrocketed from 30 percent to 80 percent. According to Matt Daniels, founder of the Alliance for Marriage, Fontroy said: "If this doesn't stop, we'll be back to slavery, when nobody knew their dad."

Martin Vaughan in the above-referenced article in *The Wall Street Journal* notes, "Under current law, marriage can have a negative impact on a person's ability to claim the earned income tax credit and welfare benefits including food stamps."

It's tragic that the new health-care bill—which is a travesty on virtually every front and should be repealed—will, in the long run, create more poverty in the name of supposedly helping the poor.

66

WHAT WAS LEFT OUT OF THE 9/11 MEMORIALS?

Originally published on September 13, 2011

Now that the dust has settled from the memorials commemorating the tenth anniversary of 9/11, we can see what was included and what was excluded.

I was pleased that the president read Scripture (from Psalm 46).

I was displeased that the mayor of New York City chose not to invite any Christian clergyman to participate, as this would supposedly violate the separation of church and state. Never mind that the founders of this country—by their words and by their actions—showed over and over again that they intended religion (by which they meant Christianity in its various stripes) to flourish, even in the public arena, on a voluntary basis. Technically, if the mayor's interpretation of the First Amendment is right, what in the world is the president doing reading from the Holy Bible—at an official function, no less?

It is good that the dead of 9/11 were honored. It is good that also honored were the many heroes of that time—such as the firemen, who rushed into the World Trade Center to save as many lives as they could. But something else was generally missing from the 9/11 commemorations, conspicuous by its absence.

If you had no idea about the history of 9/11, and you observed Sunday's commemorations, you might well think that all these poor people died in a natural disaster, not a deliberate attack. The threat of radical Islam was not mentioned (or if it was, I missed it). This is a threat that is alive today, just as it was alive on that Tuesday ten years ago.

Thereligionofpeace.com maintains a counter, keeping track of how many separate attacks jihadists have committed worldwide since 9/11. The Madrid train bombing counts as just one. The July 7, 2005, double-decker bus bombings, etc. in London count as another one. How many have there been? 17,729.[1]

Although Christians and Jews (and atheists and others) are often the targets of these attacks, usually, more than any other group, radical Islamists kill Muslims who don't share their radical views. Why are they doing this? The radical Muslims are obeying their understanding of the Koran, where it says that you are to slay the infidels wherever you find them (Surah 9:29). (Heretics may be viewed as infidels.)

It's estimated that of the 1.5 billion or so Muslims around the world, less than 15 percent commit to a radical version of Islam. The problem is that 15 percent of 1.5 billion people is still tens of millions of people.

Political correctness hinders us from naming the enemy—radical Islam. Why do they hate us? Because we won't convert. Again, not every Muslim believes the way of the terrorist. On my radio show last night, I interviewed a living Muslim hero, Dr. Zuhdi Jasser, the president of the American Islamic Forum for Democracy and host of the documentary *The Third Jihad.*

I asked Dr. Jasser about the Fort Hood shooting. Eyewitnesses said the alleged shooter cried out, "Allahu Akbar" ("Allah is the greatest," which is what radical Muslims cry out before they kill someone), as he shot and killed thirteen and wounded others. His business card had "SOA" printed on it (standing for Soldier of Allah).

Yet the Pentagon came out in 2010 with an eighty-six-page report on the Fort Hood shooting, and it didn't mention Islam, Muslim, Koran, "Allahu Akbar," etc. It didn't even mention the shooter's name (Nidal Hasan), presumably because it is a Muslim name.

How can we win in this war that we didn't ask for if we can't even name the enemy that wants to kill us?

Dr. Jasser noted, "I think [the Pentagon report] is demonstrating that we are completely wasting our time, and that we're not address-

---

1. Author's Note: a check of the statistic on thereligionofpeace.com as of July 31, 2018 shows almost double that number: "Islamic terrorists have carried out more than 33,577 deadly terror attacks since 9/11."

ing the root causes, which are the separatism of political Islam from American-type societies." He added that as a medical doctor, he has to diagnose illnesses all the time or he'll never be able to properly treat the patient. Because of political correctness, we're not treating the threat of radical Islam properly.

Thankfully, God, in His sovereignty, can convert even radical Muslims. Estimates say that more Muslims have come to faith in Jesus in the last fourteen years than in the last 1400 years.

As Faisal Malick, a former Muslim from Pakistan who now believes in Jesus, once told me, "The more Muslims that come to Christ, there's less Muslims left for the terrorists to recruit in the midst of dissolution in our world, and create more problems around the world."

67

STOP THE FALSE DICHOTOMY

Originally published on May 10, 2011

Mitch Daniels is considering the possibility of running for president. The Indiana governor said today that if he runs, his chances of beating Obama are "quite good."

Unfortunately, around the time he gave his speech to CPAC, the Conservative Political Action Conference in February, Mitch Daniels said it's best to put the social issues on the back burner and just focus on the economic ones. He said we conservatives should call for a "truce" on issues like abortion and focus instead on runaway government spending. To me, this is a false dichotomy. "Are you *either* a fiscal conservative or a social conservative?"

A lot of the runaway government spending is related to the social issues. Short version: The government has helped exacerbate the breakdown of the family. In the wake of the breakdown of the family, the government comes in to supposedly help. But they bankrupt us through shelling out for those government services. Out-of-control entitlements cause more runaway government spending than all other expenditures combined. Much of the entitlement spending has to do with fixing problems caused in part by government programs. So it all becomes a vicious cycle. Try and stop the runaway government bleeding and they liken you to the Grinch.

It's easier to do it Obama's way. Say that you oppose irresponsible government spending, but then put in your budget all sorts of unsustainable expenditures with no real brakes applied to entitlement programs. The media applauds him.

As Church Lady would observe, "How convenient!"

Whoever runs for president against President Obama needs to build a consensus of different types of conservatives. Reagan provides a great model. Reagan built a coalition, like a three-legged stool. He welcomed the social conservatives (the pro-life, pro-family values types), the strong-on-defense supporters, and the fiscal conservatives as well. If any one of these three prongs had been missing, our fortieth president might not have won election or reelection. He certainly would not have won the landslide victory he did in 1984 when he carried every state but one.

Recently, I asked (now former) Senator Jim DeMint of South Carolina about this false dichotomy between fiscal conservatism and social issues conservatism. I said, "Some people are saying, 'Let's just focus on fiscal responsibility, but forget the social issues that the values voters are concerned about, like abortion, same-sex marriage, and so forth.' What are your thoughts on this?"

He answered, "Well, we have to realize that there is a connection between fiscal issues and cultural issues. In fact, one of the biggest expenditures we have as a federal government is related to our cultural decline of children born outside of marriage and the social implications of drug use and school dropouts and unemployment and incarceration. This is related to cultural decline of social issues. So, we can't separate the two." He went on to add, "Fiscal issues are not going to work the way we want, unless we have a culture with the values and principles that make it work."

I asked a similar question of Bob Knight, a syndicated columnist and author of many books. He said it gets back to the government not interfering with the family: "The whole libertarian ethos, the idea that social issues are irrelevant—'all we want is freedom and we want smaller government'—that can't happen without strong families. It never can happen, which is why the Left has been at war with the family since its inception."

To Bob, battles over marriage matter—including battles over same-sex marriage. He told me, "I'm always amazed at the blind spot libertarians have for this truth that if you don't make marriage and families strong, you're inevitably going to have bigger government to pick up the pieces."

The tragedy is that some government policies can actually hurt the family. Let's take a specific example of the urban family during the time of the Great Society under Lyndon Johnson. LBJ declared war on poverty. Sounds commendable. But the way his administration went about it seems to have caused even more poverty in the long run by hurting the families of the poor. We've already observed how the government said in effect, "Look, Dad, if you stay in this household, we're going to give this household less money." So, they basically said it's better to be divorced or to be single. Then they said, "Mom, have more babies, and we'll give you more money."

So, all of a sudden, the government had subsidized illegitimacy. Today you have a situation where about 70 percent of children born in urban households are born to single moms, and that's a social disaster. Even most liberals would agree that the illegitimacy rate is a social disaster. That's not good for anybody, including the children—especially the children.

There is such a thing as the law of unintended consequences. I'm sure some people in some situations meant well, but it didn't work out well. We now have enough data that we should never go down this dead end again. We have to change our policies. I hope that fewer conservative politicians will fall for the lie that you can separate conservative fiscal policies from conservative social issues.

68

DOES YOUR ONE VOTE COUNT?

Originally published on November 2, 2016

Polls, shmolls. The only poll that counts in this highly fluid election is your vote. How important is your one vote? If we show up, values voters could make all the difference in this and virtually every election.

Certainly, with the make-up of the electoral college, the votes for those living in swing states may well be more substantial than such states where either party has a complete advantage.

In 2000, during the time after the national election when things still hung in the balance between George W. Bush and Al Gore, the *Washington Times* published a history piece called "Power of One." They wrote:

- 1645—One vote gives Oliver Cromwell control over England.
- 1649—One vote causes Charles [I] of England to be executed.
- 1825—One vote gives John Quincy Adams the presidency.
- 1868—One vote saves Andrew Johnson's presidency from impeaching [sic].
- 1876—One vote gives Rutherford B. Hayes the presidency.
- 1960—One vote per precinct gives John F. Kennedy the presidency.
- 2000—Enough said.[1]

What did they mean by "2000—Enough said"? I live in Broward County, Florida, the home of the "hanging chad" and "the dimpled

---

1. *Washington Times: National Weekly Edition,* November 13–19, 2000, 6.

chad" (so called because of punch-card ballots that made ambiguous whom the vote was for). Bush and Gore had a very close election in 2000. It was so close that Gore was not willing to concede until there were multiple recounts of the Florida ballots.

Every count of Florida votes and every subsequent recount—no matter how liberal the source, including the *New York Times* and the *Miami Herald*—always and consistently showed George W. Bush triumphing over Al Gore. The vote counts might have slightly varied, but not one scenario gave Gore a victory over Bush in Florida. The Supreme Court even weighed in on the count, and Bush became our forty-third president. Bill Sammon documents all this in his book, *At Any Cost.* Yet some liberals—Hillary being one of them—had the gall to say in 2002 that Bush was "selected, not elected."[2]

To me, the most amazing aspect of that election, which underscores the whole point of this piece, is that some in the media had called the state prematurely for Al Gore, *prior* to the polls in the conservative Florida panhandle closing. Panama City Beach and other places there are on Central Time, not Eastern Time, meaning an extra hour of voting time for them.

Many opportunities remained to cast one's ballot. I once heard an estimate that George W. Bush may have lost as many as 10,000 votes that way. People intending to vote for Bush, on their way to the polls, heard that Gore had already won and so turned around and didn't vote. If even a fraction of those people had voted, then maybe the Florida election would not have been so close—sparing us a month of counting and recounting.

Included also in the list above from the *Washington Times* was the "power of one vote" in the election of our third president in 1800. As Mark Beliles and I pointed out in our book, *Doubting Thomas: The Religious Life and Legacy of Thomas Jefferson* (2014), "On February 11, 1801, the House of Representatives finally determined on its 36th ballot that Jefferson would be the next president." And we added, "This was a political cliffhanger that lasted for weeks. Jefferson beat Adams handily. But Jefferson was tied with Aaron Burr; tied ballot after tied ballot cre-

---

2. Zach Montanaro, "Hillary in 2002: Bush was 'Selected' President, Not 'Elected'," *MRCTV*, October 20, 2016, mrctv.org.

ated a logjam. When Jefferson finally won, Aaron Burr became his Vice President." One vote made a huge difference.

Recently I interviewed best-selling author and speaker Bill Federer for my radio show on the subject of how important just one vote is. He told me, "Who is the king in America? Well, our founders set it up so that the people are." Federer went on to quote three historic American leaders, beginning with signer of the Constitution Gouverneur Morris—the man who spoke more than anyone during the Constitutional Convention: "The magistrate is not the king. The people are the king."[3]

Supreme Court Chief Justice John Jay said, "The people are the sovereign of this country." President Lincoln said, "The people of this country are the rightful masters of both Congresses and courts."

Federer continued, "The people being the king—not to vote is to abdicate the throne. We pledge allegiance to the flag 'and to the republic, for which it stands.' A republic is the people [as] king ruling through their representatives."

Until you cast your ballot, your voice won't be heard. So, no matter what the media say, it's not over till it's over. Your vote is extremely important, if for no other reason than that you are obeying God by exercising your lawful citizenship.

---

3. "Vocal Point—Bill Federer," *Jerry Newcombe*, October 28, 2016, jerrynewcombe.com.

69

AN APPEAL TO CHRISTIANS WHO PLAN
TO SIT OUT THIS ELECTION

Originally published on October 29, 2014

In polite society, you're not supposed to talk about politics, sex, or religion. Sorry, but this column will discuss all three, directly or indirectly.

In America, we get the kind of government we deserve. Is this the best we can do?

There certainly is a big divide in how we approach politics, even among well-meaning Christians. I was asked to speak at our church recently, and the subject given to me was: "To vote or not to vote?" Are you serious? How can we not vote? We're in such a mess because we haven't been voting our values. I believe voting is imperative for the follower of Jesus.

Jesus said that we are to render unto Caesar the things that are Caesar's and unto God the things that are God's (Mark 12:17). Surely, included in rendering unto Caesar the things that are Caesar's is voting.

It's our duty to cast a ballot. It's also our privilege. I know a man personally who risked his life with six other Cubans to flee the communist island. They rowed for forty-eight long hours in a rickety rowboat with a hole in it. One of them had to bail out water all the time. After a while, their fingers were bleeding, but they finally made it to the Bahamas. My Cuban friend is glad to be an American and is a patriot. He wouldn't think of not voting.

Historically, Christians in America applied their faith to virtually every sphere of life, including politics. While the founding fathers were not all Christians, the vast majority of them were, and virtually all of them had a Biblical worldview. As we saw before, historian Donald S. Lutz said of the founding fathers (even the unorthodox amongst them), "They knew the Bible down to their fingertips." So, for example, they divided power, since they knew man is sinful. James Madison, one of the key architects of the Constitution, noted, "All men having power ought not to be trusted." This is a Biblical perspective. Sometimes people complain that the Constitution limits the amount of power any one single branch may have. That was by design—lest we have tyranny from one man or from an oligarchy.

When we vote Biblical values, we obey what the Lord would have us do. Jesus is not on the ballot, so ultimately we must vote for a sinner. But the question is, where do those sinners stand on key issues? Too often, Christians seem to be waiting for the perfect candidates and can't bring themselves to vote for someone with many (but not all) right views. We need to vote for the available candidates with the best views, rather than waiting for the perfect candidate who's not coming.

Some Christians are so upset with the current crop of politicians that they may sit this election out. But their non-vote *is* a vote—a vote for someone with whom they would probably disagree vehemently.

There are many lesser-known candidates and amendments that will likely appear on the ballot. It behooves us to learn a Christian perspective on these before we go and vote. Where do the candidates stand on abortion? On traditional marriage? On religious freedom? On fiscal responsibility? On educational issues? All of these are addressed by the Bible.

Speaking of fiscal responsibility, Proverbs 13:22 says, "A good man leaves an inheritance for his children's children." Yet today, as one person has said, "Washington is shifting the burden of bad choices today onto the backs of our children and grandchildren." I agree with that sentiment. Who said it? Senator Barack Obama in 2006. Too bad that, as president, he has racked up a bill the repayment of which seems beyond the reach of even our grandchildren.

In this country, which had such a godly foundation, we currently have the opportunity to vote our Biblical values. But if we continue to lose our freedoms and fall prey to tyrannical government, ultimately, we will only have ourselves to blame.

My long-time pastor, the late D. James Kennedy, Ph.D., said this about Christians and politics in general: "I remember twenty years ago, a Christian said to me, 'You don't really believe that Christians should get active in politics do you?' And I said, with tongue in cheek, 'Why, of course not, we ought to leave it to the atheists, otherwise, we wouldn't have anything to complain about. And we'd really rather complain than do something, wouldn't we?'"

Look at the mess we're in because many Christians have neglected this duty. Five Houston pastors had their communications subpoenaed by the mayor because they spoke out against the bill allowing a man to use the ladies' room. The mayor demanded their emails and text messages to see if they had said anything against this bill. Commenting on that case initiated by the lesbian mayor of our nation's fourth largest city, in his *Mike Huckabee News* (October 19, 2014), Huckabee commented, "Why has this happened? It's mainly because good, church-going Christians don't vote and don't care."

It is a privilege to vote. It is our Christian duty to vote. So vote your Biblical values. If enough evangelicals and conservative Catholics showed up and voted Biblical values, we could carry this election—and virtually every election. Our nation's founders pledged their lives, their fortunes, and their sacred honor to give us our freedom. The least we could do is vote—and vote our values.

70

POLISH PEOPLE PRAY FOR PROTECTION
FROM ISLAMIC INVASION

Originally published on October 10, 2017

The Polish people have proven to be some of the greatest God-fearing, freedom-loving people on earth. Many of them proved it again just this past weekend.

An article from France24.com entitled "Polish Catholics pray at borders 'to save country'" (October 7, 2017), explains: "Thousands of Polish Catholics formed human chains on the country's borders Saturday, begging God 'to save Poland and the world' in an event many viewed as a spiritual weapon against the 'Islamisation' of Europe." The article continues: "The goal was to have as many prayer points as possible along Poland's 3,511-kilometre (2,200-mile) border with Germany, the Czech Republic, Slovakia, Ukraine, Belarus, Lithuania, Russia and the Baltic Sea." Even people in fishing boats, kayaks, and sailboats joined in the prayer meeting—forming prayer chains on Polish rivers.

The Archbishop of Krakow said the believers should pray "for the other European nations to make them understand it is necessary to return to Christian roots so that Europe would remain Europe."

The date chosen, October 7, 2017, was no coincidence. October 7 was picked because of the 1571 victory over one of the many Muslim attempts to conquer Europe, the famous Battle of Lepanto. A betting man would have thought the forces of Islam would prevail, but they did not.

Islam has been trying to take over Europe for centuries. In the last generation or so, they have made greater strides than in the previous several centuries.

Another European leader who understands the Islamic threat and has been persecuted for his hardline stance against radical Islam is Dutch political leader Geert Wilders. He told me in an interview one time that the late Libyan leader Muammar al-Qaddafi had said in effect, "We have 50 million Muslims in Europe, and we don't need one gun; we don't need one bullet; we will rule this continent in 10, 20, 30 years' time.... Europe will be ours in the near future." And what have been the results? Well, we read about them virtually every week, whether it's an attack on innocents in Berlin, in Nice, or in London.

Of course, there are many peaceful-minded Muslims, fleeing their own lands because of the implementation of strict Islamic law. I am sure it is not these Muslims that the Christians of Poland are praying for protection from.

One Catholic leader from that Eastern European nation, Marcin Dybowski, said, "Poland is in danger. We need to shield our families, our homes, our country from all kinds of threats, including the de-Christianisation of our society, which the EU's liberals want to impose on us."

Three months ago, President Trump spoke in Warsaw, also highlighting the freedom-loving nature of the Polish people. Gary Bauer wrote at the time, "Thankfully, we now have a president who is willing to defend Judeo-Christian culture." In his July 6, 2017, speech in Warsaw, the president noted, "For two centuries, Poland suffered constant and brutal attacks. But while Poland could be invaded and occupied, and its borders even erased from the map, it could never be erased from history or from your hearts. In those dark days, you [may] have lost your land but you never lost your pride."

He added, "And when the day came on June 2nd, 1979, and one million Poles gathered around Victory Square for their very first mass with their Polish Pope, that day, every communist in Warsaw must have known that their oppressive system would soon come crashing down. They must have known it at the exact moment during Pope John Paul II's sermon when a million Polish men, women, and children suddenly raised their voices in a single prayer. A million Polish people did not ask for wealth. They did not ask for privilege. Instead, one million Poles sang three simple words: 'We Want God.'"

I remember hearing Radio Moscow in the early 1980s one day refer to Solidarity, et al. as "the counter-revolutionaries" in Poland.

Dr. Paul Kengor, historian and political scientist who teaches at Grove City College and has written multiple books on Ronald Reagan and his anti-communist crusade, has written a new book, likely to be a best-seller, *A Pope and a President* (2017). It deals with our fortieth president's commitment to work with the first Polish pope in history, John Paul II, to help end the communist stranglehold in Poland. I interviewed Kengor on my radio show recently, and he tells how President Reagan and Pope John Paul II worked behind the scenes to help free the Polish people from the grip of communism. This helped lead to the end of the Cold War.[1]

Would that more Europeans might become like the Poles. I agree with Trump's point that ultimately it is their longing for God that makes them long for freedom, including the freedom from the threat of radical Islam.

---

1. "Vocal Point—Paul Kengor," *Jerry Newcombe*, June 15, 2017, jerrynewcombe.com.

71

SHOOTING AT FRC:
OVERCOMING HATE WITH LOVE

Originally published on August 16, 2012

Have we crossed a new threshold in the culture wars? On Wednesday, August 15, 2012, reports indicate that a man entered the lobby of the Family Research Council building in Washington, D.C., declaring, "I don't like your politics." In his attempt to go further into the building, he shot the building operations manager in the arm. The manager was able to pin him down.

Certainly, the building operations manager, Leo Johnson, is a hero for his courage and quick action. He prevented further bloodshed. Our thoughts and prayers go out to him and his family in the face of this tragic incident.

The reports indicate that the alleged shooter was a twenty-eight-year-old Virginia man who had been volunteering at the DC Center for the LGBT Community. Thankfully, a coalition of twenty-five gay rights groups spoke out loudly and clearly that they eschew violence, and they don't agree at all with the actions of the alleged shooter. I'm reminded of when occasional acts of violence have been perpetrated against abortion-providers. In those cases, pro-life leaders cannot get to a microphone fast enough to denounce the violence.

The day after the shooting, FRC president Tony Perkins said, "We're not going anywhere. We're not backing up, we're not shutting up. We have been called to speak the truth. We will not be intimidated. We will not be silenced" (AP, August 16, 2012).

I've been to that building many times, conducting interviews for Christian television, including with Tony Perkins, as well as with some ex-gays, among others. Hopefully, Wednesday's shooting incident is not the beginning of some new trend. But historically, persecution often follows effective Gospel work. How should we respond?

Martin Luther's hymn "A Mighty Fortress" reminds us, "The body they may kill. God's truth abideth still." There is a wider sense in which the Kingdom of Christ will prevail in our world—if we show love even in the face of hatred. As we have seen, Dr. Martin Luther King Jr. said in his wonderful letter from the Birmingham Jail (May 1963), "We must meet hate with creative love.... Let us hope there will be no more violence. But if the streets must flow with blood, let it flow with our blood in the spirit of Jesus Christ on the cross." Obviously, he dealt with much more difficult circumstances than we deal with today.

Love is the key to overcoming hate. Christ commands Christians to love even our enemies. How can we creatively love those who resort to violence against us, while still taking common-sense measures to protect the innocent, just as the FRC building manager did?

When a deranged killer murdered several Amish children a few years ago, the Amish community showed amazing love by reaching out to the widow and family of the killer. If you get a chance, watch the made-for-TV movie based on this incident, called *Amish Grace*. It's very touching.

Rev. Rob Schenck of Faith and Action in Washington, D.C., actually saw firsthand some of the love the Amish poured out to the shooter's family. He once told me, "The Amish emissaries—the elders of the Amish community—arrived at that home while I was there, to offer their forgiveness in Christ to that family.... And that extension of Christian love and forgiveness was so powerful."

Look at the example of Norma McCorvey, the "Roe" of *Roe v. Wade*, the infamous Supreme Court decision of 1973 that legalized abortion on demand. When her identity came to light in the late 1980s, she became a hated woman in some circles. But Roe now agrees with Wade in her opposition to abortion. How so? She was "won by love" through the active transforming power of love on the part of some pro-life demonstrators. She even wrote a book chronicling her story, with that very title, *Won by Love*.

We live in a time when—ironically—normal, God-fearing people who are just trying to rear their families in peace are often accused of being "haters." I wrote about this recently—that we are "living in Orwellian times," when right is called wrong and vice versa. In modern America, we're generally so removed from violent persecution it's hard to picture it. Yet Cardinal Francis George of Chicago said in 2010, "I expect to die in bed, my successor will die in prison and his successor will die a martyr in the public square."

History tells us that all the apostles except John died a martyr's death. They didn't seek it, but they didn't shrink back when the time came. They chose the next life by holding on to their integrity, rather than choosing this life but denying the Lord.

Historian Will Durant, who wrote a definitive, multivolume survey of world history, wrote about the Gospel's conquest in ancient Rome: "There is no greater drama in human record than the sight of a few Christians, scorned or oppressed by a succession of emperors, bearing all trials with a fiery tenacity, multiplying quietly, building order while their enemies generated chaos, fighting the sword with the word, brutality with hope, and at last defeating the strongest state that history has ever known. Caesar and Christ had met in the arena, and Christ had won."

It turns out that the way to overcome hate is with the love of Jesus Christ.

72

WHAT IS HATE, AND WHO DEFINES IT?
THE SPLC?

Originally published on August 23, 2017

A headline on *Drudge* (August 21, 2017) declared that Google is teaming up with "liberal groups to snuff out conservative websites." Apparently, the search-engine giant is partnering with the Southern Poverty Law Center (SPLC) and other left-wing groups to document and publicize "hate crimes and events" in America.

After the terrible events in Charlottesville, any God-fearing, rational American would welcome this news, correct? The problem, however, is that by allowing groups like the SPLC to define what is hate and who is a hater, they reveal how dangerous this development could be.

Jerry Boykin of Family Research Council, an organization once attacked by a domestic terrorist because it was listed on the SPLC "Hate Map," said, "The Southern Poverty Law Center is reckless in labeling groups as hate groups or labeling individuals as hate mongers, and they do both. They have no authority to do so."

I work for a group, D. James Kennedy Ministries, which the SPLC has falsely designated a "hate group" because we don't believe in same-sex marriage. That view doesn't make us unique. Up until the last few years, the majority of Americans did not believe in it either—nor did Barack Obama or Hillary Clinton, according to their public statements up until 2012.

Yet, according to the SPLC, we're "haters." The irony of supposing me to be a hater is that I am anything but. Daily I strive to pray the

218

Prayer of St. Francis: "Lord, make me an instrument of Your peace. Where there is hatred, let me replace it with love," and so on.

The Southern Poverty Law Center even listed the renowned surgeon Dr. Ben Carson as an "extremist of hate." Pushback caused them to relent and quietly remove him from their list. The SPLC likes to fancy itself as doing the unfinished work of the civil rights movement, which they have now linked to same-sex marriage and transgender rights, and so on.

Our ministry has produced a television special exposing the SPLC. It's called "Profit$ of Hate."[1] For our program, I interviewed Ricardo Davis, the African-American president of Georgia's Right-to-Life and State Chairman of the Constitution Party of Georgia, which is on the SPLC's hate list as an alleged anti-government group. Davis commends the SPLC for the good work they did in the waning days of the civil rights movement. But he notes that Dr. Martin Luther King's movement was undergirded by faith in God and in the Bible. In contrast, what the SPLC promotes today is often in contradiction to faith in God and in the Bible.

Davis told our viewers, "If I could say something to [SPLC co-founder] Morris Dees right now, what I would say is, 'Morris, you came alongside my father's generation to help them get out from under injustice, and it was unjust because it violated God's Word.... But now, you're on the wrong side of history.'"

Critics note that even many of the actual hate groups on the Southern Poverty Law Center's Hate Map (such as the Ku Klux Klan) have been on the wane for decades. But Morris Dees and the SPLC manage to make huge profits by scaring people into thinking that some sort of hate-monger is behind every bush in America.

Davis added, "What did Jesus say? 'What does it profit a man if he gains the whole world,' if he keeps his mailing list up to date, if he rakes in millions and millions of dollars, 'yet loses his soul?' And The Southern Poverty Law Center, in particular, is an organization that has lost the soul and energy behind the civil rights movement. The honorable thing to do would be to repent and believe the Gospel."

We should all work to end true hate in America. But defining as *hate* the politics of someone you merely disagree with just muddies the waters and further divides us as a nation.

---

1. "Profit$ of Hate: The Southern Poverty Law Center Special," djameskennedy.org.

73

FALSELY ACCUSING OTHERS OF HATE

Originally published on July 12, 2017

Perhaps the most overused word in America is *hate*. All you have to do is accuse someone who disagrees with you of hate, and that's it—guilty as charged. Former Democratic presidential candidate Howard Dean even infamously said recently that "hate speech" is not protected by the First Amendment.

This is like the modern equivalent of the horrible anti-witch hysteria in Salem in 1692–1693. If you were accused of being a witch, then you were considered guilty. Twenty were accused and executed for supposedly being witches. Thankfully, when Rev. Increase Mather returned to Massachusetts from England, he put a stop to the evil witch hunting by ordering that the Biblical standard be applied. No one could be convicted except by two or three witnesses—no more convictions by the testimony of only one witness. The killings stopped, and the jails were emptied of those falsely accused.

Today, the charge of "hater" is bandied recklessly. Christians are branded as haters simply because they may disagree with someone on some issue, with no evidence or witnesses needed, and no point of view allowed other than that of the accuser. The Southern Poverty Law Center (SPLC) of Montgomery, Alabama, has much to do with the overuse of the word *hate* in our time. Initially, during the closing days of the civil rights movement, the SPLC did some worthy work against the hate of racism. But recently the SPLC has begun to denounce pro-family groups that stand for traditional marriage—God's rules for marriage—as haters. Furthermore, the SPLC has denounced those prophets among us who are sounding the alarm on radical Islam as haters. The SPLC has put together a "Hate Map," which lumps groups like the KKK and neo-Nazis with D. James Kennedy Ministries, where I work.

Real haters bomb and shoot people. But according to the SPLC, we're haters. So are Frank Gaffney of the Center for Security Policy, Robert Spencer of jihadwatch.org (watchdogs on radical Islam), Tim Wildmon of the American Family Association, David Barton of Wall-Builders, Gary DeMar of American Vision, Liberty Counsel (led by Mat Staver), Pacific Justice Institute (led by Brad Dacus), and Tony Perkins of Family Research Council.

It's as if the SPLC practices the philosophy: we disagree with them, so we'll call them haters. At one time, they even profiled Dr. Ben Carson as a supposed hate-monger because of his Biblical beliefs on marriage and family.

The SPLC says on their website: "The Southern Poverty Law Center is a nonprofit civil rights organization dedicated to fighting hate and bigotry, and to seeking justice for the most vulnerable members of society." Sounds great, until you actually look at their map of hate.

On the map, D. James Kennedy Ministries is right there with "United Klans of America," an offshoot of the KKK. The SPLC brands us as "anti-gay." We don't agree with same-sex marriage, but we don't hate anyone, including homosexuals.

Family Research Council in Washington, D.C., is also on SPLC's map of hate. As noted, that fact led to bloodshed, when a crazed young homosexual marched in with the intention of shooting as many people as possible in August 2012. The convicted attacker later told police he chose his target from the SPLC's hate map.

He ended up shooting (not fatally, thankfully) a heroic man named Leo Johnson, who tried to stop him. That man is an African-American employee of Family Research Council. I mention his race because of the fact that the supposed civil rights champions of the SPLC now have blood on their hands—African-American blood no less. And to my knowledge, they have never apologized for this incident.

Dr. Frank Wright, host of the television program we produced exposing the SPLC, "Profit$ of Hate," sums up the problem: "The Southern

Poverty Law Center, which began well, has resorted to falsely labeling organizations that promote a Biblical view of marriage and sexuality as 'hate groups.' At the same time, they outwardly support sexual behavior that is opposed to God's design. They literally call good evil, and evil good. They're free to do that, of course. But law enforcement groups, the media, and educational institutions must no longer take seriously their pronouncements as if they were an objective, unbiased observer. The Southern Poverty Law Center is fighting for the extreme Left in the culture war."[1]

By constantly lobbing around the charge of hate, the Southern Poverty Law Center can't seem to see real hate when it rears its ugly head. The SPLC has become the proverbial boy who cried wolf, as they continue to bandy about what may well be the most overused word in America.

Despite such false accusations, as Christians we can respond best by continuing to speak the truth in love.

---

1. "Profits of Hate: The Southern Poverty Law Center Special," djameskennedy.org.

74

WHO REALLY FOSTERS HATE?

Originally published on April 16, 2013

Terrorism is in the news again as seen in the tragic bombing at the finish line of the Boston Marathon on Monday. This man-made disaster forces us to examine terrorism, as we continue to pray for the victims of the bombing.

By now, we have probably all heard about the infamous slide presented at a U.S. Army Reserve Equal Opportunity training brief on religious extremism. They have a slide with the title "Religious Extremism." First on their list of religious extremists is Evangelical Christianity (U.S. Christians). Fifth on the list is Al Qaeda. Further down on the list is Catholicism (U.S. Christians). At the end of the list is Islamaphobia.

There are millions of evangelical Christians in this country, as well as Catholics. To label them as religious extremists boggles the mind. Many of them pray daily, "Thy will be done on earth as it is in heaven." Or, "Where there is hatred, let me sow love." Where's the hate?

Some have said that the Army trainer who put this slide together traced her information back to the Southern Poverty Law Center (SPLC), based in Montgomery, Alabama. The SPLC was one of the groups that sued former (and current) Alabama Chief Justice Roy Moore for having the Ten Commandments (Exodus 20) on display at the state judiciary building in Montgomery. Prominent on SPLC's own building are words also carved in stone, attributed to Dr. Martin Luther King Jr.: "Let justice roll down..." These are words from Amos 5, also in the Bible.

Dr. King's church, Dexter Avenue Baptist, is just down the street from the judiciary building. It was in that church that the civil rights movement was born—when a group met there in the mid-1950s to deal with the injustice that had just been meted out to Rosa Parks.

The word *hate* is bandied about these days to the point that it may be losing its meaning. People motivated by love are often called haters because they don't hold to the latest politically correct view on what marriage is, or on abortion. Real hate blows people up—total strangers no less.

Meanwhile, SPLC says on their website: "The Southern Poverty Law Center is a nonprofit civil rights organization dedicated to fighting hate and bigotry, and to seeking justice for the most vulnerable members of society." Sounds great, until you look at their "Map of Hate." As we have seen, SPLC brands us (D. James Kennedy Ministries) as "anti-gay." We certainly believe what the Bible says—that all sinners (and that's all of us) can be forgiven when we repent of our sins and come to Christ and ask for forgiveness. Thousands of ex-homosexuals have found hope and change through the Gospel of Christ. Yes, we promote that at Truth in Action Ministries, and, of course, we believe that marriage is the union of one man and one woman. But we don't hate anyone.

Family Research Council in Washington, D.C., is also on SPLC's map of hate. That fact almost led to serious bloodshed. Lt. Gen. (retired) Jerry Boykin, vice president of the group, tells the details of what happened that fateful day: "August 15th, 2012, Floyd Lee Corkins walked into the lobby of Family Research Council with a backpack, a Glock 9mm, and about seventy rounds of ammunition, as well as fifteen Chick-fil-A sandwiches. And he shot a very heroic man named Leo Johnson, who tried to stop him. Leo wrestled him to the ground with one good arm, took his pistol away from him and started to shoot him, and then Leo told us later that God told him not to shoot Floyd Lee Corkins."

Boykin adds, "Now it's important to understand that he was motivated to come in and try to kill as many people as possible at Family Research Council because we had been labeled a hate group by the Southern Poverty Law Center. It's incredible that Leo stood over him bleeding after having been shot, with nobody to help him, and God told him not to shoot this man—and that's hate? I don't think so."

Why the Chick-fil-A sandwiches? Boykin says, "What Corkins said at his hearing when he plead guilty to three charges was that his intention was to kill as many people as possible that day, smear a Chick-fil-A sandwich in their face and then go on to two other organizations, both of which he had found on the Southern Poverty Law Center's website listed as hate groups. What he objected to was our stand on traditional marriage."

Tony Perkins, president of Family Research Council, says that their group regularly prays for Corkins' salvation, that he "might come to an understanding of the truth, the Gospel of Jesus Christ. I can tell you today in working with our team—there is no animosity, no bitterness. There is compassion, but understanding of the stakes of standing for religious freedom today."

Dr. King told his followers not to show hate in response to hate, but through Christ, to show love instead. On a few occasions, I interviewed Dr. Alveda King, the niece of Dr. King, who is active in pro-life work. She told me, "Well, Dr. Martin Luther King's daughter, Reverend Bernice King, marched with her bishop, Bishop Eddie Long in Atlanta late in 2004. And the theme of their march was marriage between a man and a woman and that gay rights and gay marriage was not included in the civil rights movement. Bernice said in her own words, 'I know deep within my sanctified soul that my father did not take a bullet for same-sex marriage.'"

If that were the case, would SPLC label Dr. King a hater? As it stands, the SPLC is, by their actions, denying the meaning of Dr. King's (and Amos's) words. Like the boy who cried wolf, using the word *hate* to describe someone with whose politics you disagree is wrong on every front. Real hate is what struck the finish line in Boston Monday—regardless of who turns out to be at fault.

75

THE MOST OVERUSED AND
MISUSED WORD IN OUR TIME

Originally published on August 7, 2013

Some atheists took offense recently to a military chaplain quoting the old saying popularized by Dwight Eisenhower, "In battle, they learned the great truth that there are no atheists in the foxholes." Some atheists in the military have taken issue with Ike's quote, calling it a "bigoted, religious-supremacist phrase." One of them said, "Faith-based hate is hate all the same."

Meanwhile, constitutional attorney Ken Klukowski, who wrote about this in his article, "Military Censors Christian Chaplain, Atheists Call for Punishment" (*Breitbart,* July 24, 2013), said the chaplain was completely within his First Amendment rights of free speech and religious liberty.

Obviously, since there are professed unbelievers who serve in the military, the truism that there are no atheists in foxholes is not always true. Every man or woman who serves our country in the military, regardless of religious views or the lack thereof, deserves our respect.

But I must admit that the phrase "faith-based hate" galls me because, in reality, I see so little of it. And I travel in mostly Christian circles and have for years. If I see hate, it's not based in faith in Jesus. It is *despite* professed belief in Jesus—like leftovers from an ornery disposition not yet changed by Christ.

I'm rereading *To Kill a Mockingbird,* and I note that the deep-seated racism is there, despite the professed Christianity of the townspeople.

Yet the hero of the story, Atticus Finch, is also a man of Christian faith. He says, "This case, Tom Robinson's case, is something that goes to the essence of a man's conscience—Scout, I couldn't go to church and worship God if I didn't try to help that man." He adds, "The one that doesn't abide by majority rule is a person's conscience."

In our time, the crowd increasingly accuses people of hate—people of faith acting on their consciences shaped by the Judeo-Christian tradition. *Hate* has got to be the most overused word of our time. If someone is politically incorrect in their views, they are often falsely accused of hate. According to Webster's, *hate* means "to feel great hostility or animosity toward."

Some people assume Christians are hateful because we favor traditional marriage. We favor bringing babies to term. Does that make us hateful? Does it not seem absurd to accuse conservative traditional Christians of faith-based hate simply based on our views of morality (which we believe were revealed by God in the Bible)—and which have stood the test of centuries?

Is it faith-based hate when the Salvation Army, closely followed by the Baptists and the Catholics, show up virtually always first on the scene of any disaster to help anyone in need?

Is it faith-based hate when the myriad of inner-city soup kitchens and rescue missions dish out food for the hungry out of love for Jesus? This happens daily by the millions.

Is it faith-based hate when the hundreds of pregnancy care centers lovingly provide alternatives for pregnant women, so that they can keep their babies? Many a young mother is extremely happy for those Christians who provided that lifeline to them in their time of need.

Is it faith-based hate when Christian education is provided at a greatly reduced price for inner-city children? For example, look at all the Catholic schools in the ghetto, providing a lifeline and a future hope for children in need.

Is it faith-based hate, in our day of hookups and one-night stands, when Christian abstinence groups warn people of the consequences of their lifestyles—where one night's pleasure can lead to a lifelong disease? Otherwise, someone might well say, "Why didn't anybody warn me of this?" Open rebuke, says Scripture, is better than hidden love. And no, it's not faith-based hate when someone speaks the truth in love.

When the word *hate* gets bandied about to be applied to your oppo-nents in the culture war, then it loses its meaning. Love is hate, and hate is love. The Christian ideal is to love everybody, not that we all live up to it by any means. But the idea of faith-based hate, when talking about active followers of Jesus, is an oxymoron.

76

POLITICAL CORRECTNESS HANDCUFFS US IN THE WAR AGAINST ISLAMIC JIHAD

Originally published on June 7, 2017

Maybe we should have a *Ramadan Alert*. Every time this *holy* season comes up on the calendar, the attacks by the jihadists increase. This year, Ramadan began with a bang—actually several of them, as a number of Christians in Egypt were killed on their way to a monastery. On May 26, 2017, Islamic jihadists murdered them in cold blood, insisting they renounce Jesus Christ or die. The Christians refused—God bless them—and they violently died for it.

Gary Bauer ("Special Alert," June 5, 2017) notes that about one hundred fifty people worldwide have been killed since Ramadan began on May 26. Bauer defines Ramadan as the time "when the Muslim faithful believe Allah handed down the first verses of the Koran to Muhammad."

Why are we now hearing about an increased number of attacks in the West? Robert Spencer of Jihadwatch.org, a best-selling author on all things Islamic, told me in a radio interview that it's because there are now more Muslims in the West. I asked Spencer for a statement about political correctness and the war against Islamic jihadists. He emailed me: "Certainly the politically correct unwillingness to deal honestly with the motivating ideology behind the jihad threat hamstrings our ability to respond to that threat. Governments all over the West assume many Islamic institutions are 'moderate' when they are anything but, but it would be 'Islamophobic' to consider the evidence of that fact."

I also asked him about Ramadan and why there's so much violence during that time. He wrote me: "Ramadan is the sacred month in which Muslims fast during the day and redouble their efforts to please Allah. Since warfare against unbelievers is presented in the Qur'an as a divine command, Ramadan sees more jihad violence than the rest of the year (which sees plenty)."

The amazing thing about the Islamic jihadist threat is the seemingly willful blindness on the part of so many in the West to see it. The radical Muslims can do anything and say, "This is for Allah," or "Allahu Akbar," which they often do, and the willfully blind Westerners will say there's no connection between Islam and the killing. They don't acknowledge that it's the jihadists' understanding of Islam that is the problem.

Spencer also told me: "There are in the Qur'an 100 verses advocating jihad. They do not all explicitly advocate violence, but the only context in which the Qur'an discusses jihad is warfare against unbelievers."

A few years ago, I interviewed Andrew McCarthy, the prosecutor who put away the blind sheik for the first attempted attack on the World Trade Center in 1993. At the time, McCarthy noted a disturbing little trend—the initial voicing of the politically correct notion that Islam per se (at least the jihadists' interpretation of it) had nothing to do with their violence, while we also began to hear the mantra, "Islam is a religion of peace."

McCarthy told me, "Now that seemed at the time, I thought, to be a harmless fiction because, whatever the government was saying in Washington, and even whatever the government was saying on the steps of the courthouse, we were not prevented inside the courtroom from showing exactly why the terrorists committed the acts that they committed. We were never stopped from showing the nexus between Islamic ideology, Islamic scripture, and Islamic terror. So whatever the government was saying outside the courtroom was a bunch of noise and propaganda, as far as I was concerned." But over time, this "harmless fiction" has grown to be a big problem, which today handcuffs us from dealing with a genuine threat.

McCarthy added, "It started, I think, in their minds as a harmless fiction which was designed not to alienate our natural allies in the Islamic world, that is, pro-Western, pro-American Muslims who we don't want to drive into the arms of the bad guys, and there are hundreds of millions of [Muslims]. . . . But there is a snowball effect, an avalanche effect. . . . You keep doing this sort of stuff over the years and then the next thing you do is you're purging everything that Americans need to know about Islamic ideology. You're taking Islam off the table, even though what any basic book of good intelligence, good warfare, good law enforcement would tell you is, it's important to know what the other guy thinks so that you can anticipate what he'll do next."

Today, that "harmless fiction" has grown, and it continues to blind many in the West. In the eyes of many liberals, Islamaphobia is worse than radical Islam. But Todd Starnes of *Fox News* (June 4, 2017) notes: "You can't destroy the Muslim jihadists with candlelight vigils and benefit concerts."

May the true God keep us safe and spare us from political correctness.

77

FREE SPEECH FOR ME, BUT NOT FOR THEE

Originally published on May 3, 2017

"Liberal censorship" is technically an oxymoron. But today liberal censorship is a common reality. Where once free speech reigned on college campuses and in other secular institutions (or at least it was so thought), today you have the totalitarianism of political correctness. Say the wrong thing, and you may be fired.

Dissenting Justice Samuel Alito said after the Supreme Court same-sex marriage decision in June 2015, "I assume that those who cling to old beliefs will be able to whisper their thoughts in the recesses of their homes, but if they repeat those views in public, they will risk being labeled as bigots and treated as such by governments, employers, and schools."

Ann Coulter, conservative firebrand, has proven recently that free speech is all but dead in America. Her aborted attempt last week to speak at Berkeley—the supposed birthplace of free speech in America—went up in flames. Almost literally. Young America's Foundation and the Berkeley College Republicans had invited Coulter to speak, but the school would not ensure her safety while the protesters vowed to violently shut her down. Coulter said to *The New York Times*: "It's a sad day for free speech."

As we see repeatedly, the "tolerant" folk are the most intolerant amongst us. Their attitude is simple: "Free speech for me, but not for thee."

Historically, Christianity played a seminal role in the struggle for free speech—not that Christians have always gotten it right by any means. The seventeenth-century British Puritan writer John Milton, author of *Paradise Lost,* wrote a plea for a free press, *Areopagitica.*[1] He stated, "Truth indeed came once into the world with her divine Master, and was a perfect shape most glorious to look on.... For who knows not that Truth is strong, next to the Almighty? She needs no policies, nor stratagems, nor licensings to make her victorious." God's truth stands on its own, needing no artificial man-made props. This reminds me of the quote from Church Father Tertullian, writing about AD 200: "Truth asks no favours in her cause." She doesn't need any. Truth wins out in the marketplace of ideas, because working with God's reality produces good results.

In 1777, Thomas Jefferson noted that Jesus ("the holy author of our religion") is the reason we should allow civil freedom. In his Virginia Statute for Religious Freedom, passed in 1786, Jefferson wrote: "Almighty God hath created the mind free.... All attempts to influence it by temporal punishment or burdens, or by civil incapacitations, tend only to beget habits of hypocrisy and meanness, and are a departure from the plan of the holy author of our religion, who being Lord both of body and mind, yet chose not to propagate it by coercions on either, as was his Almighty power to do."[2] Jesus gives us freedom. Who are we to deny it from others?

The alternative media continues to be a major lifeline for those in America who have dissenting views from the politically correct orthodoxy. We see a powerful example of this in *WorldNetDaily*, founded by journalist Joseph Farah. The pioneering independent online news source, WND.com, celebrates its twentieth anniversary this week. For his efforts, Southern Poverty Law Center profiles Farah as a supposed "extremist" of hate. I emailed him their outrageous, derogatory profile of him. He emailed me back, "Same old. Same old."

One of the saddest aspects of the Coulter-Berkeley story was the statement from former Democrat Chairman Howard Dean, who said, "Hate speech is not protected by the First Amendment."

Tragically, many in our society today—including liberal protesters shutting down conservatives and Christians from being able to speak—

---

1. John Milton, *Areopagitica*, 1644, gutenberg.org/ebooks/608.
2. Virginia Statute for Religious Freedom, *Monticello*, monticello.org.

do so supposedly in opposition to "hate speech." First of all, where does the First Amendment make a provision for silencing "hate speech"? And secondly, who defines what is real hate and what is not? It seems that "hate speech" is now often "speech I disagree with."

I know a brother in Christ, David Kyle Foster, who used to be a male prostitute in Hollywood. He once told me that he had probably slept with more than a thousand different men before the Lord saved him. Foster has interviewed hundreds of former homosexuals and lesbians and people struggling with all sorts of sexual issues, who found healing through the Gospel of Jesus. Up until recently, these powerful, sensitive videos were available on Vimeo, which fashions itself as a high-quality version of YouTube.

But Vimeo told Foster recently that all his videos had to be deleted because of their "hate messages."[3] Testimonials of lives set free through Christ are hate speech? That is another example of "free speech for me, but not for thee."

If only our universities and media companies could come to grips with the First Amendment as designed by our founders, how better off things would be.

---

3. "Vocal Point—David Kyle Foster," *Jerry Newcombe*, April 27, 2017, jerrynewcombe.com.

78

MIKE PENCE IN HIS OWN WORDS

Originally published on July 20, 2016

Republican presidential candidate Donald Trump has named Indiana Governor Mike Pence as his VP. Pence is notable among social conservatives. In 2008, as a Congressman from Indiana, he received the "Christian Statesman of the Year" award from the D. James Kennedy Center for Christian Statesmanship in DC.

I had the privilege of doing a television interview for the broadcast ministry of Dr. D. James Kennedy in the same month as the historic 2010 mid-term elections, which favored conservatives. Here are portions of that November 30, 2010, interview. This is Mike Pence in his own words.

ON THE EXPANSION OF THE EXECUTIVE BRANCH

I'm someone who believes that not only is this president off track, but I believe the presidency itself is off track. And I don't think that that's unique to this administration, although it's been most exaggerated by the current occupant of the oval office. It's my belief that when the founders designed the presidency, that it was principally about restraint. The chief executive of our national government was put into a position to be that advocate of the American people to essentially restrain the growth of government, to protect the rights and liberties of the people, ... to bring an attitude of a servant leader to the country.

ON THE PROBLEM OF JUDICIAL ACTIVISM

I think the purpose of the courts and every other branch of government is to practice faith with that written document as written, and that the very principle of limited government begins with believing that the founders meant what they said and said what they meant. Courts ought not to be in the business of legislating from the bench.

ON FUNDING PLANNED PARENTHOOD

I think millions of Americans would find it offensive to know that the largest abortion provider in America is also the largest recipient of federal funding under Title 10.

ON REPEALING OBAMACARE

I am of the view that House Republicans cannot rest until we repeal Obamacare lock, stock, and barrel. [Obamacare] is legislation that crosses a previously uncrossed constitutional line. It actually mandates that Americans purchase health insurance whether they want it or need it or not.... I just think it's imperative that we scrap the bill and start over with health-care reform that lowers the cost of health insurance without growing the size of government.

ON OUR NATIONAL DEBT

I think it is simply morally wrong to continue to pile a mountain range of debt on our children and grandchildren because we are unwilling to make the hard choices today to put our fiscal house in order.... We're on the verge today of leaving our children and grandchildren a less prosperous America than the one that we were born into. And we cannot allow that to stand.

ON AMERICA'S LURCH TOWARD SOCIALISM

It's my belief that as we look at America today, as we look at this struggling economy, there are people that [promote] the expansion of federal government under both political parties in recent years. And I think there is concern that we are moving farther and farther in the direction of a different kind of economy, more familiar among the social-welfare state of Europe today.

ON THE IMPACT OF SOCIALISM

When I was eighteen years old, I had the privilege of visiting then-occupied West Berlin. I traveled through Checkpoint Charlie with my brother. Now, West Berlin was this bustling city, it was bright and the stores were filled, the streets were bustling with people. In every sense in the late 1970s, it was [like] a vibrant American city. And then we walked past the tank traps and the barbed wire up to the Berlin Wall, and we went through Checkpoint Charlie, past the glare of the East German guards, and we walked into East Berlin, which was a completely different place. Gone were the bright lights of West Berlin, and replacing them was the drab, grey, leftover remains of a hollowed out East Berlin. It was an extraordinary moment in my life. The cars were vintage 1950s. Everyone seemed to be wearing the same colorless apparel. And I saw for the first time in my life as a young man of eighteen years the difference between the products of a free-market society and a socialist-state-controlled economy. It was a bright-line contrast. And where I see America today is I think we're on that wall between east and west.

CONCLUDING THOUGHT

At the end of the day, we've got to embrace policies and elect leaders who are willing to lead our country back to the principles of limited government, personal responsibility, of free market, entrepreneurial capitalism. And if we do that, then I believe we'll have a balanced future.

79

MEDIA BIAS AND TRUMP

Originally published on February 22, 2017

Here's a variation on a joke I heard recently circulating among conservatives. The Pope and Trump are out on a ship and suddenly a gust of wind causes the Pontiff's hat to fly several feet away from the boat onto the surface of the water. Trump gets out of the boat and walks on water to retrieve the miter. On a nearby boat are members of the media.

- The next day, the headline of *The New York Times* declares, "Trump Can't Swim."
- The *Washington Post* headline reads, "Trump Guilty of Water Pollution."
- The *LA Times* headline declares, "Trump Shows Off in Front of Pope."
- *USA Today* notes: "Trump Tries to Upstage Jesus."

And so it goes with the liberal media. It would appear that President Trump cannot win, no matter what he does. Has he had a rocky start to his presidency or has he been working diligently to fulfill his campaign promises? Either way, the media often colors our view of the world. Not that I think he walks on water, but is it any wonder that Trump so often takes his case to tens of millions of followers through Twitter? This is his unfiltered voice above the gatekeepers at the mainstream media.

A recent poll by *Fox News* (February 17, 2017) found that 68 percent of Americans "think the press has been 'tougher' on Trump than Obama." The poll also found that a slight majority of Americans give

Trump more credence than they do reporters: "By a slim 45 to 42 percent margin, more voters say they trust the Trump administration to 'tell the public the truth' than the reporters who cover the White House."

Meanwhile, also on February 17, 2017, Trump tweeted: "The FAKE NEWS media (failing @nytimes, @NBCNews, @ABC, @CBS, @CNN) is not my enemy, it is the enemy of the American People!" As could be expected, this tweet set off a firestorm of controversy. Senator McCain, moderate Republican leader, turned on his party's current standard-bearer and warned that when government shuts down a free press that's "how dictators get started." Of course, whenever a state actively attempts to shut down the media, that is a step toward tyranny.

But everybody knows deep down that the press is hopelessly biased. This is nothing new.

Since the early 1980s, Stanley Rothman and Robert and Linda Lichter have been studying bias among the media elite, news, and entertainment. They have found the gatekeepers to be overwhelmingly liberal, e.g., in favor of abortion rights and opposed to school prayer. One of their studies found that 86 percent of the media elite seldom or never attend church. A later survey by Lichter-Rothman found that that number was 93 percent.

To think that 93 percent of the media elite at the time of the research never darkened the door of a church or synagogue…

Hence, these are godless people imposing their godless worldview on the media-viewing populace. Gallup reports (December 24, 2013) that four in ten Americans went to church last week. Note the disparity—7 percent of the media elite, 40 percent of the American people. And it would be hard to argue that people in television have become *less* liberal since the time of Lichter-Rothman.

The majority of examples of media bias are seen not so much in what the news media covers, but rather what they choose to ignore. Perhaps this is most seen in coverage related to abortion. Over the weekend, Norma McCorvey died. She was the Jane Roe of *Roe v. Wade*, the infamous 1973 abortion decision by the Supreme Court. If she had never converted to the pro-life side of things, the media would lionize her right now. But, because she was converted to Christ and the pro-life position, the mainstream media virtually ignores her.

Here's another recent example of media bias. *Time* had a cover story (January 30, 2017) showing a defiant Trump at his inaugural. After several pages on the new president, including his aims to destroy the status quo, and on opponents who strive to undermine him, the magazine followed with an article entitled, "The President Who Loved." Who is that about? President Obama. Even in his post-presidency, the mainstream media continues what veteran CBS newsman Bernard Goldberg once called its "slobbering love affair" with Obama. Did *Time* mean to say that Obama loves, while Trump hates?

Of course, a free and independent press is essential to a free and independent country. But a conservative's free-speech rights include the opportunity to criticize the obvious bias to the left of the main gatekeepers of America's media.

80

LIBERALS ARE THE TRUE CENSORS

Originally published on March 16, 2016

There's an old story that my pastor, Dr. D. James Kennedy, used to tell. On Monday morning, the janitor found the preacher's notes. Scrawled in the margin at one spot was a handwritten note: "Argument weak— pound pulpit here!" And so it is that many times weak arguments must be bolstered with emphatic shout downs. How many times do we read of conservatives speaking at college campuses, only to be shouted down by protesters? In some cases, the conservative cannot even deliver his speech.

All ideas should be allowed in the marketplace of ideas. While the Left accuses conservatives of censorship, it seems to me that in our day, the liberals and what I call "the shock troops of tolerance" are the real censors.

Over the weekend, presidential candidate Donald Trump canceled a rally in Chicago because of a real threat of violence. Feel free to disagree with Donald. But engage in violence because you disagree with him? That's beyond the pale.

Writing for *The Washington Times* (March 13, 2016), Kelly Riddell notes, "Moveon.org is conducting fundraising activities from the Chicago protests against Donald Trump that prompted the Republican presidential front-runner to cancel a rally there Friday, and promises that more disruptions are on the way." How long can society remain free with such bare-knuckle tactics, where "might makes right"? Look at what is happening:

- If you in your conscience cannot agree to *celebrate* a same-sex "marriage," then you might be stripped of your livelihood and your money. In the case of bakers Melissa ("Sweet Cakes by Melissa") and Aaron Klein, who declined to bake a cake for a same-sex wedding, they even lost their free speech. The court put them under a gag order to prevent them from even speaking about what happened to them.

- If you disagree with man-made global warming (what they call now "climate change" even though climate always changes), watch out. Our nation's top cop, Attorney General Loretta Lynch, testified before Congress that the administration has considered taking civil action against "dissenters" like you.[1] Despite email scandals documenting that some of the leading proponents of global warming fudged the raw data, liberals want to silence dissent among scientists by punishing the dissenters.

- If you warn about radical Islam, you may find that your First Amendment rights go thus far and no farther. The brave blogger Pamela Geller is fighting in the courts to place ads revealing the link between terrorists and some of the proponents of Islam, despite facing censorship from some city governments.

- Pro-lifer David Daleiden of the Center for Medical Progress created a series of stunning videos using classic investigative journalism techniques, documenting that Planned Parenthood is trafficking in baby-body parts. But in a Houston court, Daleiden suddenly faces indictment, while Planned Parenthood gets off scot-free, at least for now. If you don't like the message, shoot the messenger.

When commenting on this overall trend, Gary Bauer noted in his "End of Day" report (March 11, 2016), "The culture war is real, my friends. The Left's assault on the First Amendment—from free speech to religious liberty—is total. Nothing is exempt from the tyrants of tolerance."

Perhaps the biggest liberal-promoted censorship of all comes in the form of political correctness. It is censorship before the fact. Censorship

---

1. Melanie Arter, "AG Lynch: DOJ Has Discussed Whether to Pursue Civil Action Against Climate Change Deniers," *CNS News*, March 9, 2016, cnsnews.com.

of speech not yet even spoken. Censorship of perceived thoughts.

An article by Erick Erickson and Bill Blankschaen in the *Daily Signal* (March 11, 2016), entitled, "The 'Compassionate Bullying' of the Left," notes, "Around the country, progressive bullies have attacked Christians for daring to put their faith ahead of the pet causes of those who feign compassion while destroying life-giving liberties. What we are seeing is a scorched-earth, take-no-prisoners approach as the wildfire burns across our land. It is not enough that Christians be quiet. Christians must be silenced and punished. Their faith cannot be respected. Legislation that ensures people are free to live and work according to their faith without fear of being punished by government must be stopped and decried as discrimination."

And why do they do this? To force people to accept what they don't agree with. Erickson says: "There is one key reason that those on the Left must force their beliefs on the rest of us: if they didn't force their craziness on us, we would never embrace it." I can't help but feel that there's a double standard on the part of the Left when it comes to this issue. "Free speech for me, but not for thee." The argument is weak— therefore, pound the podium harder and unleash those "shock troops of tolerance."

But as John Adams noted, "The liberty of the press is essential to the security of the state."

81

TRUMP'S VICTORY AND THE RELIGIOUS RIGHT

Originally published on November 16, 2016

"Clinton's loss at the hands of Donald Trump amounted to the most surprising outcome in the history of modern electoral politics." So writes David Catanese for USNews.com (November 11, 2016).

Many of the pollsters proved to be wrong after all. To his credit, Larry Sabato of the University of Virginia cried *mea culpa*, declaring, "We were wrong, ok? The entire punditry industry. The entire polling industry. The entire analyst industry. And I want to take this opportunity to take my fair share of the blame. We were wrong."

"Success," noted John F. Kennedy after he took responsibility for the fiasco that was the Bay of Pigs, "has many fathers, but failure is an orphan." Trump's surprising victory is ultimately his.

But what factors could have led the pollsters and punditry class so off base? I think a case can be made that abortion was very much on the ballot—and along those lines, since abortion was imposed on the American people by judicial fiat, the future of the Supreme Court was also key in the minds of voters.

At the outset, if anybody accuses me of being a one-issue voter— and that issue is the preborn's right to life—then I plead guilty. That issue reveals so many other aspects of where a politician stands. I feel if politicians can't get this issue right, what else can't they get right? It's so basic—especially in this day when sonograms improve all the time and document the humanity of the preborn. Yet the ruling elites treat abortion like a sacred right and rite.

I believe God has blessed America through the years. I also affirm Thomas Jefferson's view, when he said in another context, "I tremble for my country when I reflect that God is just; that his justice cannot sleep forever." How can God continue to bless us when we have now killed up to sixty million preborn children since *Roe v. Wade?*

But, of course, abortion has many supporters. Writing for Gallup (May 29, 2015), Lydia Saad noted, "Americans divide 50 percent 'pro-choice,' 44 percent 'pro-life' on abortion.... This is the first time since 2008 that the pro-choice position has had a statistically significant lead in Americans' abortion views." Yet, voting-wise, it didn't work out that way last Tuesday.

Hillary Clinton and Planned Parenthood wanted to repeal the Hyde Amendment—the 1976 measure named after the late pro-life Illinois Congressman Henry Hyde—which denies federal funding for abortions. Some pro-lifers estimate that that measure has saved at least two million babies. I once interviewed Henry Hyde for TV. He said, "There is no constitutional justification for *Roe v. Wade.* No one had ever seen a right of privacy—or whatever other distortion the Court found to justify its decision—for two hundred years."

The platforms of the two major political parties this year were diametrically opposed to each other on this issue of life. And this issue played a key role in terms of what types of judges would be appointed and approved. Since personnel is policy, choosing Mike Pence—a solid Christian conservative—as his running mate told millions of potential voters that Trump meant business.

After the election, on my radio show I asked Bill Federer, "What role did Christian conservatives play in the outcome?" He said, "I think it was crucial. Several different groups were trying to educate pastors."

One of those was Tony Perkins, the president of Family Research Council in Washington, D.C. Perkins "served as a platform delegate from Louisiana." He sent out a release after the election, noting the importance of the platform and the actual votes: "The Republican Party's platform positions on unborn human life and religious liberty [were] the bridge between Donald Trump and Christian conservatives."

Perkins added, "Nearly 60 percent of Trump voters were more likely to vote for him because the platform is very clear on life and religious liberty. It was the party platform that brokered the deal between Trump and Christian conservatives — a deal that was sealed in the final debate when Trump vividly described a partial-birth abortion and pledged to appoint pro-life justices." And Perkins noted, "If there's one overwhelming message everyone should have heard on Tuesday, it's this: the media, the courts, and the Left don't speak for the American people."

Eric J. Scheidler, Executive Director of the Pro-Life Action League, sent out a post-election statement: "Voters rejected Hillary Clinton's radical support for taxpayer-funded abortion. Now it's time to withdraw all our tax dollars from Planned Parenthood, the nation's largest abortion chain. This will be our number-one priority in the first 100 days of the Trump administration."

Thus, Donald Trump was able to build a successful coalition, which included the religious right. I'm reminded of how, after the conservative victories of the 2010 midterm elections, Ralph Reed of the Faith & Freedom Coalition declared, "Those who ignore or disregard social conservative voters and their issues do so at their own peril."

Anybody who thought the religious right was dead in this country should think again in light of last week's election.

82

TEN REBUTTALS TO THE LEFT'S
MELTDOWN OVER TRUMP-PENCE

Originally published on December 7, 2016

A month after the Trump-Pence victory, the Left's meltdown doesn't seem to be slowing down. For example, a *Drudge Report* headline declared (December 3, 2016), "Madonna Still Can't Cope...'Ashamed To Be American'..." Protests on Inauguration Day may generate more fireworks on the twentieth of January than on the Fourth of July.

But here are ten reasons I'm glad Trump-Pence won. Not only was Hillary repudiated, but so also was Obama's record, which she had promised to continue.

1. The mainstream media proved wrong.

These days, we're hearing all the time about "fake news." The biggest example of fake news was the reporting that Hillary had won and the election was over. The election of 2016 will be studied for years to come to see how the pundits could have gotten it so wrong.

2. Political correctness took a drubbing.

Several times during the campaign, Donald Trump said things that normally would have sunk a candidate. Some of those things were indefensible. But in the big picture, the American people are sick and tired of this form of liberal censorship. "I refuse to be politically correct," said Trump. "The current politically correct response cripples our ability to talk and think and act clearly."

3. The election identified Islamic jihad as the problem it truly is.

After jihadist attacks, Trump boldly connected the dots and said the

247

politically incorrect thing: there is a link between some Muslims killing innocents and their Islamic ideology. You can't defeat an enemy you refuse to name.

4. The Christians in the Middle East have a better chance of survival and justice.

President Obama has virtually ignored the plight of Christians in the Middle East, those slaughtered by ISIS and other Islamic jihadist groups. The Arab Spring has become the Christian Winter. Secretary of State Hillary Clinton shares much of the blame for that. Christians in Syria and other countries are the proverbial canary in the coal mine.

5. Religious freedom in America has a greater chance of a revival.

The Obama administration has virtually declared war on the Judeo-Christian ethic, especially when it comes to traditional marriage. This is a zero-sum game when it comes to religious liberty. It is an either/or: gay rights or religious freedom. How ironic that Christians are losing religious freedom in a country founded by Christians for religious freedom, which they extended to all.

6. It's the economy, stupid.

People have suffered under this economy. No wonder Bernie Sanders appealed to so many young people, with promises of free college education and other freebies. Millions of millennials live at home, saddled with debt and no hope of getting good jobs. Executive orders to fight on behalf of phony environmental concerns have made the Obama economy run like a car with the emergency brake on.

7. We can hopefully repeal Obamacare.

Obamacare, imploding under its own weight, contributes to the weak economy, forcing many companies to curtail the number of hours their employees can work. The Affordable Care Act is not so affordable after all. The marketplace always does better at running things than does the government. Let the insurance companies compete across state lines while retaining care for those with pre-existing conditions.

8. The poor will suffer less.

To paraphrase Abraham Lincoln, it's a good thing the Left loves the poor—they've made so many of them. The Left often invokes the name of the poor. They claim to do so much of what they do to help the poor. But it appears the Left just wants the poor vote. Leftist policies to help the poor have routinely proved to fail the poor because they degrade the families of the poor. And the family, by God's design, has repeatedly proved to be the key to upward mobility.

9. America has a greater chance of freeing itself from the scourge of abortion.

President Washington said that America can never hope to receive God's blessings if we defy His rules. With about sixty million unborn babies aborted, how can we claim, "God bless America"? Why should He? Abortion was very much on the ballot, and thankfully the pro-life side prevailed.[1]

10. We can hope for a Supreme Court that will actually follow the Constitution.

The final reason I'm grateful that Trump-Pence prevailed is because of the promise that future justices chosen for the Supreme Court would be in the mode of Antonin Scalia, meaning that we the people would retain more rule over ourselves, rather than becoming merely the serfs of our "robed masters," who invent new rights and ignore the Constitution.

Sorry, but let Madonna and the others weep. I won't gloat, but I am thankful that the American people rose up and said enough is enough of the Obama/Clinton agenda.

---

1. In his First Inaugural Address, April 30, 1789, George Washington said, "The propitious smiles of Heaven can never be expected on a nation that disregards the eternal rules of order and right, which Heaven itself has ordained."

83

FIDEL CASTRO
BEFORE THE JUDGMENT SEAT

Originally published on November 30, 2016

"It is appointed for men to die once, and after that comes judgment."
So declares the Bible (Hebrews 9:27 RSV). As everyone knows by now,
Fidel Castro's time to die came over the weekend.

The Left chooses to idolize the wrong people, and Castro is no exception. I see people on occasion wearing Che Guevara shirts, and I think
to myself, "What happened? Is your Adolf Hitler shirt in the wash?"

How many millions of people experienced premature death and untold misery because of Fidel Castro? Initially, Cubans had high hopes
for Castro because he successfully defeated the military dictator, Fulgencio Batista. But Castro chose to align with the communists in the
name of "the people."

I once interviewed Rafael Cruz, the father of Ted. Rafael fought
against Batista's forces. They jailed and tortured him for it. Like many
Cubans, Cruz initially had high hopes for Castro, only to be sorely
disappointed.

Long before it occurred in the Cuban Revolution, George Orwell's
Animal Farm (1945) told Castro's story. In that parable, the drunken
human who runs the farm so mistreats the talking animals that they
rebel and pull off a revolution. They even manage to kill the human.
One of their rules is "All animals are equal." But over time, they modify
that rule to "All animals are equal, but some animals are more equal
than others." Pretty soon, the pigs are running everything and living

very well, while day-to-day life for the rest of the animals is worse than it was under the cruel farmer.

I remember once seeing a TV segment on the lifestyle of Fidel Castro and his inner circle. They lived lavishly, while normal Cubans suffered under the communism Castro imposed. Imagine. The Cuban people live in a very degraded and perpetually depressed economy even as the Castros enjoy luxurious parties. Indeed, some are more equal than others.

Joseph Farah, founder of *WorldNetDaily*, once told me in an interview on socialism that it seems that "every generation has to relearn this lesson" that socialism fails and ushers in nothing but death and misery: "We saw Fidel Castro in the 1960s come to power in Cuba, promising utopia, once again, and it deteriorated very rapidly into a tyrannical police state. And it's never recovered. And Cuba was a fairly prosperous country before."

Dr. Paul Kengor is a professor of political science and history at Grove City College and a widely syndicated columnist and best-selling author. Among his books on communism is *The Communist* (2012), about Obama's mentor, Frank Marshall Davis, who was Communist Party USA member #47544. Kengor wrote me: "We have just witnessed the death of the world's longest-running communist menace and dictator. He was horribly destructive to the people of Cuba and held the potential to literally kill tens to hundreds of millions of people worldwide if he had gotten what he wanted in October 1962—namely, to unleash nuclear Armageddon. Fidel wanted to fire those nuclear missiles in October 1962. Thankfully, the Soviets wouldn't let him."

Writing for *The American Spectator* (November 27, 2016), Kengor notes, "*The Black Book of Communism*, the seminal Harvard University Press work (Kramer, ed. 1999), which specialized in trying to get accurate data on the enormous volume of deaths produced by communist tyrants, states that in the 1960s alone, when Fidel and his brother Raul (Cuba's current leader) established their complete control, with the help of their murdering buddy Che Guevara, an estimated 30,000 people were arrested in Cuba for political reasons and 7,000 to 10,000 were believed to have been executed. Even then, that was merely the start."

Armando Valladares, the famous Cuban patriot who spent twenty-two years in one of Fidel Castro's gulags in Cuba and authored *Against All Hope* (1986), said of the communist occupation, "Every night there were firing squads." Note that this was only four years after the takeover. Valladares reflects on those he saw killed, many of whom were Christians: "I thought about all of those men who marched to the firing squads with a smile on their lips; I thought about the integrity of those martyrs who had died shouting, 'Viva Cuba Libre. Viva Christ the King. Down with Communism.' And I was ashamed to feel so frightened.... My heart rose up to God, and I fervently prayed for Him to help me stand up to this brutality, and do what I had to do. I felt that God heard my prayer." By 1963, the soldiers gagged such condemned men before shooting them, lest other courageous souls might hear their cries of "Long live Christ the King" and "Down with Communism."

Well, now the long-awaited time has come. Castro is dead. Meanwhile, Christ the King reigns for eternity.

84

THE COMING BATTLE OVER
THE SUPREME COURT

Originally published on July 6, 2016

Here's a true Rip Van Winkle story: Jeremiah Denton, an American pilot captured in Vietnam in 1965, returned home when he was released in 1973 to a very different country. Consider the differences between the United States of 1965 and that of 1973. During those eight years, the floodgates of pornography opened. Abortion became legal and was becoming widespread. Many marriages floundered and the divorce rate skyrocketed. Thankfully, positive civil rights made gains, but despite that, morality began to tank.

Millions were beginning to live in sin, only they resented anyone calling it that. The gay movement started up and began marching down the streets. They lagged just a couple of years behind the women's liberation movement, which also took to the streets.

Denton once told me in a television interview, "When I came home.... and saw all these signs—X-rated movies, massage parlors, these dumpy-looking places—and I asked [my wife] Jane, 'What are those?' And then saw the magazines on the magazine racks in the Naval Hospital, I was shocked." He added, "I couldn't believe that my country—a country which had succeeded in getting 'One nation under God' placed back in the Pledge—had gotten to this place." Denton later went on to serve his country as a U.S. Senator to fight on behalf of Judeo-Christian principles, long before his death in 2014.

The Supreme Court had a lot to do with many of those changes, including pornography and abortion rights. During those eight pivotal years, we went from one nation under God to a nation that had basically lost its moral compass. Judicial activism refers to judges making laws from the bench, something they are not constitutionally charged to do—and I would argue, not permitted to do. But since when has the law ever stopped those intent on breaking the law anyway?

In America today, we are now virtually ruled by the Court. Every year we have to wait until the end of June or thereabouts to know the latest that our robed masters will hand down to us, as they come down from Mount Olympus, if you will, with their rulings.

The founders never intended this. *Federalist #81*, for example, makes it clear that the courts would be the weakest of the three branches of government. As a nation, we have launched adrift on a sea of relativism—and the high court bears much of the blame for that. The founding fathers gave us a Constitution to govern us. It was predicated on the Declaration of Independence, which said our rights come from God. Therefore, our laws should be in accordance with "the laws of nature and of nature's God." The mainstream disregard Natural Law today.

The next president could well set the course of the Supreme Court of the United States (SCOTUS) for at least a generation or two. Some members of the high court are older than eighty. The next president will likely get to choose at least two or three justices.

Our founding document, the Declaration of Independence, upon which the Constitution is predicated, tells us we have the right to "life, liberty, and the pursuit of happiness." But many court decisions are taking away these very things.

Which candidate do you want to see choose the members of the Supreme Court? Where would the judges they choose stand on issues like life, marriage, religious liberty, property rights, and the Second Amendment? Those who hold to the notion that the Constitution is a "living document" are able to read into it whatever they want it to say. Jefferson could see early on that the germ of the dissolution of the Constitution was that it could become "a thing of wax" to be twisted this way and that in the hands of some of these justices. Those who hold to the notion that the framers cared about what they actually wrote are those who make the best justices on the Supreme Court. Of course, the founders were far from perfect and knew the Constitution would need amending from time to time—as happened in the mid-nineteenth century to outlaw slavery forever.

What types of judges will the next president choose and the Senate confirm? Will they move us toward freedom or toward tyranny? Will they recognize religious liberty or continue to strip it away? I think the courts are the most critical issue of this election.

If a Rip Van Winkle fell into a long, deep sleep today, what type of America would he wake up to in 2024? To a large degree, we the people will determine that answer on November 8th. For the sake of the next generation or two, let's make it count.

85

HOW SCALIA STOOD STRONG FOR DECADES

Originally published on February 17, 2016

A great man has died, Antonin Scalia. Imagine his great homecoming to be with his Lord, whom he ultimately served.

If there is not a battle royal over the appointment of his successor, then it would appear that the Republican Party has no pulse. Such a battle will be about what the future of America is to be—Constitution or no Constitution? Appointed by Ronald Reagan in 1986, Scalia stood fully for the Constitution, including its original intent.

Growing up in modern America, we assume that it's just natural for the Supreme Court justices to impose their opinions on the rest of us, to effectively legislate from the bench. After all, judicial activism has been on display in the courts at least since the 1940s.

We tend to forget that activist courts reinterpreted the First Amendment's prohibition on the governmental establishment of religion to mean the separation of church and state—even, in effect, the separation of *God* and state. The Supreme Court gave us abortion on demand, opened the floodgates of pornography, and even same-sex marriage—despite the expressed will of the people. All of these things fly in the face of our history. For example, our first president said we could never hope to be a happy nation unless we imitate Jesus.

What did the founders think of the idea of legislating from the bench? They were against it. They said that the legislative branch (covered in Article I) is the most important branch in our country since it is closest to the people. They delegated powers to the executive branch

(Article II) and to the courts (Article III). Clearly, the founders cared more about the legislature than the judiciary. Article I of the Constitution deals with the legislature in 2,266 words. In contrast, Article III, which deals with the judiciary, contains only 375 words.

Brave Scalia tenaciously fought with wit, charm, and a great deal of courage, for the people to retain the powers (through their legislators) that the Constitution recognized. Twenty years ago, Justice Scalia gave a speech at a prayer breakfast for the First Baptist Church of Jackson, Mississippi, where he famously said, "We are fools for Christ."[1] Those familiar with the New Testament knew that Scalia simply quoted the apostle Paul in his first letter to the Christians in Corinth, where he said that to those who are perishing, the cross of Christ is foolishness. Paul adds that we may appear to be fools in the eyes of the world. But God's so-called "foolishness" is wiser than man's "wisdom."

In that speech, Scalia noted how unbelievers today sneer at the idea of Christ's resurrection—a miracle—therefore, in conflict with reason: "Reason and intellect are not to be laid aside where matters of religion are concerned. What is irrational to reject is the possibility of miracles and the resurrection of Jesus Christ." But to "the worldly wise," noted Scalia, "everything from Easter morning to the Ascension had to be made up by the groveling enthusiasts as part of their plan to get themselves martyred."

Scalia endured year after year, decision after decision, in contradiction to the prevailing wisdom of the dominant rulers in our culture—as seen in the major law schools, law firms, the Washington elite, and the mainstream media.

I once had the privilege to interview Robert Bork, nominated to serve on the Supreme Court by Reagan, until a massive smear campaign "borked" him, adding a word to our political lexicon. I asked him why supposedly conservative justices often turn liberal after a few years in the Court. He replied, "The Court is part of the intellectual class and it responds to the intellectual class. If, when you go one way, you get praised by all of *New York Times* and the *Washington Post* and the NBC and CBS and ABC, that's kind of seductive. But if you go the other way, you get criticized and over time that, I think, has some effect on some justices."

---

1. "Scalia's Sermonette," *Notre Dame Law Review*, June 1, 1999, scholarship.law.nd.edu.

So how was it that Scalia was able to endure the perpetual criticism? His Christian commitment. Going back to his remarks at the Jackson prayer breakfast, he said that the "view of Christians taken by modern society" is a derogatory one. He added, "We are fools for Christ's sake. We must pray for the courage to endure the scorn of the modern world." No wonder Scalia could tell the graduating class of William and Mary in 1996, "The only thing in the world not for sale is character."

Scalia will be missed. He has left a huge hole in our national politics. May God grant that it be filled well.

86

SO MUCH FOR THE CONSTITUTION

Originally published on July 1, 2015

In 1819, Jefferson spoke out against judicial activism, saying, "The Constitution is a mere thing of wax in the hands of the judiciary, which they may twist and shape into any form they please."

Recently we have seen judicial activism on steroids at the Supreme Court. That is especially true in their hubris-laden decision to set aside "the laws of nature and of nature's God," declaring that same-sex marriage is now the law of the land in all fifty states. Period. We-a-slim-majority-of-the-Court have spoken. And there it is. To me, the big issue boils down to authority. By what authority did a majority do this?

As Chief Justice Roberts himself said, you can celebrate this decision if you want to, but the bottom line is it had nothing to do with the Constitution. If the Constitution means whatever the justices want it to say, then the nation is like a great ship set adrift without a rudder—or worse, with a rudder forcing us to go on our inexorable way toward a great precipice.

Those who applaud such an imposition of power may not be so enthusiastic if another arbitrary authority arises which doesn't share their values. ISIS marked the Supreme Court's decision over the weekend by throwing alleged homosexuals off tall buildings in Syria, as crowds below cheered on. I'm sure those poor victims received no due process.

The United States of America has been a great and noble experiment. How can sinful man govern sinful man in a way that protects freedom, including for those who don't share the same values? Power had to be balanced and parceled out, lest we ended up with a monarchy or an oligarchy, a rule by the few. This was the genius of the American system. It gave us great freedoms. But now, instead, the government has so collected power that we're essentially in a scenario of "might makes right."

Justice Samuel Alito dissented in this case, noting, "The system of federalism established by our Constitution provides a way for people with different beliefs to live together in a single nation.... By imposing its own views on the entire country, the majority [of this Court] facilitates the marginalization of the many Americans who have traditional ideas." He added, "If a bare majority of Justices can invent a new right and impose that right on the rest of the country, the only real limit on what future majorities will be able to do is their own sense of what those with political power and cultural influence are willing to tolerate. Even enthusiastic supporters of same-sex marriage should worry about the scope of the power that today's majority claims."

Scalia noted in his dissent, "Today's decree says that my Ruler, and the Ruler of 320 million Americans coast-to-coast, is a majority of the nine lawyers on the Supreme Court."

In short, what matters now is who's got the power—in this case, one man, Justice Anthony Kennedy. In a different context, satirist Tom Lehrer sang: "Might makes right, until they see the light..." That is such a dangerous place to be, for the annals of history are filled with the bloody trail of abuses of power, even among so-called enlightened people.

One of the greatest books summarizing the history of the twentieth century—the bloodiest century on record because of the anti-God views of so many leaders, i.e., Stalin, Hitler, Mao, Pol Pot, etc.—is *Modern Times* (1983) by the excellent British historian Paul Johnson.

He notes that at the end of the nineteenth century, many intellectuals claimed that God was dead. This created an incredible vacuum. Johnson writes, "The history of modern times is in great part the history of how that vacuum had been filled.... In place of religious belief, there would be secular ideology.... Above all, the Will to Power would produce a new kind of messiah, uninhibited by any religious sanctions whatever.... The end of the old order, with an unguided world adrift in a relativistic universe, was a summons to such gangster-statesmen to emerge."

Anthony Kennedy's decision on Friday, written in the voice of a philosopher-king, rather than a judge, divorced marriage from the norms of history, world civilization, and God.

Justice Clarence Thomas wrote in his dissenting opinion, "Aside from undermining the political processes that protect our liberty, the majority's decision threatens the religious liberty our Nation has long sought to protect." Thus, they have turned the Constitution on its head, granting a right not found there that will trump rights explicitly spelled out there.

In 1821, Jefferson warned, "The germ of dissolution of our federal government is in...the federal judiciary."

I can only take comfort in the fact that, as Dr. Alveda King reminds us, God will have the final word. Said the apostle Paul, "Let God be true, and every man a liar" (Romans 3:4).

A particular concern to Christians about this decision is that the highest court in the land has basically nullified the Biblical view of marriage as being consonant with American law. If you disagree with same-sex marriage, keep your opinions to yourself. It might cost you your job or your livelihood.

Again, quoting Alito's dissent: "I assume that those who cling to old beliefs will be able to whisper their thoughts in the recesses of their homes, but if they repeat those views in public, they will risk being labeled as bigots and treated as such by governments, employers, and schools." So much for the freedom to disagree with the prevailing politically correct ethic.

87

HAVE "WE THE PEOPLE" STOPPED
BEING "OUR OWN RULERS"?

Originally published on October 14, 2015

Once the Supreme Court has ruled, that's it. Case closed. Right? Not necessarily. Last week (October 8, 2015) a group of scholars issued a "Statement Calling for Constitutional Resistance to *Obergefell v. Hodges*" in reference to the Supreme Court's same-sex marriage decision. The statement begins, "We are scholars and informed citizens deeply concerned by the edict of the Supreme Court of the United States in *Obergefell v. Hodges* wherein the Court decreed, by the narrowest of margins, that every state in the country must redefine marriage to include same-sex relationships." The statement says, "If *Obergefell* is accepted as binding law, the consequences will be grave." Here is my summary of those grave consequences:

- Denigration of the time-honored building block of society, and the best means for bearing and rearing children
- Dissent against same-sex marriage will be punished
- It opens a Pandora's box on what constitutes a marriage
- The decision undermines "we the people"

Consider again what Justice Alito said about the second point above in his dissent of *Obergefell*—that dissent against same-sex marriage will be punished: "I assume that those who cling to old beliefs will be able to whisper their thoughts in the recesses of their homes, but if they repeat those views in public, they will risk being labeled as bigots and treated as such by governments, employers, and schools."

The statement notes that the whims of five lawyers cannot amend the Constitution, when it declares, "We stand with James Madison and Abraham Lincoln in recognizing that the Constitution is not whatever a majority of Supreme Court justices say it is." The signers of the statement also call upon all officials to uphold the Constitution, rather than "the will of five members of the Supreme Court." They should "refuse to accept *Obergefell* as binding precedent for all but the specific plaintiffs in that case."

By my count, the statement has currently garnered the signatures of sixty-four scholars, affiliated with such schools as Princeton, Notre Dame, Vanderbilt, Boston College, Villanova, University of Oxford, LSU Law Center, Pepperdine, and Regent School of Law.

Dr. Robert George of Princeton leads the charge. *New York Times Magazine* once called Dr. George "this country's most influential conservative Christian thinker." I've had the privilege of interviewing Dr. George a few times through the years. As he explained in one of those interviews, "Marriage is the conjugal union of a husband and wife. That's the foundation of the family, and it's the family that's the foundation of every other institution in society." George went on to say, "Everything else ultimately depends on it. It's the family that produces what every other institution in society needs, but cannot produce itself. Every institution needs basically decent, hardworking, conscientious, honest people who will treat each other with respect, who will show up for work on time, who won't be drunk or on drugs, who will pay taxes, who will carry the burdens of caring for those who cannot care for themselves."

And he added, "If [the legal system] really had to rely on the threat of punishment to get anybody ever to do anything that was honorable and right, well, it wouldn't work. The political system needs such people, but ... they will be produced by one institution and one institution only, and that's the family."

But now the high court has undermined the legal and traditional definition of marriage, and thus, the family. And they have done so on highly questionable grounds. The statement cites several examples challenging the validity of the ruling from the four dissenting justices in the *Obergefell* case.

Did the founders of our country intend for us to be governed by judicial fiat? Not at all. We call attention again to *Federalist #81* by Alexander Hamilton, for example. It says the courts are to be the weakest of the three branches of government.

The statement draws heavily on the example of President Lincoln. It cites portions of his First Inaugural Address, where he spoke eloquently against judicial tyranny. Lincoln eschewed the idea that "we the people" should be ruled by "we the judges." I'm sure he had the *Dred Scott* decision of 1857 in mind. In effect, that awful decision held that "once a slave, always a slave." Lincoln disagreed with the premise underlying *Dred Scott*—that the Supreme Court has the constitutional authority to sovereignly determine the meaning of the Constitution, which amounts to the power to just make up law.

As noted before, he said: "If the policy of the Government upon vital questions affecting the whole people is to be irrevocably fixed by decisions of the Supreme Court...the people will have ceased to be their own rulers." In other words, he didn't buy the premise upon which judicial activism was built. Nor should we, say these scholars. Hear. Hear.

88

THE CHRISTIAN AND CIVIL DISOBEDIENCE

Originally published on September 9, 2015

Recent events have called into question the issue of obeying the government in all ways—even in all circumstances. In the 13th chapter of Romans, Paul says that God has given us the government as a minister of righteousness. It is our duty to obey it. But we also see in Scripture that on occasion, when the government calls for one to disobey God, then civil disobedience is in order.

There's a great lesson to learn from one aspect of World War II related to distortions of Romans 13. With no implication of calling anybody a Nazi, consider this lengthy lesson, wherein the Nazis quoted Scripture in order to demand unquestioning obedience. On April 9, 1940, without any warning or provocation, the Germans invaded Norway. It was an unexpected battle and an unfair fight, with four hundred thousand German Wehrmacht versus a nation not expecting it. This nightmare lasted until May 1945.

There were, of course, Norwegian collaborators—Norwegians who sold their soul to get ahead during the reign of the Nazis. Foremost amongst them was Vidkun Quisling. His name has been adopted into the dictionary: a quisling is a traitor.

When the Nazis took over Norway, a country full of "pure Aryans," they expected the Norwegians to fully participate in their attempts to glorify the "master race" and purge the "undesirables" from humanity, such as Jews, Gypsies, and Slavs. The Norwegians would have nothing to do with this. So they resisted, usually in every peaceful way they could. Much of the battle was fought over distributing accurate information.[1]

The Norges Hjemmefront Museum in Oslo is dedicated to the resistance movement of World War II. A plaque there in English reads: "In Norway, Nazi ideology was defeated by the democratic forces rooted in a national, Christian culture." While the Nazis won militarily (until the end of the war), they never came close to winning the hearts and minds of the people.

Normally, in those days, the churches were full. But during the war, something happened to cause the churches to go empty. The Norwegian bishops and priests, desiring to be faithful to God and the Scriptures, resisted the Nazi efforts to control the churches and the content of sermons. The clergy reasoned that if they all resisted together as one, nothing could happen to them. The Nazis arrested all of them and sent them to concentration camps. Most never returned. Many Norwegian Christians met in private homes secretly for worship and avoided the churches during the war.

The same thing happened with the schoolteachers. The Nazis took over the curriculum of the schools. The teachers resisted as one group. The Nazis arrested them also and sent them to concentration camps. Most never returned.

The museum contains a 1941 book, written in Norwegian, used in the schools by the Nazis.[2] In it, they quote Scripture: "What are those called in Romans 13:1 who God has set over us? Have you considered that your parents, your school teachers (your principal), policemen, police chief, judges, the priest, the bishop, the county commission, the state government, are the authorities who are installed by God, and that you owe them obedience?" Then it says, "Overall, we owe the Führer and the government obedience. If you set yourself up against the authorities and against the state, you are standing against God's structure and are subject to punishment."

Talk about the devil quoting Scripture. In reality, the Führer was hostile toward Christianity. Hitler once declared, "The heaviest blow

---

1. Jerry Newcombe, "The Alternative Media—A Lifeline of Freedom," *Jerry Newcombe*, May 6, 2015, jerrynewcombe.com.

2. Sigmund Feyling, *Life and Doctrine: Christian Teaching with Study Questions*, 1941.

that ever struck humanity was the coming of Christianity. Bolshevism is Christianity's illegitimate child. Both are inventions of the Jew." But he was happy to have his minions twist the Christian Scriptures for his own ends.

God's Word is pure and right. But that doesn't mean evil people intent on achieving goals contrary to the message of Scripture can't distort it. There's a time and a place for everything under the sun, including (on occasion) civil disobedience.

Recently I came across an unpublished letter by D. James Kennedy (November 29, 1988), in which he addressed this issue: "The basic Bible principles, I believe, are these: 1) All authority is from God. 2) All human authority is delegated from God. 3) No human authority can countermand the authority of God. 4) If such anti-biblical laws are passed, Christians must in conscience disobey them. 5) They must be prepared to suffer the consequences of their actions."

Then he solidifies the whole point: "The very existence of Christianity depends upon Christians obeying these principles. Had they not done so, Christianity, which was outlawed first in Israel and then in the Roman Empire, would have ceased to exist many centuries ago."

89

DARWIN AND WWI

Originally published on September 3, 2014

Quick quiz: What started World War I? An anarchist in Serbia shot and killed a visiting Austrian leader. But why would that shooting a hundred years ago trigger the killing of millions, including one out of two young Frenchmen, in what we now know as World War I?

In his 1997 book, *A History of the American People*, British historian Paul Johnson writes, "The Great War of 1914–18 was the primal tragedy of modern world civilization, the main reason why the twentieth century turned into a disastrous epoch for mankind" (Johnson 1997, 642).

A series of conflicting European alliances led to the bloodbath when the tinderbox ignited. Johnson explains how the shooting of the Archduke Franz-Ferdinand of Austria (June 28, 1914) led to "the Austrian ultimatum to Serbia, the Russian decision to support the Serbs, the French decision to support Russia, the German decision to support Austria and fight a two-front war against Russia and France, and Germany's consequential decision to send its armies through Belgium to enforce quick defeat of the French, and so the involvement of Britain and its dominion allies in support of Belgium" (Johnson 1997, 642).

World War I led to the deaths of millions of people—with millions more dying of a flu epidemic in the immediate wake of its devastation. Consider other consequences of WWI:

- The Russian Revolution, i.e., the collapse of czarist Russia and the rise of the Soviet Union, leading to the death of twenty to forty million Russian people (in peacetime).

- The end of the Ottoman Empire, which led a later secularized Turkey in 1924 that abolished the caliphate (not necessarily a bad development). Those events impact even our current situation. Al-Baghdadi, leader of the murderous ISIS/ISIL at the time of this writing, is viewed by his followers as the new caliph for the Muslim people.

- World War II. The winners after WWI made the armistice conditions so terribly difficult for the Germans in the Versailles Treaty that they sowed the seeds for WWII at the end of WWI. World War II soaked the globe in blood, killing some fifty-five million people.

- In the wake of WWII, Chairman Mao turned China into an atheistic communist state, killing some seventy-two million Chinese in the process. This led to the fall of Vietnam, Laos, and Cambodia.

By any measure, World War I was a disaster for humanity, underscoring the depravity of man. But could there be an additional factor in the causes of World War I that conventional history has overlooked? Dr. John West, senior fellow at the Discovery Institute of Seattle, says, "Historians continue to debate the causes of World War I, which were complex." West directed a new film, *The Biology of the Second Reich*, which highlights a link between Darwinism and the Great War. West states, "Social Darwinism was certainly one of the key issues that exerted a profound influence on German militarism before, during, and after the conflict."

The film can be seen online at darwintohitler.com, a website that deals with the "impact of Social Darwinism in Germany." The historian behind the website is the key guest in the video, Dr. Richard Weikart, a first-rate historian on twentieth-century Germany. Weikart wrote *From Darwin to Hitler: Evolutionary Ethics, Eugenics, and Racism in Germany* (2004), which shows the not-so-missing link between evolution and the rise of the Nazi scheme to clean up the gene pool (as they saw it), in order to create a master race of pure Aryans. Jews need not apply. Nor Gypsies, Slavs, dissenting Christians, etc.

Weikart is Professor of History at California State University, Stanislaus. I interviewed him for our 2006 TV special, hosted by the late D. James Kennedy, "Darwin's Deadly Legacy." Said Weikart, "Natural selection was the guiding idea for Hitler and the Nazis....The term [*selection*] was related directly to Darwinian terminology that when you went to the camps, you went through a selection process. They were selecting this person to survive and this person to go to the gas chambers."

The new film on Darwin and WWI quotes Charles Darwin: "The support which I receive from Germany is my chief ground for hoping that our views will ultimately prevail." The film shows the link between Darwinism and German militarism, including the genocide the Germans committed against a tribe in one of their African colonies.

The film quotes Hitler, who later set out to finish the work begun in WWI: "The law of selection exists in the world, and the stronger and healthier has received from nature the right to live. Woe to anyone who is weak, who does not stand his ground! He may not expect help from anyone."

Weikart notes that neither Darwin nor his immediate followers were anti-Semitic per se. But their ideas made possible anti-Semitism and inhumanity against many other peoples as well. A hundred years later, we're still living with the consequences of some of those ideas, including their indirect contribution to World War I.

PART III

RECOVERING OUR RELIGIOUS LIBERTY
IN THE FACE OF A MILITANT SECULARISM

90

SILENCE IS GOLDEN

Originally published on October 18, 2010

School prayer is in the news again. Sort of. A federal appeals court last Friday upheld a 2007 Illinois law mandating a moment of silence at the beginning of the school day. Educators and legislators alike said it has a calming effect on the students.

A long-time atheist, Rob Sherman, took on the Illinois law on behalf of his daughter Dawn, who is now a seventeen-year-old senior. Initially, they were successful. The court held the law unconstitutional. But now, a three-judge panel of the Seventh Circuit Court of Appeals has overturned that decision. Sherman and Sherman vowed to appeal. I find it ironic that Rob Sherman, the atheist activist, accuses the judges of "judicial activism."

Judicial activism?

Conservatives have pointed out for years that judicial activism threw prayer out of public schools in the first place. *Judicial activism* is when the Supreme Court in its infinite wisdom in the early 1960s repeatedly threw out school prayer in one form or another.

Opponents to this Illinois law said that it was just another attempt to get school prayer back in. The panel did not agree and therefore said the law is okay.

But my point is that we have gone too far the other way. We have become so afraid of anything that smacks of school prayer that we have gone to the opposite extreme.

What would be so wrong with school prayer? Think about it.

In America, the school day began in prayer for the first three hundred years of its existence. And, no, the First Amendment wasn't under assault because of it. But there has been a gradual assault on common sense and common courtesy since school prayer has been banned. God has been kicked out of schools, and in His place have come the metal detectors.

One of the three critical Supreme Court decisions on prayer centered around then-fourteen-year-old William J. Murray in the Baltimore Public Schools. His mother Madalyn Murray O'Hair was the nation's leading atheist for years. Bill told me that in the early 1960s, his divorced mother tried to immigrate with her children to the Soviet Union. She thought the atheists had ushered in the millennium, if you will—the workers' paradise. But the Soviet officials in Russia told her to return home, that she could do more good for the cause back home.

Very upset by this turn of events, by the time she came home, the school year had already started. As she took William in late for school one day in a Baltimore public school, she was angry to see and hear the school children reciting the Lord's Prayer. "What the —— is this?" she asked. She sued, with Bill as the chief plaintiff, and won.

All these years later, William J. Murray, around whom that pivotal case revolved, is now an evangelical minister. He totally disagrees with what he and his mother did. He favors school prayer today. I interviewed him for Christian television, where he said, "I would like people to take a look at the Baltimore public schools today vs. what they were when I went to those schools in 1963 and my mother took prayer out of the schools. We didn't have armed guards in the hallways then when we had God in the classroom. But I'll guarantee you [now] there are armed guards. In fact, the city school system of Baltimore now has its own armed police force."

David Barton, walking encyclopedia on America's spiritual roots, who is lately a frequent guest on Glenn Beck's television program, says this of the founding fathers: "On the floor of the Constitutional Convention, they talked about that a nation accounts to God for its stands. Prior to 1962, our official stand was that God was welcome in the affairs of the nation. In 1962, for the first time, we told God He was not welcome in the lives of our students or in our classrooms, that we wanted Him to stay out."

When he was president, even Bill Clinton—no conservative—said that the public schools should not be religion-free zones.

George Washington said in his Farewell Address, "Of all the dispositions and habits that lead to political prosperity, religion and morality are indispensable supports." So even if the Illinois moment-of-silence law simply inches ever so slightly in the direction of school prayer, I welcome it. Silence is golden.

91

MISREADING JEFFERSON ON CHURCH AND STATE

Originally published on November 4, 2014

Unless you've been living in a cave lately, you might have noticed an ongoing onslaught against our Judeo-Christian traditions and beliefs. It's happening on virtually every front in our culture—in schools, in the media and movies, and in the public arena.

Many elitists today interpret the First Amendment in such a way as to turn it into a "search and destroy mission for any sneaky vestiges of religion left in the public square," as one Christian law professor put it. That's what separation of church and state means nowadays.

Virtually all of this is done, consciously or unconsciously, in the name of Thomas Jefferson. After all, it was he who gave us the phrase "separation of church and state." But what he meant by the phrase and what the ACLU and their allies mean are two different things.

First of all, Jefferson wasn't even in the country when the founders wrote the Constitution. He was in France, serving as our ambassador. Nor was Jefferson directly involved in the crafting of the First Amendment, which reads, "Congress shall make no law respecting an establishment of religion or prohibiting the free exercise thereof."

In 1947, the Supreme Court took an obscure letter of Jefferson's, written to the Baptists of Danbury, Connecticut, in which he quoted the First Amendment and said that it built "a wall of separation between church and state." Prior to that 1947 decision, there were few cases regarding the establishment clause. After it, floodgates seemed to open—eventually washing away things like school prayer and Bible reading, which had gone on for centuries, beginning in the colonies, and the posting of the Ten Commandments in public. And now, it never stops.

Todd Starnes of *Fox News* documents the current war against all things Christian in the public arena is his new book *God Less America*. I interviewed Todd recently on our television program and mentioned how the idea of "God-less America" is an oxymoron, since our national birth certificate, the Declaration of Independence (written by Jefferson, of course), says that our rights come from the Creator. Todd responded, "The atheist and the secularist, they really truly want God to be removed from the public marketplace of ideas." And what happens if they are successful? Todd says, consider "the nations throughout history, where man has been in charge [and removed those God-given rights]....Those become dictatorships. Those become [tyrannies]."

The irony of this anti-God crusade is that it is done in the name of Jefferson. Why is that ironic? Everybody knows he was an atheist or closet unbeliever, right? Well, not so fast.

I just cowrote a book on Jefferson and his faith with Dr. Mark Beliles, who lives in and pastors a church in Charlottesville, not far from Monticello. Dr. Beliles has been researching our third president for years and has uncovered some important things that are not well known. Together we produced the book, *Doubting Thomas? The Religious Life and Legacy of Thomas Jefferson* (2014). The book deals with five distinct religious phases in Jefferson's life.

In his most believing phase, Thomas Jefferson helped start a church in 1777, the Calvinistical Reformed Church of Charlottesville, with the evangelical Rev. Charles Clay as minister. Jefferson even wrote the church's founding document with the stated desire for "Gospel knowledge." He also donated more money than any other layman for that church. This was a year after he wrote the Declaration and the same year as the Virginia Statute for Religious Freedom.

The book contains two sermons of Rev. Clay, never before in print. They are evangelical (and evangelistic), and Jefferson helped support this man's ministry.

Later, Thomas Jefferson *privately* shared with people growing doubts (and then unbelief) about the Trinity, the divinity of Jesus, and the trustworthiness of the entire Bible. But to take the Thomas Jefferson of 1813 who denied the Trinity and superimpose his thoughts onto the Thomas Jefferson of 1776 and 1777, when he helped create a local orthodox church, is anachronistic—and bad history. But that's what is done today.

Thus, Thomas Jefferson was not a lifelong skeptic. Secondly, he did not believe in the separation of God and state. Even the above-mentioned letter from which we get the phrase "separation of church and state" ends with President Jefferson appealing to the Baptists to pray for him and promising he'll pray for them—to God. If the ACLU and their minions were correct, the very source of "the separation of church and state" violates "the separation of church and state"!

It boils down to interpretation. Jefferson and the other founders did not want a national denomination. That is clear. But that doesn't mean they did not want godly influence to hold some sway in government. Far from it. They cherished the influence of "religion and morality."

When Jefferson was president, he attended Christian worship services regularly on Sunday mornings. Where? In the U.S. Capitol building. But, "What about the separation of church and state?" someone might ask. Again, Jefferson didn't believe in the separation of God and state.

One view he never abandoned was that our rights are God-given. Etched in stone at his Memorial are these words: "Can the liberties of a nation be secure when we have removed a conviction that these liberties are the gift of God?" The answer is no. In short, the Thomas Jefferson of the ACLU is an historical fiction. *Doubting Thomas* seeks to set the record straight.

92

GOD AND THE CONSTITUTION

Originally published on November 11, 2014

Some skeptics today like to argue that the founding fathers purposefully left God out of the Constitution. They say that a "godless Constitution" was the intended design of the document—and they're wrong. First of all, the authors of the Constitution not only mention God, they even mention that Jesus is God. They do this in the ratification clause. This was done "in the Year of Our Lord" 1787.

Some skeptics object. Yet law professor John Eidsmoe, author of the book *Christianity and the Constitution,* notes in response to their objection, "Saying this [ratification] clause is not really part of the Constitution is like saying the attestation clause is not part of a will."

The general response of the skeptic is to dismiss the "Year of Our Lord" as just a custom. Custom, shmustom. The leaders of the French Revolution, who really did espouse a *secular* Enlightenment philosophy, changed their calendar a couple of years after the writing of America's Constitution in order to explicitly repudiate Christianity, so that time would no longer be measured "in the Year of Our Lord." (About a dozen years later, Napoleon restored the Christian calendar.)

To understand America's founders, we should realize what Dr. Michael Novak of American Enterprise Institute said. He observed that thinkers we call men of the "Enlightenment" are really of two sorts—those who believed in God and those who didn't.

The French Revolution was history's first secular revolution—and, incidentally, spilled rivers of blood. They chose to follow the unbelieving thinkers of the "Enlightenment"—e.g., Voltaire, Diderot, Rousseau, and David Hume. But our founders quoted those men of the "Enlightenment" who believed in the Lord—e.g., Montesquieu, John Locke, and Sir William Blackstone.

In his *The Spirit of Laws*, Baron Montesquieu wrote, "We shall see that we owe to Christianity, in government, a certain political law, and in war a certain law of nations—benefits which human nature can never sufficiently acknowledge."

John Locke not only wrote his *Second Treatise of Civil Government*, which was influential to our nation's founders; but he also wrote *The Reasonableness of Christianity.*

Sir William Blackstone, the great British jurist, was important to our founders and is still quoted by the Supreme Court. Blackstone wrote of "the law of nature and the law of revelation"—akin to "the laws of Nature and of Nature's God" in our Declaration of Independence.

The two key founding documents in American history are the Declaration of Independence and the Constitution. The first explains *why* we exist as a nation. Not only does the Declaration mention God four times, most importantly, it says that our rights come from the Creator.

The Constitution explains *how* we exist as a nation—how we function. The Constitution is predicated on the Declaration. When skeptics claim the Constitution doesn't mention God (which it does, in the ratification clause), they ignore that the latter is predicated on the former.

Fifty-five men assembled in what we now call the Constitutional Convention. Research shows that fifty to fifty-two of those men were members in good standing of Trinitarian churches. Many of them were even presidents and founders of Bible societies.

Certainly, Benjamin Franklin was not a Trinitarian, nor a member of such a church. Yet after weeks of wheel spinning at the Convention, on June 28, 1787, Dr. Franklin delivered a speech, asking them how it is that they had forgotten to seek God's help.

He said, "In the beginning of the contest with Great Britain, when we were sensible of danger, we had daily prayer in this room for divine protection. Our prayers, Sir, were heard, and they were graciously answered. All of us who were engaged in the struggle must have observed frequent instances of a superintending Providence in our favor." He went on to say, "I have lived, Sir, a long time, and the longer I live, the more convincing proofs I see of this truth—that God governs in the affairs of men. And if a sparrow cannot fall to the ground without His notice, is it probable that an empire can rise without His aid?"

He asked that they pray. The Convention accepted a variation of his request. So on July fourth, they all attended worship together at a local Christian church and prayed together. After they met, much of the acrimony died down and they were able to produce the Constitution. And again, Franklin was one of the *least* religiously orthodox of our nation's founding fathers.

Some of today's skeptics say that *any* mention of God in government is "unconstitutional." That ironically would make the Constitution itself "unconstitutional." I don't think so.

93

HOUSTON, WE HAVE A PROBLEM

Originally published on July 5, 2011

Political correctness in modern America continues to run amok. The latest front is at the Veterans Administration's Houston National Cemetery. Can someone pray there in the name of Jesus at a public event? Apparently not. According to reports about Arleen Ocasio, the director of that facility, she insists on seeing a written copy of prayers in advance, so she can approve or disallow them.

So, for example, local Nazarene pastor Rev. Scott Rainey was asked to say a prayer at a Memorial Day service there. Director Ocasio told him to send in writing what he was going to say. He complied. She got back to him and said it was "well written," but he couldn't say it—or pray it—because it was not "all inclusive" as a prayer. Translation: Since he wanted to end his prayer, as he is wont to do, in the name of Jesus Christ, he could not pray—at least not that way.

Keith Ethridge, director of the VA National Chaplain Center, said in an official statement, "Prayer is a very personal and sacred moment. To honor veterans as they are laid to rest, VA chaplains always pray and preside over religious services according to the veteran's faith tradition and the family wishes."

Praying in the name of Jesus is not "inclusive" enough. (Note: always only Jesus is offensive, apparently.) Rainey respectfully sought permission from the VA to override the Houston director's decision. The VA said no.

So, on his behalf, enter First Liberty,[1] a legal organization based in the greater Dallas area fighting for religious freedom. First Liberty filed suit and won a last-minute injunction. The judge ruled that prayer is free speech, has First Amendment protection, and should not be censored. Rev. Rainey was able to pray in the name of Jesus after all.

First Liberty has now filed suit on behalf of three local veterans groups against the cemetery for similar anti-religious discrimination. The three groups are the Veterans of Foreign Wars District 4, The American Legion Post 586, and the National Memorial Ladies. Scott Rainey is also a part of the lawsuit so that his future prayers won't be subjected to censorship.

The lawsuit claims, "Defendants are engaging in unlawful religious viewpoint discrimination against Plaintiffs by…banning certain religious words such as 'God' and 'Jesus,' censoring the content of prayer, and banning religious speech and expression from burial rituals when prior approval for such religious expression is not sought."

I called the Houston office and spoke with cemetery representative Melody Hardwick. She referred any questions related to the litigation to the U.S. Attorney's office. She also sent me a fax from the national VA's office (cited above) on their policy, which noted that the VA has a thousand chaplains throughout the country.

Meanwhile, she denied that viewpoint discrimination takes place at the Houston facility, but that they defer to the wishes of the family of the deceased. She said her own father was buried there on November 6, 2010 (at a time when Director Ocasio was in charge of the cemetery), and it was a "lovely Christian service."

One of the complaints against the Houston National Cemetery is that they apparently shut down the chapel and changed it into essentially a storage facility. Hardwick said that the graveyard is being expanded, and as construction was going on, the chapel was temporarily shut down as a chapel. But that was not and is not a permanent move, she said. Jeff Mateer, general counsel of First Liberty, says that's not true. He told me the chapel was closed prior to any construction.

Meanwhile, one man who spoke on behalf of First Liberty's lawsuit against the cemetery and its director was sixty-six-year-old Vietnam

---

1. At the time this column was written, what is now First Liberty was called Liberty Institute.

veteran Nobleton Jones, Honor Guard Junior Vice Command. He said, "On March 15, Director Ocasio told me that I couldn't say 'May God grant you grace, mercy and peace' to grieving families."

How did he react to the news? "That makes me feel smaller, even after I spent my time in the military, fighting so that people should be able to say that.... I did all this for my country and you are going to tell me what I can and can't say?"

As a student of American history, I find it fascinating that the first thing George Washington did as Commander in chief, when he received the Declaration of Independence on July 9, 1776 (mail was slow back then), was to systematize the placement of chaplains throughout the regiments, with assurance of a decent wage.

Speaking of himself in the third person, Washington said once about his army, "The General hopes and trusts, that every officer and man, will endeavour so to live, and act, as becomes a Christian Soldier, defending the dearest Rights and Liberties of his country." I have no doubt where the father of our country would stand on this issue.

Just this week, on the Fourth of July, about a thousand (according to *The Associated Press*) peaceful protesters gathered at the cemetery. U.S. Congressman Ted Poe, representing that area, attended. He said, "Really, this cemetery doesn't belong to the VA.... It belongs to those buried here and their families." The Houston Area Pastors' Council organized the rally. The rally cry was for religious freedom and for Ocasio to step down. Our founders gave us freedom *of* religion. But some today apparently only want to impose freedom *from* religion.

94

MUST OUR CHAPLAINS BE POLITICALLY CORRECT TOO?

Originally published on August 1, 2013

Recently, a chaplain got in trouble for quoting the old saying popularized by Dwight Eisenhower, "In battle, they learned the great truth that there are no atheists in the foxholes."

As we saw before, some atheists involved in the military have taken issue with Ike's quote, calling it a "bigoted, religious-supremacist phrase." One of them said, "Faith based hate, is hate all the same."

"Faith based hate"? Sounds like an oxymoron to me. Certainly, those atheists in the military—for whose service we should all be grateful—are an exception to Eisenhower's general rule. But I'm curious. Were our nation's founding fathers engaged in Christian "supremacism" and "faith based hate" when they said such things as the following? Consider just a sampling:

Thomas Jefferson said, "Of all the systems of morality, ancient or modern, which have come under my observation, none appear to me so pure as that of Jesus" (To William Canby, September 18, 1813).

On May 12, 1779, some Delaware Indian chiefs brought their sons to George Washington, seeking to have them taught by the colonists. Our first president said, "You do well to wish to learn our arts and ways of life, and above all, the religion of Jesus Christ." I saw a website where they claim this quote is questionable. It is not. You can see it for yourself in John Rhodehamel's, *George Washington: Writings* (1997, 351).

Samuel Adams, lightning rod of the American War for Independence, wrote the following in his famous "The Rights of the Colonists" (1772). Said Samuel Adams, "The right to freedom being the gift of God Almighty, the rights of the Colonists as Christians may best be understood by reading and carefully studying the institutions of The Great Law Giver and the Head of the Christian Church, which are to be found clearly written and promulgated in the New Testament."

During the Constitutional Convention, in the hot Philadelphia summer of 1787, tempers often flared. The proceedings seemed to be grinding to a halt. Then on June 28, the oldest man in the room, Benjamin Franklin, got up and made a passionate plea for prayer. It's a great speech. As we have seen, he said, "I have lived, Sir, a long time, and the longer I live, the more convincing proofs I see of this truth—that God Governs in the affairs of men. And if a sparrow cannot fall to the ground without His notice, is it probable that an empire can rise without His aid?" Acting on his idea, the founders prayed together as they attended worship at a July fourth service.

John Jay, first Chief Justice of the Supreme Court, said, "At a party in Paris, once, the question fell on religious matters. In the course of it, one of them asked me if I believed in Christ? I answered that I did, and that I thanked God that I did" (April 23, 1811).

James Madison, who helped shepherd the Constitution, wrote, "Whilst we assert for ourselves a freedom to embrace, to profess and to observe the Religion which we believe to be of divine origin, we cannot deny an equal freedom to those whose minds have not yet yielded to the evidence which has convinced us" (Memorial and Remonstrance, June 20, 1785). In other words, just because you don't happen to believe the Christian faith as we do, writes Madison, doesn't mean you will be punished for not believing. Here in America, thanks to the Christian views of most of our founders, there is freedom to believe and to not believe.

But today it seems as if those who have faith are being singled out to be punished. It seems as if some of today's secularists, like the militant atheists trying to punish the good chaplain, are trying to remake America into some sort of secular wasteland.

Our nation's birth certificate—our reason for being, expressed in the Declaration of Independence—says our rights come from the Creator.

Such rights can't be taken away—even by politically correct elites out to punish a lowly chaplain.

95

WHEN CHAPLAINS CAN'T DISCUSS THE BIBLE

Originally published on May 27, 2015

I believe the military keeps America safe. In turn, the military has had a spiritual shield held over it from before we were even a country—because of the chaplains. But today, chaplains are under enormous pressure to fully embrace political correctness.

Meet Lt. Commander Wes Modder, a chaplain in the U.S. Navy. About fifteen years ago, the Navy thought so highly of him that they used him in a video to recruit potential chaplains. He has ministered to sailors, Marines, and Navy Seals. Today, Chaplain Modder is fighting for his military career because he refused to bow the knee to political correctness.[1]

Sadly, this is not an isolated case. Lt. Gen. (Ret.) Jerry Boykin, Vice President of Family Research Council, told me in a 2013 interview, "I talked to [chaplains] privately about the pressure that they are under. Many of them are under pressure to perform same-sex marriages and most of the ones that I have talked to, . . . when the time comes that they are told to do it, . . . they're going to refuse."

Kelly Shackelford, the founder and director of First Liberty[2], fights for religious liberty in the courts and in the court of public opinion. His group fights against the anti-Christian legal organizations that try to strip away any Christian influence (including that of chaplains) from the public arena. He says such secularist groups are working "to

---

1. "Chaplain Modder Case," *First Liberty*, firstliberty.org.
2. At the time this column was written, what is now First Liberty was called Liberty Institute.

288

really change our country to something it never was and I hope never will be."

He adds, "They think that society would be better if religion was sort of relegated to people's homes or their churches or synagogue but not brought out in public. Well, that has never been the approach in this country; that wasn't the approach of the founders, that's not what our Constitution says and, hopefully, we can continue to win these cases so that it doesn't become what this country is about and how it's based."

The founders of America were very clear that God was important to the American cause. Our national charter, the Declaration of Independence, says our rights come from the Creator. They appealed their cause "to the Supreme Judge of the World for the Rectitude of our Intentions." It also says the founders had a "firm reliance on the protection of Divine Providence."

When George Washington, then Commander-in-Chief of the continental forces, first read the Declaration to his troops on July 9, 1776, he decreed that the military should retain chaplains and place them throughout the troops. In his order, he declared, "The blessing and protection of Heaven are at all times necessary but especially so in times of public distress and danger." But today, we seem to be turning our back on God.

Lately, command is pressuring military chaplains to make their prayers more "inclusive." Translation: Don't pray in Jesus's name. Kelly Shackelford told me, "These attacks that we're seeing are not usually against the Muslim faith, they're not usually against the Buddhist faith. They're not against the Jewish faith. They're attacks against Christianity in particular."

Lately, they are also exerting pressure to accept modern views of sexuality, as opposed to traditional views taught in the Bible. The widespread acceptance of those novel views has wreaked havoc on society—ultimately causing the breakdown of the family, the rise of crime, runaway venereal diseases, fatherless homes, rampant divorce, untold misery, etc. In the military, as in society, conflicts over standards of sexual morality are bound to lead to conflict.

As an example, superiors relieved Chaplain Wes Modder of his duties. Why? Because during counseling sessions with some young sailors, he privately expressed his disagreement with premarital sex and homo-sexual practice, in accordance with the Bible and his sending denomination, the Assemblies of God. The sailors complained to Chaplain Modder's higher ups, who summarily relieved him of his duties, threatening to kick him out of the Navy and cut off his pension—after nineteen years of stellar military service.

Mike Berry, First Liberty's Director of Military Affairs, said, "Knowing what I know about Chaplain Modder, reading his service record, seeing the awards he's received, the decorations he's received, the accolades, the fitness reports, and evaluations, the letters of recommendation—and to see these allegations and accusations that... the Navy is trying to use against him, I can't comprehend how this is happening to this American hero." The news shocked Wes Modder: "I feel betrayed. I feel dishonored for my fifteen years, almost twenty total of my service to my country."

Says Shackelford, whose legal group is defending Modder in this case, "The chaplains are under a lot of pressure to bow their knee to the government instead of to the proper One that they should be bowing [to]."

96

NO BIBLES ALLOWED IN A HOSPITAL?

Originally published on December 9, 2011

A leading military hospital was poised to implement an anti-Bible policy that would have been spiritually devastating. Thankfully, once light was shone on the policy, common sense prevailed, and the policy was quashed.

Since 1909, Walter Reed General Hospital in Washington, D.C., has cared for injured Army personnel. Later it was named Walter Reed Army Medical Center. Recently, they moved to Bethesda, Maryland, and became Walter Reed National Military Medical Center, expanding their mission beyond just the Army.

As the new facility was opening, the Navy issued a four-page memo with new guidelines for the new hospital. Amazingly, the guidelines stated, "No religious items (including Bibles, reading material, and/or artifacts) are allowed to be given away or used during a visit."

How far will political correctness in this country go? Would some bureaucrats try to keep the world's most loved (and hated) book from providing consolation for wounded soldiers or their grieving families? Thankfully, active Christians managed to get the policy reversed.

Tony Perkins, president of Family Research Council, a conservative pro-family think tank in Washington, D.C., sounded the alarm on December 2, 2011: "The new orders are buried in a four-page document about patient care, which an Army officer forwarded to us in disbelief. Effective immediately, families, friends, and even pastors will have to check their beliefs at the door to visit one of the largest military hospitals in the United States."

When Family Research Council learned of these new guidelines, they alerted officials on Capitol Hill, including Rep. Steven King of Iowa. So Congressman King went to the House floor late last week and declared, "Mr. Speaker, these military men and women who are recovering at Walter Reed and Bethesda have given their all for America. . . . They've defended and taken an oath to the Constitution, and here they are. The people that come to visit them can't bring a religious artifact? They can't bring a Bible? . . . A priest can't walk in with the Eucharist and offer communion to a patient who might be on their deathbed because it's prohibited in this memo from the Department of the Navy?"

After alerting their readers on this issue, Family Research Council could report success on December 5, 2011: "After working with concerned leaders like Rep. Steve King (R-Iowa) and talking with staff at Walter Reed, we were assured that the Navy was rescinding the policy."

Indeed, the Walter Reed website itself states (as of this writing, December 9, 2011): "Bibles and other religious materials have always been and will remain available for patient use at Walter Reed National Military Medical Center. The visitation policy as written . . . was incorrect . . . and should have been more thoroughly reviewed before its release. It has been rescinded. . . . We apologize for any confusion the policy may have caused."

But my question is, Why in the world would such a policy be issued in the first place? In a nation with our spiritual foundation, where our national motto still happens to be "In God We Trust," why would any such guidelines be written at all? Even a cursory reading of our nation's founding shows how incredibly out of step such anti-religious measures are with our roots.

The founders of America did not intend for America to have a national denomination, and they desired that the sacred right of conscience not be violated. But that did not mean they wanted the public realm to be religion-free zones. Far from it.

George Washington said in his First Inaugural Address that the first thing we ought to do as a new nation was to give thanks to God. He said in his Farewell Address that "religion and morality" were "indispensable supports" to our "political prosperity."

Even Ben Franklin, who was not orthodox in his beliefs, was the one who made an impassioned plea for the founders to pray when they were writing the Constitution and had hit some major impasses. As noted, he declared on June 28, 1787, during the Convention, "We have been assured, Sir, in the Sacred Writings, that 'except the Lord build the House, they labor in vain that build it.' I firmly believe this; and I also believe that without his concurring aid we shall succeed in this political building no better than the Builders of Babel: We shall be divided by our partial local interests; our projects will be confounded, and we ourselves shall become a reproach and bye word down to future ages." The Convention adopted a variation of Franklin's request for prayer, the founders prayed together (on July fourth), and they finished the Constitution.

Like Franklin, Thomas Jefferson was also not necessarily an orthodox Christian. Yet he made common references to God. He said that the moral teaching of Jesus was the best there is. He also had the Bible used as a textbook in Virginia schools (at all levels) that he helped found.

In short, it's a myth that the founders of America (even the non-orthodox ones) intended for our nation to be run as an essentially atheistic state. Yet here we are, some 225 years later and, if the elites could have had their way, the Bible would be banned from even a military hospital.

Long before he became our first president, note what George Washington declared to his troops when he first took over the army on July 4, 1775 (speaking of himself in the third person): "The General most earnestly requires and expects a due observance of those articles of war established for the government of the army, which forbid profane cursing, swearing, and drunkenness. And in like manner he requires and expects of all officers and soldiers, not engaged in actual duty, a punctual attendance on Divine service, to implore the blessing of Heaven upon the means used for our safety and defense."

I'll take the founders' vision for America over the politically correct version any day.

97

THE IRONY OF CALIFORNIA'S OUSTING OF CAMPUS CHRISTIAN GROUPS

Originally published on September 7, 2014

A disturbing story came and went, barely noticed a few weeks ago. California's twenty-three state universities are unceremoniously booting InterVarsity Christian Fellowship off their campuses. The process begins with "derecognizing" these as legitimate campus groups.

Why? Though everyone is welcome at their ministry events, IVCF reserves leadership only for those committed to their goals and creed, just as a homosexual group would presumably reserve leadership for gays or those who affirm its pro-gay agenda. Or a Muslim group for Muslims.

InterVarsity Christian Fellowship is a network of campus ministries. It is evangelical in orientation and has been around at least since the 1940s. IVCF personally touched me during my undergrad college years through their chapter at Tulane in the 1970s.

Theoretically, college is a place where students engage in and entertain robust discussion over a plethora of opinions in the marketplace of ideas. But political correctness is strangling that. Consider that the Christian church arguably created the phenomenon of the university, c. AD 1200 (to reconcile Greek philosophy with Christian theology), and Christianity created arguably the most notable universities the world over—e.g., Sorbonne, Oxford, Cambridge, Harvard, Yale, Princeton, William and Mary, Notre Dame, etc. Why then, are only Christian ideas—in the name of tolerance—prohibited on some of our campuses?

A friend of mine works in one of the California colleges in question. He wrote to me about this IVCF story: "Universities are allowed to implement 'all-comers' policies, which means that no campus organization can discriminate on the basis of religion or ideology. So, not only would a straight person be theoretically allowed to join a gay group, but someone who considers homosexuality a sin could theoretically be a member or even leader of such as group, and the group could not discriminate against them based on their beliefs." He adds, "This is absurd, of course. In reality, this 'all-comers' policy is being used primarily to discriminate against Christian organizations, who are truthful enough not to lie about the fact that, of course, they are going to discriminate on the basis of religion."

Apparently, if you sincerely hold conservative religious views, you have no place on the campus, at least as recognized by the school. This is because of a perversion of the notions of "tolerance" and "diversity." The late Dr. D. James Kennedy said, "We Christians do believe in and practice a tolerance, but remember this: Tolerance is the last virtue of a completely immoral society." Once in a while, protesters would come out and surround Dr. Kennedy's church to remonstrate. I said to him one such time, "Oh look, here come the 'shock troops of tolerance' again!"

I once interviewed Rabbi Daniel Lapin for our TV special, *What If Jesus Had Never Been Born?* He said, "There is a cultural struggle in America today. It is between those who are comfortable with God's divine blueprint for society, and that includes serious devoted Christians and Orthodox Jews. And on the other side, those who are fanatic extremists, who are determined to rip every element of traditional Judeo-Christian faith out of the village square."

How ironic this California campus story is, in light of that state's history. California owes a huge debt to Christianity, and to the Catholic Church in particular. That debt includes their first schools. Santa Clara, a Franciscan mission (1777), was California's first college. Father Junipero Serra (d. 1784) was responsible for beginning these missions and that school, and he is buried at the mission in Carmel by the Sea, the Mission San Carlos Borromeo de Carmelo. I visited that mission and took a photo of his library—the first library in the entire state.[1]

European settlement of California began with Spanish Catholic leaders creating a network of missions from the south (San Diego) stretching all the way to San Francisco (named after the thirteenth-century saint from Assisi). Los Angeles (whose original name meant "The Town of Our Lady the Queen of the Angels of the River Porciúncula") was one of those twenty-one missions. Each mission was roughly the distance of a day's horseback ride from the last one. From the mission at one end to the furthest mission at the other end is about six hundred miles.

California is known for its wine industry. Why did wine production begin, ever so small, in that state? For the purpose of providing communion wine. Even the state's capital refers to the Catholic celebration of Holy Communion—i.e., Sacramento.

The irony of the anti-Christian campaign in the name of "diversity" is that Christianity is and will continue to be the source of true diversity. For example, IVCF chapters are often remarkably diverse in terms of the socio-economic and racial backgrounds of their attendees. I don't think true diversity could be described any better than what St. John says of the worshipers he saw in heaven: "After this I looked and there before me was a great multitude that no one could count, from every nation, tribe, people and language, standing before the throne and in front of the Lamb" (Revelation 7:9). St. John would no longer have any welcome at California's schools.

---

1. The University of California began on the initiative of Reverend Samuel Hopkins Willey, chaplain of California's Constitutional Convention, coming to realization at Berkeley in 1855 through his leadership. Dorothy Dimmick, *The Making of American California: A Providential Approach* (Gilroy, CA: Dorothy Dimmick, 1990), 244–245. Nordskog Publishing Inc. holds the rights to this book and sells the remaining copies in circulation on "Jerry's Bookshelf" at nordskogpublishing.com.

98

SECULAR FUNDAMENTALISTS RULE
AGAINST PUBLIC CROSS

Originally published on January 6, 2011

The secular fundamentalists are at it again. This time they are suing to remove a fifty-seven-year-old cross in San Diego that serves as a veterans memorial.

A three-judge panel in the Ninth Circuit Court of Appeals in the San Francisco area has found the tall concrete cross at Mt. Soledad to be unconstitutional. The ACLU filed suit on behalf of a Jewish veterans group to remove the symbol. Rather than remove the cross on behalf of this group, why couldn't a Star of David have been added? Could it be that at the core of this lawsuit was not a wish to see all religions honored, but a campaign to secularize public life?

The secular fundamentalists have their own vision for America, and it's a lot closer to that of the failed Soviet Union—where they outlawed God and demolished churches or turned them into museums—than it is to the vision of the founders of America. Our nation's founders wanted no one church to dominate the other churches or to rule over the government. They also wanted religion—that is, Christianity—to flourish on a voluntary basis. Eventually, that tolerance toward various Christian denominations extended to other religions or those of no religion. In short, the founders gave us freedom of religion. But the secular fundamentalists are moving us toward freedom *from* religion.

There's a huge difference. Freedom *of* religion gives freedom to all, regardless of what they believe. Freedom *from* religion discriminates against the believer. Plus, in any country where they have officially established atheism, anyone who disagrees with the ruling party (or usually dictator) is on the outs—even if he too is an atheist.

Stalin, the arch-atheist, had Leon Trotsky, another arch-atheist, the communist co-architect of the Soviet Union—hunted down all across the globe. Finally, in our hemisphere, one of Stalin's followers managed to jam an ice pick into Trotsky's brain.

Ideas have consequences. Why can't we learn from the failed Soviet Union and see it for what it is: a seventy-year nightmare of bloodshed unleashed by official atheism?

America is predicated on one thing: our rights come from God. That's what the Declaration of Independence says. The Constitution is predicated on the Declaration. Our 1776 birth certificate explains *why* we exist. The Constitution then explains *how* our government is to work. When rights come from God, they are non-negotiable.

But the secular fundamentalists do everything they can to strip away our Judeo-Christian heritage. They've been quite successful at it. Now many of our schools have become something even Bill Clinton spoke against: "religion-free zones." A valedictorian can thank any power or person or force he or she wants to—unless it's the G-word, or worse—the J-word. One valedictorian actually had her microphone cut off in the middle of her speech because the authorities feared she was going to thank Jesus Christ for His help. Score another one for the secular fundamentalists.

If the secular fundamentalists were successful in their goal to purge any reference to God or our Judeo-Christian heritage from public life, then eventually they would have to scrub the Constitution itself. That document mentions God. It even acknowledges the deity of Jesus Christ. "How so?" you ask. It is signed, "in the year of our Lord," as in our Lord Jesus Christ. "But that's just a tradition," you might say. "It doesn't mean anything." If the fact that our Western calendar is based on the birth of Jesus means nothing, then how come the atheistic leaders of the French Revolution decided to toss out the calendar and make the year 1791 into Year 1 of the Republic? To get even further away from any Judeo-Christian influences, the revolutionaries even abandoned the seven-day week (with its built-in Sabbaths—Saturday for Jews and the

Lord's Day for the Christians) for a ten-day week. Thankfully, Napoleon undid all these things.

The secular fundamentalists had their way in the French Revolution, and the streets of Paris ran red with human blood. The secular fundamentalists had their way in the Soviet Union and in China and in Cambodia, etc., and *The Black Book of Communism* (Kramer, ed. 1999) documents the atrocities of one hundred million people killed by the twentieth-century communists.

The scrubbing of all Judeo-Christian symbols from the public square is just another attack on our civilization from the secular fundamentalists. What's next? The crosses at Arlington?

99

WILL NYC IMPLEMENT THE ABC PRINCIPLE—
ANYTHING BUT CHRIST?

Originally published on January 23, 2012

A terrible decision in New York City could have a chilling impact on religious liberty. If it spread to other cities, it could be devastating. Because of a court's ruling against one particular small church of the Bronx, Mayor Michael Bloomberg has now decreed that come February 12, 2012, the city must evict all churches and fellowships meeting in public schools. This will impact 160 churches, congregations, and fellowships.

These churches generally have great relationships with the community. Many of them offer important services to the needy, and they even provide revenue for the city. But it seems that among some today, the ABC principle trumps other considerations. ABC, as in, Anything But Christ.

This case goes back several years. In the name of "the separation of church and state," the educational establishment of New York City decided that churches could not meet in schools for worship. They could meet in schools for discussions or sports events, but not divine services. So one small church, the Bronx Household of Faith, filed suit with the help of the Alliance Defending Freedom,[1] a legal group that fights against anti-religious bigotry in the courts and beyond. As long as the litigation continued, that church and other churches have been able to meet in schools.

---

1. At the time this column was written, what is now Alliance Defending Freedom was called Alliance Defense Fund.

Greg Baylor, an attorney with the Alliance Defending Freedom, said recently, "Unfortunately, even though they had a temporary injunction that allowed them to meet in the public schools, the New York City education officials kept fighting them in the courts. They were insistent upon their objective of keeping out the churches. And they eventually persuaded the U.S. Court of Appeals for the 2nd Circuit, which is headquartered in New York City, to say 'Yes, you school districts can keep out churches who want to engage in religious worship services.'"

After the Appeals Court decision, the ADF appealed the case to the Supreme Court, which declined to take the case. The Supreme Court receives thousands of requests every year—I remember hearing in a recent year, it was about eight thousand. They turn down the vast majority of requests, only agreeing to a small number of cases—between eighty and a hundred. That means they turn down about 99.9 percent of the requests for appeals. Therefore, no one should read too much into the Supreme Court's refusal to take on any case. It's not on the same level as an out-and-out Supreme Court ruling on a particular issue. Mayor Bloomberg is reading way too much into the Supreme Court's decision not to hear the appeal.

So here we are in a country founded for religious freedom—where residents of our largest city are about to lose theirs.

George Washington said, "If I could have entertained the slightest apprehension that the Constitution framed by the Convention, where I had the honor to preside, might possibly endanger the religious rights of any ecclesiastical Society, certainly I would never have placed my signature to it." (Washington, *The Writings of Washington*, Vol. XXX, May 10, 1789, 321) So George Washington would not agree with Mayor Bloomberg's decision.

John Adams famously said our Constitution only applies to people when they are "moral and religious." So John Adams would not agree with Mayor Bloomberg's decision.

As president, Thomas Jefferson attended church every week at the U.S. Capitol. Clearly, he had no problem with government buildings being allowed for worship. So Thomas Jefferson would not agree with Mayor Bloomberg's decision.

As we can see, the mayor's decision does not fit with our history or traditions or law. (The church had even won at the District Court level.)

Some congregations are so small and limited in their resources that they might end up folding if this decision goes through. Imagine the net impact if this terrible decision doesn't get overturned. Today, New York. Tomorrow, California. Next day, perhaps your town. Cultural trends often spread from New York City to the rest of the country. Think of all the churches in our land that meet in schools. The church I happen to be a part of meets in a school.

Thankfully, the legislative body for the state of New York is considering an emergency bill that would address the issue statewide, thus overruling the mayor's decision. New Yorkers for Constitutional Freedom have been pushing for this.

Even if the mayor's edict goes into full effect (heaven forbid), the kingdom of God will continue—after all, we're talking about the religion of the catacombs. But it's just so ironic that this kind of thing could seriously be considered in a nation whose motto is still "In God We Trust."

100

WHAT WOULD THE FRAMERS THINK OF
EVICTING CHURCHES FROM NYC SCHOOLS?

Originally published on April 9, 2014

A new court ruling has determined that churches can no longer rent public school facilities.

The City of New York can evict churches from the schools. Despite the good they do in the community, they could be out in the cold.

Writing for *Facts & Trends* (April 3, 2014), Bob Smietana observes, "The 2–1 ruling from the Second Circuit Court is the latest twist in a long-running legal battle between the Bronx Household of Faith and the Board of Education of the City of New York."

Indeed, this is not new. This is the latest decision in an on-going battle that the Alliance Defending Freedom (ADF) has been fighting for years. In fact, I can remember interviewing Rev. Bob Hall, the church's founding pastor, as far back as the 1990s on this case for a religious-freedom TV special, hosted by the late Dr. D. James Kennedy.

Jordan Lorence, one of the ADF attorneys fighting on behalf of the churches, said that the city officials trying to oust the churches are treating Christianity as if it were asbestos. The amazing thing about all this is how contrary such a move is to our national spiritual heritage. Consider a short review.

First of all, the idea of schools for the masses, which eventually became public schools, is a result of the desire to teach the Bible. About a dozen years after the Puritans founded Boston, they passed "the Old Deluder Satan Act." They stated that it is one of the chief ends of that "old deluder Satan" to keep people from the Word of God. Therefore, people need to read the Bible for themselves. Therefore, they need to read. Therefore, we need to have schools to teach them how to read. This is the origin of schools for the masses in the American experience.

America was founded by different colonists, the vast majority of whom came for religious freedom. They were all Christians of one stripe or another. They eventually learned to work together when Mother England threatened their rights.

When we became a country, we agreed that we would not allow any one denomination (all being Christian) to lord it over the others. The very first freedom guaranteed in the Bill of Rights was the freedom of religion. The framers wrote, "Congress shall make no law respecting an establishment of religion or prohibiting the free exercise thereof."

Liberals today talk about the "freedom of worship." But, as we see in this case in New York, they don't even grant that. Freedom of religion includes freedom of worship, but much more.

We have seen that George Washington famously said in his Farewell Address that we can't maintain national morality apart from religion. John Adams said our Constitution was made only for a moral and religious people and will not work for any other.

But, someone might say, Thomas Jefferson and James Madison wouldn't agree. They wanted to make sure that the state would be free from any corrupting influence of the church. Oh really? When President Jefferson lived in Washington, D.C., he regularly attended services at the U.S. Capitol. Christian worship services were held there on Sunday mornings until the 1880s.

I had the privilege of interviewing Dr. James H. Hutson of the Library of Congress about the founders and religion. He is the author of *Religion and the Founding of the American Republic* (Library of Congress, 1998), as well as *The Founders on Religion: A Book of Quotations* (Princeton, 2005). In the latter book, Hutson writes of Jefferson that he "'constantly attended public worship' in the House of Representatives, once riding through a cloudburst to arrive on time. In retirement he regularly patronized worship services at the Albemarle County Court House." Hutson adds, "As president, James Madison followed Jefferson's example by attending services in the House."

Dr. Hutson notes that as Jefferson was on his way to church one Sunday, someone challenged him as to why he would go, since he supposedly didn't "believe a word in it." Jefferson replied, "No nation has ever yet existed or been governed without religion. Nor can be. The Christian religion is the best religion that has been given to man and I as chief Magistrate of this nation am bound to give it the sanction of my example. Good morning, Sir." (Hutson, *The Founders on Religion,* 2005, 192–193). I have been challenged before as to the accuracy of this statement. I didn't make it up. It comes from a Princeton University Press book, written by a key archivist of the Library of Congress.

Only by divorcing ourselves from our nation's true roots can courts come up with such decisions. Thankfully, the Alliance Defending Freedom (cofounded by the late Dr. Kennedy and others) is appealing this decision. The churches will continue—after all, we're talking about the religion of the catacombs. But will New York City continue to feel the blessings the churches bring?

101

THE SEPARATION OF GOD AND STATE?

Originally published on May 14, 2013

Virtually every week there is some outrageous story of an alleged violation of the separation of church and state. They're becoming so frequent that they are often met with a collective yawn. The crazy thing about all this is how removed it is from the clear intent of the founders themselves, as seen in their documents, in their actions, and in their words.

A lot of times when the pro-religious-freedom side fights back, we win. That's because the Constitution and the history are on our side. But fighting back takes a lot of courage and energy. And many people would rather just go with the flow and turn the other cheek, which is understandable. Yet over time, we find our liberties being chipped away piece by piece.

First Liberty[1] of Plano, Texas, is one of those groups that fight for Christian expression in the public arena. They reported just the other day (May 9, 2013) on a victory of some brave high-school cheerleaders, standing up for religious freedom.

Kountze, Texas has a population of 2,123 according to the 2010 census. The high-school cheerleaders in this small town in the eastern part of the state have had the custom of writing encouraging Bible verses on the banners the players run through. But the Freedom From Religion Foundation (based in Wisconsin) complained and threatened to sue, so last fall the superintendent stopped the practice. But with the help

---

1. At the time this column was written, what is now First Liberty was called Liberty Institute.

of First Liberty, the cheerleaders won a victory in court to resume the practice. The legal group noted, "[First Liberty] is proud of these young women for taking a bold stand."

Stepping back, let me ask a question in this case: Where's the church? Where's the state? Why is it that any sort of Christian expression in the public arena is not allowed, but virtually every other expression is allowed?

There is no question that we can find lots of evidence that the founders wanted the separation of the institution of the church from the institution of the state. They did not want to have a national state-church, as was most often the case in Europe. They saw the persecution often meted out to dissenters in such a scenario. Here in America, the various denominations were forced to work with each other to prevent that from happening. They stated in the first right listed in the Bill of Rights that there would be no establishment of religion by the federal government and no denying the free exercise of religion. Thus, they ensured a separation of the institution of the church from that of the state, at the federal level. But there is zero, zip, nada evidence for the idea that they wanted us to have the separation of God and state—which is what we have in effect today.

The very men who gave us the Bill of Rights asked President Washington to declare a national day of thanksgiving—to God—for the right to peaceably create our government. Washington complied, and he made his proclamation on October 3, 1789. He even made an oblique reference to Jesus ("the ruler of the nations," based on Psalm 2 and Revelation 12) in that proclamation. It was understood for the first one hundred fifty years of American history under the Constitution that the establishment clause did not mean to separate God and state—which is what, in effect, we have now.

Changes of interpretation began in 1947, when the Supreme Court used an obscure letter from Thomas Jefferson to the Baptists of Danbury, Connecticut, as the final arbiter of what the establishment clause meant. On January 1, 1802, Jefferson wrote to the Baptists, "Believing with you that religion is a matter which lies solely between man and his God, that he owes account to none other for faith or his worship, that the legislative powers of government reach actions only, and not opinions, I contemplate with solemn reverence that act of the whole American people which declared that their legislature should 'make no law respecting an establishment of religion, or prohibiting the free exercise thereof,' thus building a wall of separation between Church and State."

First of all, why should Jefferson be the final arbiter of what the establishment clause means?

Jefferson was in France when the Constitution was written. He was back in the U.S. when the Bill of Rights was written, but he didn't directly participate in the process. Why wouldn't Madison or Washington or Fisher Ames (who wrote the final wording of the First Amendment) be better sources to turn to? Secondly, such a wall was intended to protect everyone—including believers.

Interestingly, even if we considered the Supreme Court correct in making Jefferson the final arbiter of the understanding of the First Amendment, then Jefferson himself would have to be understood as violating the separation of church and state *in the very letter that gave us the phrase*. How so? He ends the letter by asking them to pray for him, as he will commit to pray for them: "I reciprocate your kind prayers for the protection and blessing of the common Father and Creator of man, and tender you for yourselves and your religious association, assurances of my high respect and esteem."

That's ridiculous. It's about as ridiculous as saying the Constitution is unconstitutional because it mentions God in the signature, where it says that it was "done in the year of our Lord" 1787. It's about as ridiculous as saying cheerleaders in a small Texas town can't have Bible verses on their run-through banners.

Author's Note: Victory at the Texas Supreme Court, February 2, 2016, by 8–0, the SCOTUS ruled in favor of freedom *of* religion, not freedom *from* religion.

102

IS THE BIBLE LIKE "ASBESTOS" IN THE PUBLIC SCHOOL?

Originally published on February 3, 2016

It is amazing that people today want to treat anything from the Bible as if it were asbestos, to borrow a line from Christian attorney Jordan Lorence, if it somehow shows up in a public school. Historically, the push to teach the Bible gave birth to education for the masses in the first place. This was the forerunner to the public school. How ironic.

A seemingly minor conflict in a small Texas public high school is symptomatic of a major conflict in society at large. Specifically, can cheerleaders in a public school adorn banners with Bible verses? The Freedom From Religion Foundation based in Wisconsin says no and filed a complaint to censor such banners. But First Liberty[1], based in Texas, says yes.

The case began in Kountze, Texas—population, 2,123. On Friday, January 29, the Texas Supreme Court ruled in favor of the cheerleaders, 8–0.

I spoke recently with Hiram Sasser, the lead attorney for First Liberty in the case, on my radio show.[2] He told me that Justice Guzman's opinion provides support for the private beliefs and speech of the cheerleaders. Sasser said that the cheerleaders at Kountze are "a private student club." They buy their own uniforms and materials. With their money, they pay for the banners and the paint to adorn the banners with up-

---

1. At the time this column was written, what is now First Liberty was called Liberty Institute.

2. "Vocal Point—Hiram Sassar," *Jerry Newcombe*, February 1, 2016, jerrynewcombe.com.

lifting messages from the Bible. For example, they have a banner with Paul's exhortation from Philippians 4:13, "I can do all things through Christ which strengthens me." They prefer to have uplifting messages, rather than the typical "Kill the Tigers" type cheerleading banners.

To Sasser, the essence of the case is that the cheerleaders were losing their free exercise of religion rights guaranteed in the Constitution. But doesn't this violate the establishment clause? Sasser told my listeners, "The establishment clause regulates government speech—when the government is speaking. That is when the establishment clause applies. . . . But when it comes to private speech, the establishment clause doesn't even apply. . . . Private speech has an affirmative protection under the free exercise clause." He added, "Then the only question is whether the government is allowed to censor speech because it's religious. Thankfully, the U.S. Supreme Court has answered that question four different times over the past twenty-five years. . . . It is unlawful censorship and no, the government may not censor speech simply because it's religious."

But administrators and teachers in the public school system often discriminate against religion, and especially Christianity, today. Some of them, perhaps, think they're upholding settled law. Sasser pointed out that settled law, as seen in Supreme Court decisions, consistently upholds the free exercise of religious rights of students. When little Johnny says his grace at his meal, he does not "establish" religion, even in the public school cafeteria. Rather, it is unlawful to prohibit him from doing that.

The Freedom From Religion Foundation began this case. Now the ACLU is continuing it. They will likely appeal, as they represent the school district, which has dug in its heels and is trying to disallow the banners. That is to say, the ACLU and the school district are engaging in what the Supreme Court called censorship.

But who cares about cheerleaders' banners in a small town in Texas? The world is on fire. We have a huge election campaign underway. Well, this case is important because it gets to the heart of what we are as a society. The founders of America envisioned a self-governing people, for which morality was a precondition. That morality would come through the Bible and through private, voluntary involvement in churches.

The founders recognized freedom *of* religion. What groups like the Freedom From Religion Foundation want to mandate is, as their name explicitly suggests, freedom *from* religion.

As we consider whom to vote for in the primaries, especially for president and for senators, we must consider the issue of judges. The whole anti-Christian campaign of the last fifty years in America came on us in large part through judges. The president appoints our federal judges. The Senate confirms or rejects them. As you go to the poll, consider the question, What types of judges would the candidate choose? That is a huge issue.

The Supreme Court once ruled, "It can hardly be argued that either students or teachers shed their constitutional rights to freedom of speech or expression at the schoolhouse gate" (*Tinker v. Des Moines,* 1969). That remains true despite the persistent efforts of anti-Christian groups to treat the Bible like asbestos in the public school.

103

THE IRONY OF BANNING GOD
FROM THE PUBLIC SQUARE

Originally published on February 10, 2016

Last week I wrote a column noting that authorities are unconstitutionally attempting to ban the Bible in the public schools far too often—and even treating it like asbestos, to borrow a line from Christian attorney Jordan Lorence. A reader responded to that article negatively, raising the common objection, that the founders supposedly intended a secular government, one that was free from Biblical influence. The reader wrote, "Once you see that ideas and our capacity for reason are the most important tools we possess, maybe you will understand that the Bible is like 'asbestos' in the public school."

Such claims, that the founders intended to banish God from the public square, come frequently enough that they deserve some further analysis. The claims are ironic, since the founders said our rights come from the Creator.

First, the reader's assertion here implies that Christianity and reason must conflict. The founders didn't see it that way. They had an affinity for the writings of John Locke, and one of his books was *The Reasonableness of Christianity.*

Samuel Adams reflected the common notion that "the laws of nature and of nature's God" were in harmony when he said, "'Thou shall do no injury to thy neighbor,' is the voice of nature and reason, and it is confirmed by written revelation."

In 1793, President Washington wrote to a church in Baltimore, "We have abundant reason to rejoice that in this Land the light of truth and reason has triumphed over the power of bigotry and superstition, and that every person may here worship God according to the dictates of his own heart." There was no perceived conflict between faith and rational thought.

Our fourth president, James Madison, a key architect of the Constitution, said, "Religion, or the duty we owe to our Creator, and manner of discharging it, can be directed only by reason and conviction, not by force or violence." Again, faith and reason worked in tandem.

But what about the schools and the idea that religion—really, Christianity—were unwelcome to our nation's settlers and founders? Education for the masses began in earnest in America with the Puritans in Boston in the 1640s when they passed "The Old Deluder Satan Act." They said it was one of the chief goals of "that old deluder Satan" to keep people in darkness by keeping them from the Word of God. Therefore, they established schools so the children would be able to read for themselves. The Bible gave birth to the forerunners of the public schools.

In one way or another, the Bible was the chief textbook in colonial America. *The New England Primer* taught many of the founders their ABCs using Biblical doctrines:

A—In Adam's Fall, we sinned all.
B—Thy life to mend, this book [the Bible] attend.
C—Christ crucified, for sinner's died.

John Hancock, John Adams, Samuel Adams, Ben Franklin, Roger Sherman—they were all weaned on this stuff.

The founders passed the Northwest Ordinance in 1787 (under the Articles of Confederation) and then reaffirmed it in 1789 (under the Constitution). The whole point of this legislation was that as new territories were converted into states, they sought conformity to a few basic principles. Article III of the Northwest Ordinance mentions schooling. What did the founders think about education or its content? Were the schools to be "religion-free zones"? In their own words, the same men who gave us the First Amendment, which today is often being distorted to exclude any Christian expression in the public arena, wrote: "Religion, morality, and knowledge, being necessary for good government and the happiness of mankind, schools and the means of education shall forever be encouraged." In a day when 99.8 percent of people were professing Christians—granted, not all professors are possessors—*religion* meant Christianity. Why should children go to school, according to our nation's founders? To learn about God and about morality—and gain knowledge too.

Today, we have an exactly opposite situation. Religion, specifically Christianity, is treated in too many public schools as if it were illegal. Stories about this are commonplace.

Yet our second president, John Adams, in his Inaugural Address, spoke positively of "a veneration for the religion of a people who profess and call themselves Christians." He said, "A decent respect for Christianity [is] among the best recommendations for the public service."

Remove the Christian base from our freedoms—something our founders never advocated—and ultimately we will lose the freedoms themselves. As radio host Janet Parshall once told me in a TV interview, "If we extrapolate out of the human experience Christianity, what's left? Well, I think that the answer to that question has to be the basic sin nature of man."

104

SUPREME COURT CAKE DECISION
ALIGNS WITH MOST AMERICANS

Originally published on June 13, 2018

To hear some liberals discuss the Colorado baker case last week, you would have thought it was "Cake-ageddon." The effect of the Supreme Court's ruling is that Jack Phillips will not be forced, against his conscience, to bake a cake for a same-sex wedding. *Fox News* contributor Pat Caddell noted that many reacted to the decision with hysteria until they learned that it was a 7 to 2 ruling.

What I find fascinating about the Court's ruling is that it aligned very well with the findings of a poll Pat Caddell, formerly a pollster with the Carter Administration, conducted of the American people in August 2015 after the Supreme Court's decision in favor of same-sex marriage. The gist of the survey dealt with the attitudes of the American people on religious liberty and gay rights on cases like the Colorado baker. Should the baker, the photographer, or the florist be forced by law to participate in that which violates his or her conscience? The results of the findings were that most Americans want to see both religious liberty and the rights of gay people.

In cases not involving sexuality, this issue would be obvious. As one colleague noted, "Should a black printer be forced against his will to print up fliers for the KKK? Should an Orthodox Jewish deli owner be forced to serve ham sandwiches?" Yet the absolutists favoring same-sex rights allowed for no freedom of conscience in this area.

The *Washington Examiner* wrote up the findings of Caddell's 2015 poll (August 5, 2015) in an article by Paul Bedard.[1] Caddell asked this question, which has direct implications in the Christian baker case: "Suppose a Christian wedding photographer has deeply held religious beliefs opposing same-sex marriage. If a same-sex couple wanted to hire the photographer for their wedding, should the photographer have the right to say no?"

Based on the media and the cultural push for absolute hegemony of gay rights in this area, one might assume the answer would be "no" only for a relatively few benighted souls, clinging to their old-time religion. The answer, though, was actually *82 percent*. Four out of five Americans would not like to see the photographer forced against her will to have to violate her conscience on the altar of political correctness.

Furthermore, Caddell wrote of his survey findings, "More than two thirds (68 percent) disagreed that the federal and state government should be able to require by law a private citizen to provide a service or their property for an event that is contrary to their religious beliefs. Only 18 percent agreed. Indeed, 51 percent strongly disagreed with this."

Some have argued that the Christian baker and candlestick maker were only hiding their innate anti-gay bigotry behind a religious facade. But a majority of the American people don't see it that way. Caddell reports: "When asked whether it should be up to the federal government to determine what constitutes legitimate religious beliefs, only 11 percent agreed and a massive 79 percent disagreed. Indeed, even two-thirds of those on the 'left' of the segmentation disagreed."

This was indeed where the Supreme Court came down hardest on the Colorado Civil Rights Commission, for attacking Jack Phillips's religious beliefs as illegitimate.

Sometimes gay rights and religious liberty are viewed as a zero-sum game. One wins; the other loses. There is no middle ground. But what Caddell found is that a majority of Americans favor a middle ground.

So, what if one had to choose between the two? "When asked which was more important, by a 4 to 1 ratio, voters said protecting religious liberty (31 percent) over protecting gay and lesbian rights (8 percent)," Caddell found. After last Monday's decision, I interviewed Caddell on

1. Paul Bedard, "Poll: Truce sought between LGBT, religion, but gays lose in 'cultural war' 4–1," *Washington Examiner*, August 5, 2015, washingtonexaminer.com.

my radio show.[2] He told me, "The majority wanted both [religious liberty and gay rights], but if you forced a decision on this to an absolute choice, those who chose were overwhelmingly on the side of religious freedom."

Again, while uncomfortable being forced to choose between the two polarities, Cadell notes, the American people view religious freedom as "the most fundamental of rights. This country exists for that reason. We have never had religious wars in this country. Even more than the freedom of speech, the right of religious freedom is bedrock in the American character and American history."

Dr. Frank Wright, president of D. James Kennedy Ministries, wrote after last Monday's decision, "Thus, the fight for religious liberty continues. Today's decision is a victory, to be sure—but a very limited one. The fact that we must wait for future Supreme Court decisions to declare that the First Amendment is still in effect shows that our judicial system is out of control."

---

2. "Vocal Point—Pat Caddell," *Jerry Newcombe*, June 6, 2018, jerrynewcombe.com.

105

NO GOD, NO AMERICAN FREEDOM

Originally published on March 3, 2015

On Friday morning, February 27, 2015, I saw Chris Cuomo pontificating on TV with fellow CNN host, Michael Smerconish. Speaking about CPAC, at one point Cuomo seemed to suggest that a majority of those attending the Conservative-PAC meeting in Washington, D.C., favored establishing Christianity as the national religion.

Cuomo then said that here we are, in modern America, dealing with religious extremism abroad—he's presumably referring to ISIS, the Islamic State—yet we have our own extremists here in America too. He seemed to mean those whacko Christians who want to impose a theocracy on the rest of us. Cuomo also said that the founders left God's name out of the Constitution by design. Ergo, our framers established a secular nation by design.

This is similar to his claims a few weeks ago that our rights in America are not derived from God. The founders were clear that there shall be no established religion at the federal level in this country, and I'm positive the majority of CPAC members agree with that point. But God *is* the source of our rights in this country. We have a national birth certificate—the Declaration of Independence—which states that our rights come from the Creator. It is the duty of governments to respect those God-given rights. Because the King of England messed with those rights—and Jefferson provided a laundry list of such oppression—then, Jefferson reasoned, the king had essentially "unkinged" himself. Jefferson's motto was "Resistance to tyrants is obedience to God."

In his book *A History of the American People* (1997), Paul Johnson notes, "America had been founded primarily for religious purposes, and the Great Awakening had been the original dynamic of the continental movement for independence. The Americans were overwhelmingly church-going, much more so than the English, whose rule they rejected. There is no question that the Declaration of Independence was, to those who signed it, a religious as well as a secular act" (Johnson, *A History of the American People*, 1999, 204–205).

When the founders met in what we now call the Constitutional Convention eleven years later, they dated that document "in the year of our Lord" 1787 and in the twelfth year of Independence. The Constitution is predicated on the Declaration—which mentions God four times.

As we have seen, in 1955, President Eisenhower said this: "Without God, there could be no American form of Government, nor an American way of life. Recognition of the Supreme Being is the first—the most basic—expression of Americanism. Thus the founding fathers of America saw it, and thus with God's help, it will continue to be."

Did the founders suddenly cast off their religiosity at the Constitutional Convention? Alexander Hamilton was there, and he noted of the document they produced, "For my own part, I sincerely esteem it a system which without the finger of God, never could have been suggested and agreed upon by such a diversity of interests."

In one sense, Cuomo and all of us who love freedom can thank one person above all others for the freedom to speak our minds (even if what we speak is wrong). That would be: Jesus, whom Jefferson refers to as "the holy author of our religion."

Thomas Jefferson wrote the document often viewed as a key forerunner to the First Amendment, with its guarantees of no established church at the national level and of freedom of religion. Jefferson's document (written 1777, passed 1786) is the Virginia Statute for Religious Freedom. Note the theological basis for such freedom. As noted before, he writes: "Almighty God hath created the mind free.... All attempts to influence it by temporal punishments... are a departure from the plan of the holy author of our religion, who being lord both of body and mind, yet chose not to propagate it by coercions on either, as was in his Almighty power to do, but to exalt it by its influence on reason alone."

In other words, Jesus, "the holy author of our religion," could have forced His way on people to believe, but instead, He offers a choice. Who are we to offer less?

I do not believe America should be an authoritarian theocracy. But it is disingenuous of modern secularists like Chris Cuomo to say that those of us trying to preserve what's left of our Christian heritage actually want to create such a theocracy.

Nonetheless, without God, there would be no America and no American freedom.

106

THE NON-JESUS RELIGION

Originally published on November 6, 2013

The Supreme Court has heard arguments this week about whether prayers at government meetings—for example, a town council—can include the name of Jesus. The case is *Galloway v. City of Greece* (which is a suburb of Rochester, New York), and it will likely be decided in the summer, or possibly spring, of 2014. The case could potentially have strong ramifications for this nation, especially in light of our extensive Christian heritage.

Jesus told His followers to pray in His name. That's why people pray "in Jesus's name. Amen" Or, as is often heard in the *Book of Common Prayer* from the Anglican Church, which was very influential in the founding of America, "through the merits of Jesus Christ our Lord. Amen." George Washington was an avid reader of the *Book of Common Prayer*.

Different judicial circuits have ruled in ways that contradict each other on this issue—hence, the Supreme Court's hearing to clarify the matter.

One could ask why prayers occur (much less prayers in the name of Jesus) at government settings in the first place. We would do well to remember that, historically, legislative sessions or town councils often began in prayer and mostly in Jesus's name.

When the ACLU challenged the notion of chaplains—paid by the state to offer prayers, Christian or otherwise—the case went all the way to the Supreme Court in the 1980s. The prayers won. The ACLU lost.

In *Marsh v. Chambers,* the Court affirmed that we had chaplains before we were a nation.

Our tradition of praying in Jesus's name in public shouldn't surprise us, since at the time of our Independence, 99.8 percent of colonists were professing Christians.[1]

The same Congress that gave us the First Amendment, now used to suppress prayers and other religious expressions, was made up of men who hired chaplains for the Senate and the House of Representatives. The U.S. Capitol Building hosted Christian worship services on Sundays from its beginning until the 1880s. Presidents Jefferson and Madison often attended these.

The first time the Continental Congress met, they discussed whether they should open the next day's proceedings in prayer (September 7, 1774). Virtually all were Christian, but different Christian groups can pray in different ways. Samuel Adams said he was no "bigot." He could hear a prayer from a man who loved his God and his country. So they opened with a lengthy Bible reading (Psalm 35) and fervent prayer in Jesus's name from a local Episcopal minister, Jacob Duché.

We note again that George Washington told the Delaware Indian chiefs when they brought their sons to learn the Englishmen's ways, "You do well to wish to learn our arts and ways of life, and above all, the religion of Jesus Christ." (May 12, 1779). Washington went on to say, "Congress will do everything they can to assist you in this wise intention." (Rhodehamel, ed., *George Washington: Writings*, 1997, 351.)

Thomas Jefferson, in whose name comes so much of the cleansing of anything religious—no, anything Christian—from the public square, would be shocked at this. For all his heterodox views later in life, he regularly (perhaps daily) read the teachings of Jesus Christ for his own edification. Jefferson said, "Of all the systems of morality, ancient or modern, which have come under my observation, none appear to me so pure as that of Jesus" (to William Canby, September 18, 1813).

My friend constitutional attorney David Gibbs III of the National Center for Life and Liberty is fighting in this current case for the government not to concede to the ACLU to censor prayers. David told me, "What the ACLU is arguing is that praying in Jesus's name is establish-

---

1. Benjamin Hart, "The Wall That Protestantism Built," *Policy Review* Number 46, Fall 1988, 44.

ing a religion. The reality is that their goal is to establish a non-Jesus religion." David noted the ACLU is advancing cases only against prayer in Jesus's name, not in any other tradition. David adds, "Do we really want judges deciding what words are okay and what words are not okay in religious prayers? The ACLU is bullying government officials by threat of expensive lawsuits to eliminate traditions that have been happening since our government's founding."

I remember when a liberal lady called a conservative talk show during the HHS Mandate controversy. She advocated that Christians be forced to fund abortions, even though it violates their consciences. She said, "If you don't like it, then go off and start your own country." Wow, lady, I think we did. It's called the United States of America. And because we began with that Christian base, people of all faiths or no faith are welcome here.

But why should those who continue the tradition to pray in Jesus's name, yes, even in official government meetings, have their prayers censored?[2]

---

2. Author's Note: In 2014, the U.S. Supreme Court ruled (5–4) that the prayers in Jesus's name were allowed after all. In their ruling, they even cited *America's God and Country* by Bill Federer (also author of this book's Foreword).

107

TRYING TO BANISH GOD FROM CHARITY, A JUDEO-CHRISTIAN INVENTION

Originally published on July 16, 2013

There is a strong link between faith, the Christian faith in particular (in all of its various stripes), and doing good—including feeding the hungry, clothing the naked, and providing shelter. It has been true in the past, and it is true in the present. This is a mandate that comes from Jesus Himself, and the impact of Christian charity on civilization has been enormous and positive. What the church does, it will continue to do and should do without any assistance from the government. In some cases, it does this despite resistance from the government.

Before Jesus, charity was virtually non-existent. The late Dr. D. James Kennedy once said, "The world before Christianity was like the Russian tundra—quite cold and inhospitable." The great historian Will Durant said this about charity in ancient Rome, the greatest of the civilizations of antiquity: "Charity found little scope in this frugal life. Hospitality survived as a mutual convenience at a time when inns were poor and far between; but the sympathetic Polybius reports that 'in Rome no one ever gives away anything to anyone if he can help it'—doubtless an exaggeration."

Of course, the ancient Hebrews had the law from God to love our neighbor as ourselves (Leviticus 19:18). Jesus expanded on this point (John 13:34), and His disciples spread these transforming ideas around the world (2 John 1:6).

People today consider the label "Samaritan" as a good-doer. In Je-

324

sus's day, a Samaritan was an outcast and looked down upon. When Christ told the parable of the Good Samaritan, He chose an alleged antagonist as the protagonist and imbued new meaning into the word "Samaritan."

But some in our society want to cut off charity from its ultimate source. U.S. Senator Mary Landrieu of Louisiana (D) introduced a new piece of legislation last week to rectify what she sees as a wrong. She calls this the "Freedom to Pray Act." She sees a corrective needed to make sure God isn't banished from charity. The other side sees this as a way the government would supposedly mandate religion. (AP, July 12, 2013).

Regardless of the specifics of this particular legislation, it raises some important issues. Are charities that receive any government assistance allowed to pray? Are they allowed to pray in the name of Jesus? Are they allowed to encourage (or force) church attendance?

I remember years ago at a business where I worked, a notice posted on the bulletin board sought volunteers for a suicide hotline. But the ad said that if you're religious, you need not apply. As I recall, the very name of the outreach had the word Samaritan in it. Wow. They would not only cut off many potential faithful volunteers, they would also cut off those seeking to kill themselves from a message of hope that could change their lives. How tragic.

In the First Amendment, the founders of America proscribed a national denomination. No one specific religious group could lord it over the others and bind our consciences. But that's a far cry from saying the founders intended that government banish God and Christian prayers from the public square and that a state-assisted charity must be secular.

In his Farewell Address, as we have seen, George Washington declared, "Of all the dispositions and habits which lead to political prosperity, religion and morality are indispensable supports. In vain would that man claim the tribute of patriotism, who should labor to subvert these great pillars of human happiness." Yet we have many today busily subverting these pillars. Washington added, "And let us with caution indulge the supposition that morality can be maintained without religion." This would include the morality of charitable giving and living.

For almost twenty years I've been an active volunteer with a Christian food-distribution ministry. A few years ago, I remember when our leader decided we would no longer receive any kind of government assistance because it came with strings attached. There was a threat along these lines: we couldn't pray, but if we did, we certainly couldn't pray in the name of Jesus. It wasn't worth receiving anything from the government when the very heart and soul of what we were doing would be cut out of it. Thankfully, the Lord continues to provide the means for us to help from voluntary sources.

I suppose such conflicts will continue to arise, especially as some continue to promote a vision of America where they completely banish God and the Christian faith from the public square, even in our charities. Yet charity is God's idea and an assignment for the church.

108

AWAY WITH THE MANGER?

Originally published on December 20, 2016

Communities routinely displayed manger scenes in public places before the anti-Christian crusade that the Supreme Court unleashed starting in the 1960s and 1970s with its anti-God-in-public type of decisions. Subsequently, the Supreme Court ruled in *Lynch v. Donnelly* (1984) in a case out of Pawtucket, Rhode Island, that if enough reindeer and other secular symbols of the season surrounded a manger scene, the government could allow it on public property. The legal activist group the ACLU (American Civil Liberties Union) initiated many of these anti-God cases.

Apparently, the ACLU's favorite Christmas carol is "Away With the Manger." But they're not alone. The Freedom From Religion Foundation (FFRF) also sues to keep crèche scenes out of public venues, as they did recently in a small town in the motor state. On December 16, 2016, as Liberty Counsel reports, the city restored a Nativity scene in Menominee, Michigan, through Liberty's pro bono "defense to reinstate the City's long-standing Christmas tradition of displaying a Nativity scene in a city park." They note that the town took down the Nativity because of FFRF complaints, but Liberty Counsel intervened, encouraging the town to "add secular items to the display." And so the town plans to reinstate the manger scene.

The question is, Are manger scenes in public places constitutional? I spoke recently on my radio show "Vocal Point" with Thomas Brejcha, the founder and director of the Christian Legal Group the

Thomas More Society.[1] Brejcha told me manger scenes in public are "absolutely constitutional if they're done the right way. The key is that these are privately funded and privately sponsored Nativity scenes— that really amount to free speech on the part of private citizens in what we would call a 'traditional or designated public forum'." He added, "Our First Amendment is pretty clear about it. If you allow somebody to get up on their soapbox and proclaim their politics, well, you cannot discriminate against another citizen that gets up on his or her soapbox and preaches his or her religious faith. In both cases the content of the speech is free speech and as such is protected by our constitution."

Thus, if political rallies or other examples of free speech are allowed in a public setting, including rotundas in state capitols, then religious speech can't be legally discriminated against in those settings. According to Brejcha: "It's the denial of free speech that is wrong and not the folks who want to put up a Nativity scene. [A Nativity scene] is a kind of symbolic speech—very powerful speech—and it ought to be promoted."

What does the Nativity scene communicate? That God so loved the world, that He gave His only begotten Son, that whoever believes in Him should not perish, but have everlasting life.

The Thomas More Society is now working with a group also out of Chicago, the American Nativity Scene (ANS). Brejcha told our listeners about the ANS, "They're blessed to have a benefactor who anonymously provides Nativity sets to anyone who will agree to put them up and take care of them in any public space." The provision of a professional-looking, life-size manger scene is made free to those willing to commit to getting it up in a city square or even better yet, a place near or on the state capitol rotunda. The ANS's website explains the logistics, including the need for a local carpenter to make the stable for the set and for its off-season storage. The ANS website states that during the Christmas seasons of 2014 and 2015, they "shipped over 120 Nativity Scenes to 24 different states across this great country. . . . Many of these Nativity Scenes were placed in public parks, libraries, farm roads and government buildings."

---

1. "Vocal Point—Thomas Brejcha," *Jerry Newcombe*, December 16, 2016, jerrynewcombe.com.

Tom Brejcha said they are focusing on getting as many manger scenes as possible at state capitol buildings in future Christmases. So far, through Christmas 2016, ANS has been able to get such Nativity sets in eleven state capitols, with thirty-nine to go. He also said that if anybody hits any legal snag from the atheist-type groups, the Thomas More Society will defend them for free. Thankfully, other Christian legal groups, such as Liberty Counsel, also provide legal assistance on religious liberty matters.

As the ANS notes, a recent poll by *The Washington Times* found that 72 percent of Americans "agreed that religious scenes displayed on PUBLIC property by PRIVATE individuals should be allowed as our Constitution allows" (emphasis theirs).

Thus, while the atheist activists and their sympathizers may try to sing "Away WITH the Manger," Lord-willing, in future years we may just see more privately sponsored manger scenes popping up in various cities and towns (including state capitols) to remind us of the true reason for the season.

109

TEN REASONS STATE-SANCTIONED ATHEISM IS OUT OF STEP WITH OUR AMERICAN TRADITIONS

Originally published on June 1, 2016

The University of Miami has now announced a chair for the study of atheism. In another recent story, an atheist group is suing a sheriff because of his pro-God statements on his Facebook page (Constitution.com, May 19, 2016). No one can deny the rise of the shrill atheistic voices of our time.

But dare I say that the idea of state-*sanctioned* and in some cases state-*mandated* atheism is absolutely out of step with the traditions of America? Here are ten reasons why:

1. At the time of our founding, 99.8 percent of the population were professing Christians. Ben Franklin, himself a bit of a skeptic, said in 1794 when writing about America, "Atheism is unknown there, infidelity rare and secret; so that persons may live to a great age in that country without having their piety shocked by meeting with either an atheist or an infidel."

2. The founding fathers (not just the settlers, like the Pilgrims—whom even the ACLU will admit were Christians) hired chaplains to say prayers—virtually always in the name of Jesus—for the military and the legislature. The tradition of prayers at the opening of the legislature goes back to 1619 when the Jamestown colony had the first congress of any kind in America.

3. The symbol of America's founding is the Liberty Bell. And as everyone should know, it has a Bible verse on it—"Proclaim liberty throughout all the land and unto all the inhabitants thereof" (Leviticus 25:10 KJV).

4. The foundational education of the founders was Christian— even those who later may have lost their faith or some aspects of it. As Dr. Donald S. Lutz, author of *The Origins of American Constitutionalism* (1988), once told me, they all knew the Bible "down to their fingertips." To those who are Biblically literate, the influence can easily be seen.

5. Originally, all the colleges in North America were thoroughly Christian. Those who attended Harvard, for example, learned at an institution with the motto (in Latin) "Truth for Christ and His Church." Only centuries later did the Harvard trustees sever truth from Christ and His church. Madison learned his wise politics from the then-thoroughly Presbyterian College of New Jersey. We know it today as Princeton.

6. Since 1956, our national motto has been "In God We Trust." But sometimes you wouldn't know that. It was suggested by Francis Scott Key, who wrote our National Anthem. The first verse, beginning with "Oh say, can you see..." is well-known. But, as we have seen, here is the fourth verse, which I wish we would sing more often:

> Blest with vict'ry and peace, may the Heavn'n-rescued land
> Praise the Pow'r that hath made and preserved us a nation!
> Then conquer we must, when our cause it is just,
> And this be our motto, "In God is our trust!"

7. Every state constitution mentioned God. Most of them still do. For example, here is the opening to the constitution for my home state: "We, the People of the State of Illinois— grateful to Almighty God for the civil, political and religious liberty which He has permitted us to enjoy and seeking His blessing upon our endeavors..."

8. Since the days of Abraham Lincoln, drawing on the tradition of the Pilgrims, we have an annual holiday based on the

concept of giving thanks to God. Washington was the first president to declare a day of Thanksgiving on the suggestion of Congress—the same Congress that wrote the First Amendment, the words of which are sometimes twisted today to mean state-sanctioned atheism. Washington said in that October 3, 1789, proclamation, "It is the duty of all nations to acknowledge the providence of Almighty God, to obey His will..."

9. God is carved in stone all over our nation's capital. For instance, there are three Bible verses in Lincoln's Second Inaugural Address chiseled at the Lincoln Memorial. If the atheists continue their jihad against God, would we have to sandblast the name of God off the monuments?

10. The single biggest reason that state-sanctioned atheism is out of keeping with our American tradition comes from our national birth certificate. The Declaration of Independence says that our rights come from the Creator. Therefore, they are not up for grabs. In contrast, what the state gives, the state can remove.

How have we come to the place in society where those who hold Biblical views are marked out to be fired or discriminated against if their views leak out in the public square? What is happening today is literally an exaltation of atheism over belief.

In America, atheists are free to share their unbelief. Great. I just wish they would extend that freedom to the very traditions that extended that freedom to them in the first place—the Judeo-Christian heritage.

110

WHICH VIEW OF HEAVEN WILL PREVAIL? THE DIFFERENCE CAN MEAN HELL ON EARTH

Originally published on March 29, 2017

Last week, British-born jihadist Khalid Masood ran over innocent people in London on the bridge close to Big Ben and then stabbed a police officer to death before being killed by police. Where is Khalid Masood's soul right now? Presumably, he thought he was taking a shortcut to Paradise.

After 9/11, I once asked Christian leader Dr. D. James Kennedy this question: "Islamic militants believe that suicide missions give them a one-way ticket to heaven—to Paradise. What will actually happen to them?" He told me, "These suicide bombers are taught that they will be taken immediately into Paradise, where…lovely virgins will await them. The fact is that they will discover that the same kind of inferno they have created in these buildings will be awaiting them in hell."

For this column, I reached out for a statement from Robert Spencer of jihadwatch.org. He wrote me the following:

- The Qur'an promises virgins in Paradise: "And fair women with large eyes, the likenesses of pearls well-protected, as reward for what they used to do." (Qur'an 56:22–24)
- What does one have to do to get them? The Qur'an offers one guarantee of Paradise: to those who "kill and are killed" for Allah (9:111).
- The number seventy-two for the virgins of Paradise comes

from the Hadith: "None is made to enter Paradise by Allah Most High except Allah Most High shall marry him to seventy-two wives, two of them from the wide-eyed maidens of Paradise and seventy of them his inheritance from the People of Hellfire, not one of them but her attraction never lags nor his arousal ever wanes." (Ibn Majah; Ibn Adi's *Kamil*; al-Bayhaqi's *al-Ba'th wal-Nushur*)

- It's a nonstop orgy: "The Prophet said: 'The believer will be given tremendous strength in Paradise for sexual intercourse.' It was questioned: 'O prophet of Allah! can he do that?' He said: 'He will be given the strength of one hundred persons.'" (Tirmidhi 2536)

The Pulitzer Prize-winning book *The Looming Tower: Al-Qaeda and the Road to 9/11* by Lawrence Wright (2006) observed, "Martyrdom promised such young men an ideal alternative to a life that was so sparing in its rewards. A glorious death beckoned to the sinner, who would be forgiven, it is said, with the first spurt of blood, and he would behold his place in Paradise even before his death.... The martyr who is poor will be crowned in heaven with a jewel more valuable than the earth itself. And for those young men who came from cultures where women are shuttered away and rendered unattainable for someone without prospects, martyrdom offers the conjugal pleasures of seventy-two virgins" (Wright, *The Looming Tower*, 2006, 123).

Wright quotes Osama bin Laden, who said, "This is jihad!... This is the way we want to go to heaven!"

Several years ago I spoke with another Masood. This one is not a murderer. Steven Masood grew up as a sincere Muslim in Pakistan. He even had the entire Qur'an memorized by the age of ten. He inferred from something he read in the Qur'an that if he were a really good Muslim, he would know the Bible. So he got a copy and started reading it and ended up becoming a believer in Jesus. He said, "In the Gospels, I found Jesus said, 'I am the way.' So, here is a Muslim who was trying for many years, asking God, 'Show me the way.' So, I had to give in. I said, 'Lord, thank You for showing me the way.' And I accepted Him." This caused a rift with his parents, and Steven had to escape Pakistan to stay alive.

I once asked Steven Masood about jihadists who think they're going to heaven. He said: "They believe that, 'Well, if we are killed, we will go straight into Paradise. It's much easier for us to go into Paradise that way than by performing all the ritual performance and everything and still not knowing that we are going to Paradise of [Allah] or not.'"

Steven Masood founded jesustomuslims.org. He said, "The Great Commission of our Lord includes the Muslims too, that they should know about Christ, not only that He is just a prophet of God, but He is more than a prophet. He's the Word of God, the Spirit of God. And God sent Him as a Savior into this world and that assurance is available to a Muslim too."

I wish more Muslims would listen to the likes of Steven Masood and eschew the terrible misdeeds of someone like Khalid Masood. Khalid died apart from the grace of Jesus Christ. Therefore, do not the words of Dante apply to him? "Abandon all hope, ye who enter here."

111

PRAY FOR THE PERSECUTED CHURCH—
ABROAD AND AT HOME

Originally published on November 8, 2017

Sunday, November 12, 2017, has been designated as the International Day of Prayer for the Persecuted Church. I planned to write about this topic and focus on anti-Christian persecution overseas at this time. And then came the tragedy—the mass shooting on Sunday at a church in Texas that killed twenty-six and wounded twenty. Media described the murderer as one who "preached atheism" and "hated religious people."

Of course, killing Christians just because they are Christians is the exception in America. However, in about sixty countries on earth, for millions of professing Christians it is dangerous to be a practicing believer in Jesus. Yet God is using Christian martyrdom to grow the church.

"We are witnessing an astonishing escalation in Christian persecution like we have rarely seen since the first century," writes Johnnie Moore in his new book *The Martyr's Oath: Living for the Jesus They're Willing to Die For* (2017). Johnnie wrote a book a few years ago that was a bestseller, called *Defying ISIS*. After writing that first book, he was able to raise $25 million on behalf of the persecuted church.

In a radio interview with him about his new book,[1] Moore told me he got involved in this because, as a college student at Liberty University, he witnessed an unusual (to him) graduation ceremony in India. Moore said, "There were two thousand graduates to this Bible school...and

---

1. "Vocal Point—Johnnie Moore," *Jerry Newcombe*, October 16, 2017, jerrynewcombe.com.

yet, before they got their diploma and a bicycle and a one-way train ticket to an unreached place of their choice, they had an extra step. They had to actually stand up and take a 'Martyr's Oath.' They had to pledge that if they had to die for their faith, they would be willing to die for their faith."

"I AM A FOLLOWER OF JESUS. I believe he lived and walked among us, was crucified for our sins, and was raised from the dead, according to the Scriptures," begins the "Martyr's Oath," which Moore includes in the appendix of his book. This is the type of pledge that the Indian bishop administered. The oath continues, "I believe he is the King of the earth, who will come back for his church. . . . As he has given his life for me, so I am willing to give my life for him. I will use every breath I possess to boldly proclaim his gospel."

Moore reflected on how this struck him at the time: "Here I was, a sheltered American, never having been exposed to such a thing. And all of a sudden, I was in the heart of the persecuted church. And I felt like I was standing in the book of Acts." He notes that persecution of Christians has often been the norm in history, not the exception.

Moore told of a Muslim couple that converted to Jesus and left Syria for a neighboring country. One of their relatives wrote, saying he knew what they had done (leaving Islam), and he knew where they lived. When he caught up with them, he would crucify them unless they recanted. Moore said the couple wrote back to the relative, answering that they were glad to know Jesus and were willing to die for Him—but that they were not worthy to die in the same manner as He did.

"There've always been crucifixions of Christians because it's the obvious thing to do if you hate them and you want to get rid of them." So said the late Dr. David Barrett, a leading church statistician and researcher, who was the founding editor of the massive *World Christian Encyclopedia* (2001), in a Christian TV interview I did years ago.

Barrett said, "Martyrdom is a continuing phenomenon, affecting roughly one in every two hundred Christians. Sometime or other in their lives, that number of people will be murdered for their faith or they will lose their lives. And it's been the same right from the beginning. People tend to think that martyrdom belongs to the early church—the first three centuries. But it went on after that, and it is going on [at] exactly the same rate today—0.5 percent per annum."

Barrett even told a humorous story, where he once addressed a large group of Southern Baptists. During an open-mic session, a very wealthy industrialist asked, "What is the single most significant way I can help promote world evangelization?" Barrett answered, "Well, the main factor, as I see it, is martyrdom." This elicited laughs from the audience, but the industrialist didn't laugh. After a few moments, he asked what the second most important way is.

It is good to pray for the persecuted church and do what we can to help them. Not just one day of the year, but throughout the year as well.

112

INSIDE THE COPTIC CHURCH BOMBINGS

Originally published on April 19, 2017

As we all know, on Palm Sunday, two bombings at Coptic Churches in Egypt killed nearly fifty persons and injured one hundred twenty others. I heard about two of my relatives-in-law who were near enough to hear and feel the blast at St. Mark's Cathedral in Alexandria.[1] Even though they had returned for a vacation to their native Alexandria and had even been married at St. Mark's, they are thankful that they providentially chose to worship at *another* church that particular morning.

An email to me from Coptic Solidarity includes this comment from one of their experts on what happened at St. Mark's: "The Alexandria suicide bomber detonated himself outside the church. The videos (I've seen) show him trying to enter through a side gate, but the (Coptic) guard man told him to pass thru the metal detector set up by the police a few meters away. As the detector buzzed, he stepped back one step and detonated himself. All 17 victims were on the street around him, including 4 police. Some Muslims walking by were also killed."

He added, "Timing wise, the service had ended and the Pope [Coptic Pope Tawadros II, the head of the Coptic Church] just left the altar to a resting room in the back of the building. The security set up was especially higher than usual because of the presence of the Pope. That wasn't the case in Tanta where the terrorist managed to enter a seat in front rows."

---

1. "Raw: Video Shows Moment of Egypt Bomb Blast," *Associated Press*, December 13, 2016, youtube.com.

In Tanta, fifty-six miles north of Cairo, the powerful explosion that ripped through the Palm Sunday service at about the same time at St. George's Coptic Cathedral killed over three-dozen worshipers. Photos show the bloody mess on the floor and remaining pews of the church. Here again is radical Islam at work.

What exactly are "Coptic Christians"? Lindsay Vessey of Coptic Solidarity once told my radio audience, "Coptic Christians are the indigenous Christians of Egypt. So when St. Mark the Apostle brought the Gospel to Egypt, the church that was started there became known as the Coptic Orthodox Church. This is one of the oldest elements of Christianity we have in the world today.... They are also the largest Christian minority in the Middle East. They make up about 10 percent of the Egyptian population."[2]

After the bombings, I spoke on my radio show with Bishop Julian Dobbs of the Convocation of Anglicans in North America. He has many Coptic friends and has visited many Christians in Egypt. He is a board member of the Barnabas Fund, a group dedicated to helping the worldwide, persecuted church. Dobbs told me, "The church has been very strong in Egypt, and we're thankful to the Lord for it. However, Christians are in the minority, and that places Christianity in Egypt under significant pressure. We saw it recently with the Palm Sunday attacks, but we also see it with regard to Christians in Egypt having decreased freedoms to choose and change their religion, to have Christianity recorded on their identity cards. All of these things are significant challenges to the body of Christ in that nation."[3]

He added, "We often see these attacks around the holidays.... As Christians gathered to declare 'Hosanna! Blessed is he who comes in the name of the Lord' on Palm Sunday, Islamic jihadists attacked churches in two Egyptian cities.... The death toll continues to rise. The injuries are horrific."

What has been the response in the West for the most part? A collective yawn. Even Piers Morgan, a liberal British host (formerly on CNN), expressed his concerns about this story and its scant coverage in the West: "You know, if you look at what ISIS really stands for, what

2. "Vocal Point—Lindsay Vessey," *Jerry Newcombe*, January 8, 2015, jerrynewcombe.com.

3. "Vocal Point—Bishop Julian Dobbs," *Jerry Newcombe*, April 17, 2017, jerrynewcombe.com.

they are carrying out in the Middle East, and in Egypt in particular, it's a kind of genocidal attack on Christians and Christianity. They want Christianity eradicated.... This is the kind of story that ought to be dominating cable news, in America. It should be dominating headlines around the world. The press in America should be full of headlines about this."[4]

Roman Catholic Pope Francis I, who is scheduled to visit Egypt, has not canceled his plans (to my knowledge, as of this writing).

Coptic Solidarity wants the Egyptian government, led by President El-Sisi, to do more to protect the Christians. A day after the bombings, they declared, "Under Mr. El-Sisi's rule, the Egyptian state has failed to protect its Coptic citizens. In response to Sunday's attacks, President El-Sisi has declared a three-month emergency period and few other largely symbolic measures."[5]

It's scary to think that just by attending church on a Sunday morning, you may be taking your life into your own hands. But such is the reality for many Christians in the Middle East in the shadow of radical Islam. Lord, have mercy.

---

4. Carlos Garcia, "Piers Morgan slams mainstream media for ignoring ISIS attack on Egyptian Christians," *The Blaze*, April 10, 2017, theblaze.com.

5. Lindsay Vessey, "Coptic Solidarity Condemns Palm Sunday Pogrom of Egypt's Copts, Demands International Inquiry," *Coptic Solidarity*, April 10, 2017, copticsolidarity.org.

113

LAND OF THE FREE?
NOT WITH SAME-SEX MARRIAGE

Originally published on April 29, 2015

The other day I sang the National Anthem with a group. When we got to the part about "the land of the free," I got as far as "the land of the—." But I froze with the word *free* on my lips.

I thought about what I had read earlier that very day. A bureaucrat in these United States ruled that a good Christian family of seven must face bankruptcy because they supposedly caused a lesbian couple $135,000 worth of pain and suffering. In fact, a complaint by one of the lesbians was that she "felt mentally raped, dirty, and shameful." And what was this terrible deed that was done? The bakers declined to make a wedding cake to celebrate the lesbian couple's "wedding"—because the bakers' religious convictions would not allow them to.

As Tony Perkins of Family Research Council says of the case, "If you thought it was expensive to buy a wedding cake, try *not* baking one!"

At the center of the controversy are Melissa and Aaron Klein, whom I have interviewed for Christian television on *Kennedy Classics*. They are the founders of the now virtually bankrupt "Sweet Cakes by Melissa." Ever since she was a child, Melissa Klein of Gresham, Oregon (near Portland), wanted to make beautiful, ornate, customized wedding cakes to help celebrate the big day in a couple's life. She poured her heart and soul into making those cakes extra special. Her husband Aaron said, "We did quite a few weddings. I'd probably say about 150–160 weddings a year. It was Oregon-based. We delivered...about a 700-mile range, and we had people that were willing to pay for that delivery because they wanted our cakes that badly."

But in the new politically correct America, their sweet success was soon to turn sour. In early 2013, when a lesbian customer—a repeat customer no less—wanted them to bake the cake for her same-sex "marriage," the Kleins respectfully declined. While there were plenty of bakers around town available to bake a wedding cake for the lesbian couple, they filed a complaint with Oregon's Bureau of Labor and Industries against the Kleins.

A campaign to drive customers and vendors away from Sweet Cakes by Melissa spread like a blazing fire, and the family had to close up shop. Now, maybe once or twice a month, Melissa makes a cake from home. But the business is basically gone.

What really stings Melissa is the reaction against them personally: "We've been accused of or called a hater, a bigot, every name that you can possibly think of in the book. At first, I won't lie—it really hurt. Then it really hit me hard because it was like, 'How am I a hater?' Just because I don't want to do something, do I not have rights to say what I want to do and what I don't want to do? I shouldn't have to be forced to do something that violates my religious beliefs especially."

Now the Kleins face the huge fine they have been ordered to pay to the lesbian couple—$135,000 for "emotional damages." This could bankrupt the couple and their five children.

Some well-wishers set up a GoFundMe page for the Kleins and $109,000 was reported to have poured in before GoFundMe pulled the account because the Kleins are supposedly in violation of the law.

At the time of this writing, their pro bono attorney is Anna Harmon of the Alliance Defending Freedom, a consortium of attorneys fighting for religious liberty. D. James Kennedy and others founded it in 1994. Harmon told me, "The state of Oregon has brought the full force of the law down on these people for simply deciding to stand by their religious beliefs. A person should be allowed under the Constitution to work in the marketplace and make a living without fear of having to go against what they believe in their heart of hearts to be true."

Aaron has been forced into finding other work, now driving a garbage truck to help make ends meet for their family, which includes five children. He notes, "The Constitution guarantees my religious freedom. It does not guarantee your right to force your beliefs down my throat, and that's realistically speaking what's going on here."

Tragically, the Kleins are part of a growing number of such victims—at least three hundred, according to columnist Dr. Michael Brown. This includes bakers, florists, photographers, and now even an Indiana pizza-shop owner. These shops do not discriminate against gay people per se. They draw the line at catering an event that violates their religious beliefs. Rob Schwarzwalder of Family Research Council[1] has come up with a number of excellent analogies that will cause us all to think.

Here they are, to quote Schwarzwalder:

- Should a Muslim butcher be compelled by law to serve pork products?
- Should a gay baker be required by law to decorate a cake with Bible verses against homosexuality?
- Should a Jewish deli be mandated by law to remain open on Friday evenings?
- Should a Catholic hospital be obligated by law to provide abortions?
- Should an African-American florist be told by law that she must provide flowers for a Klan-themed wedding?
- Should an Asian-American videographer be held legally responsible to film a movie full of anti-Asian racism?
- Should an Amish family be required by law to send its children to high school (current law allows them to stop their kids' education after eighth grade)?
- Should a Seventh Day Adventist school be forced by law to include meat in its students' lunches?
- Should a Jehovah's Witness be coerced by law to have a blood transfusion if he is ill?

The Supreme Court has now heard oral arguments on same-sex "marriage," which is at odds with religious freedom. Tragically, the militant agenda of those promoting it are changing things so that America is no longer the land of the free.

---

1. Now with Regent University.

114

HIDING FROM THE CROSS LIKE DRACULA

Originally published on January 21, 2015

I try to make it a practice to vet the circulating emails I receive before I forward them. I think one of the best sources to vet email rumors is truthorfiction.com. They seem to lack a political bias one way or another, and they are discerning in terms of religious rumors. They don't throw the baby out with the bathwater—particularly the baby in the manger.

The other day I received an email that I thought worth checking out. It claimed that in a chapel in a VA hospital, administrators had covered up Christian symbols because of a federal order to do so. In the *chapel*. So I checked this out with truthorfiction.com, and there it was labeled as "Truth!"

This online rumor clearinghouse notes of the VA hospital in Iron Mountain, Michigan, "The hospital was told that Christian symbols, statues and religious items inside the chapel were no longer permitted. This according to a June 3, 2014, article by *Christian Today*."

Truthorfiction.com went on to observe, "In order to comply with the regulation statues, crucifix and an altar 'were encircled with a curtain at the Iron Mountain chapel after an inspection by the National Chaplain Center discovered the unauthorized items.'"

The policy went into effect in 2008, and under the Obama Administration since 2009 things have only gotten worse. I remember when Obama spoke at Georgetown one time, and he demanded that they cover over "IHS" in the background in that Catholic building. I'll bet

90 percent of *Christians* don't even know what IHS stands for. I had to take New Testament Greek to find out myself. "IHS" are three letters in the Greek language: Iota, Eta, and Sigma, and they are the first three letters of the name of Jesus in Greek. The English equivalent would be "J-E-S." It simply means Jesus.

It would appear that some in our government today seem to follow the ABC principle—Anything But Christ. Like Dracula, they recoil at the sight of the cross. America's founders gave us freedom of religion. Liberals today like to limit that liberty to "freedom of worship." Yet apparently at services at the VA chapels, even the freedom to worship has been truncated. To what God may they pray? "To Whom It May Concern"? What an insult to the Christian veterans of whatever stripe. No one is forcing anyone to bow down to that cross in the chapel or to worship the God of the cross.

How far we have fallen as a nation. When he was Commander-in-Chief of the Continental Army, General George Washington insisted on hiring military chaplains systematically. Here were paid Christian clergymen to pray for and serve the troops in an explicitly Christian way.

But leftists today take "the separation of church and state" to ridiculous lengths. They often do this in the name of Thomas Jefferson. A letter written January 1, 1802, by Thomas Jefferson, is the source of the phrase "a wall of separation between Church and State." He wrote this letter in response to the Danbury Baptists, who cheered him on as president and as a champion of religious freedom. The Baptists closed their letter, "And may the Lord preserve you safe from every evil and bring you at last to his Heavenly Kingdom through Jesus Christ our Glorious Mediator."

Jefferson's obscure letter of reply to the Danbury Baptists changed history because, in 1947, the U.S. Supreme Court took it as the Rosetta Stone of the First Amendment. No longer was that first right in our Bill of Rights understood to mean that in these United States there would be no national denomination, which is what it actually intended. Now, instead, "Congress shall make no law respecting an establishment of religion" meant that the government must erect a strict wall separating church and state.

Ironically, if the liberals were right, Jefferson violated the separation of church and state in the very letter that gave us the separation of church and state, since he closes his reply with this: "I reciprocate your kind prayers for the protection and blessing of the common Father and Creator of man, and tender you for yourselves and your religious association, assurances of my high respect and esteem." Prayers? To Father and Creator? By a president?

We seem to have a case of national amnesia today. And that can be seen by what apparently we cannot see in some of our VA hospital chapels of late.

115

AMERICA WITHOUT RELIGIOUS
FREEDOM IS UNTHINKABLE

Originally published on July 7, 2015

To conceive of America apart from religious liberty is almost unthinkable. But recent events have shown us the unthinkable may be
right around the corner, with long-established religious rights brushed
away—despite weak judicial assurances to the contrary.

I think it's worthwhile to take a look at how important Christian
liberty was to America's settlers and founders. For many of them, it was
the reason they sacrificed everything to come here.

It was not easy undertaking this "errand into the wilderness," to use
a phrase from the Puritan Cotton Mather, who wrote *The Great Works
of Christ in America* (1702). The first winter the Pilgrims experienced
here (1620–1621) half of their number died. But they were free to worship Jesus without restrictions on their conscience, which is what they
sought here.

Ten years later, Rev. John Winthrop led thousands of Puritans, and
they founded Boston in 1630. Before even disembarking, Winthrop
preached a classic sermon, "A Model of Christian Charity," where he
said, quoting the words of Christ, "We shall be a 'city on a hill'."

John Winthrop had a sizable estate, which he spent to help further
the colony. Mather related to us, "Many were the afflictions of this
righteous man! He lost much of his estate in a ship, and in an house,
quickly after his coming to New England, besides the prodigious expense of it in the difficulties of his coming hither."

This uprooting from their homes and their wider families must have been traumatic, but it was all worth it. For example, months later, when the Puritans finally began to settle in the New World, Winthrop wrote his wife, who could not go with them initially because she was pregnant. Despite a harsh winter that killed off many of their number and despite all the difficulties that they faced, here is what he said to her: "We here enjoy God and Jesus Christ, and is not this enough?"

In 1636, Roger Williams, who felt some of the measures of his fellow Puritans oppressive, established Providence (named after God), Rhode Island. Williams intended to provide a safe haven for people to worship however they saw fit. His charter for the new colony stated, "No person within the said colony, at any time hereafter, shall be anywise molested, punished, disquieted, or called in question for any differences in opinion in matters of religion...but that all persons may...enjoy their own judgments and consciences in matters of religious concernments."

Catholics founded Maryland to practice their religion.

In the 1670s and 1680s, Quakers founded a haven for Christians of all kinds. The Quaker William Penn laid this foundation, and to this day, Pennsylvania, named in honor of his father, enshrines the family name. Penn created what he called a "Holy Experiment," allowing for Christians of all denominations to worship freely as they saw fit.

And on it goes. Freedom to worship according to the dictates of conscience was a huge motivating factor in the creation of America. But, it didn't stop when the settling era stopped and the founding fathers entered the stage.

In 1789, George Washington said in a letter to the United Baptist Churches in Virginia, "If I could have entertained the slightest apprehension, that the Constitution framed in the Convention, where I had the honor to preside, might possibly endanger the religious rights of any ecclesiastical Society, certainly I would never have placed my signature to it."

In his Virginia Statute for Religious Freedom, Thomas Jefferson said that to force people to believe in something they don't believe in is a "departure from the plan of the holy author of our religion"—that is, Jesus. Jesus gives us the freedom to believe or not. The state should not determine what people may or may not believe. That's un-Christian, argued Jefferson.

James Madison said, "Whilst we assert for ourselves a freedom to embrace, to profess and to observe the Religion which we believe to be of divine origin, we cannot deny an equal freedom to those whose minds have not yet yielded to the evidence which has convinced us." Therefore, to God shall people give an account someday, but not to the state.

Senator Daniel Webster, one of the great orators in nineteenth-century American politics, summed up how religious freedom helped build this country: "Finally, let us not forget the religious character of our origin. Our fathers were brought hither by their high veneration for the Christian religion. They journeyed by its light and labored in its hope. They sought to incorporate its principles with the elements of their society, and to diffuse its influence through all their institutions, civil, political, or literary."

An America without religious freedom is frankly un-American.

EPILOGUE

ON THE PURSUIT OF HAPPINESS:
JOY IS A STATE OF MIND

Originally published on October 3, 2017

Millions of Americans spend much of their time on what they think will make them happy. And being happy turns out to be good for you. *Time* reports, "It's official: happiness really can make you healthier" (October 2, 2017).

The God-given right of "the pursuit of happiness" is even in our national birth certificate the Declaration of Independence. But many people don't find happiness and joy. Why not? Perhaps because they are seeking them in all the wrong places. Indeed, happiness seems to elude a lot of Americans. Jim Carrey, the accomplished comedian and movie star, once said, "I think everybody should get rich and famous and do everything they ever dreamed of so they can see that it's not the answer."

The apostle Paul gave an interesting model for true happiness. He encouraged us to "rejoice in the Lord always: and again I say, Rejoice" (Philippians 4:4 KJV).

There's a notable quote from *Hamlet*: "There is nothing either good or bad, but thinking makes it so." He wasn't saying that morality was relative—the whole play is premised on the outrageously wrong murder of the namesake's father by his brother to grab royal power. Rather, Hamlet was saying that how he thinks about his circumstances is more important than the circumstances themselves.

Christian pastor Chuck Swindoll put it this way: "Life is 10 percent circumstances, 90 percent how we react to those circumstances."

Many people think the source of happiness is eating forbidden fruit. The late Pastor Dave Breese once wrote a book about Satan's "believable lies" (1987). He notes, "In our time, both the world and the church seem to have conspired to present the gracious Creator of the universe as a tyrant. The image that many have of him is that of a despot in heaven looking down at people having fun, quickly moving to break up the game. Believing this Satanic distortion, modern Adams and Eves quickly turn from grateful appreciation of their wide privileges to a fatal resentment of the few things that are forbidden to them."

I think a perfect example of finding joy through obeying God versus disobeying Him can be seen in the conversion of St. Augustine. His classic book (written about AD 400) *The Confessions of St. Augustine* autobiographically chronicles Augustine's journey from sinner to saint. As a young man, Augustine prayed, "Give me chastity and continence, but not yet!" On the subject of lust, Augustine said [speaking to God], "I broke your laws, but I did not escape your scourges. For what mortal man can do that?" He goes on, describing his state at age sixteen: "Then it was that the madness of lust, licensed by human shamelessness but forbidden by your laws, took me completely under its scepter, and I clutched it with both hands."

But his mom Saint Monica was a woman of prayer who prayed diligently for him. Later in life, he penned how miserable he felt as a slave to sin: "The enemy had control of my will, and out of it he fashioned a chain and fettered me with it. For in truth lust is made out of a perverse will, and when lust is served, it becomes habit, and when habit is not resisted, it becomes necessity. By such links, joined one to another, as it were—for this reason I have called it a chain—a harsh bondage held me fast.... Unhappy man that I was! Who would deliver me from the body of this death, unless your grace through Jesus Christ our Lord?"

This all resolved one day while he was in the backyard of a friend: "And lo, I heard from a nearby house, a voice like that of a boy or a girl, I know not which, chanting and repeating over and over, 'Take up and read. Take up and read.'"

He opened a scroll at hand—Paul's letter to the Romans (13:34): "I snatched it up, opened it, and read in silence the chapter on which my eyes first fell: "Not in rioting and drunkenness, not in chambering and impurities, not in strife and envying; but put you on the Lord Jesus Christ, and make not provision for the flesh in its lusts." No further wished I to read, nor was there need to do so. Instantly, in truth, at the end of this sentence, as if before a peaceful light streaming into my heart, all the dark shadows of doubt fled away."

St. Augustine was converted and discovered true joy, and he affirmed: "You have made us for Yourself, Oh God, and our hearts are restless until they find their rest in You."

The oldest city in North America is on the east coast, named in honor of this man: St. Augustine, Florida. On the west coast in the greater Los Angeles area is Santa Monica, named after Augustine's mother. The vast majority of Americans live between these two cities named in honor of these great Christian luminaries.

How do you spell JOY? Someone put it this way: Jesus first, Others second, Yourself last. It works every time.

REFERENCES

Alinsky, Saul. 1971. *Rules for Radicals*. New York: Random House.

Barrett, David B., ed. 2001. *World Christian Encyclopedia*. Oxford: Oxford University Press.

Beevor, Antony. 1998. *Stalingrad*. New York: Viking.

Beliles, Mark A., and Jerry Newcombe. 2014. *Doubting Thomas: The Religious Life and Legacy of Thomas Jefferson*. New York: Morgan James Faith.

Bradford, William. 2008. *Of Plimouth Plantation from the Original Manuscript*. Berwyn Heights, MD: Heritage Books. Many editions are available including free online.

Breese, Dave. 1987. *Satan's Ten Most Believable Lies*. Chicago: Moody Press.

Federer, William J. 2000. *America's God and Country: Encyclopedia of Quotations*. St. Louis, MO: Amerisearch, Inc.

Fiore, Jordan D., ed. 1985. *Mourt's Relation: A Journal of the Pilgrims of Plymouth*. Plymouth, MA: Plymouth Rock Foundation. Many online versions are available.

Franklin, Benjamin, Frank Woodworth Pine, ed. 1916. *Autobiography of Benjamin Franklin*. New York: Henry Holt and Company. Also available at gutenberg.org.

Gragg, Rod. 2014. *The Pilgrim Chronicles: An Eyewitness History of the Pilgrims and the Founding of Plymouth Colony*. Washington, D.C.: Regnery History.

Horn, Jonathan. 2015. *The Man Who Would Not Be Washington: Robert E. Lee's Civil War and His Decision that Changed American History*. New York: Scribner.

Hua, Du. 2012. *The Escapes and My Journey to Freedom*. Bloomington, IN: AuthorHouse.

Hutson, James H. 1998. *Religion and the Founding of the American Republic*. Washington, D.C.: Library of Congress.

———— 2005. *The Founders on Religion: A Book of Quotations*. Princeton: Princeton University Press.

Johnson, Paul. 1983. *Modern Times: The World from the Twenties to the Nineties*. New York: Harper Collins.

———— 1997. *A History of the American People*. New York: Harper Collins.

Kengor, Paul. 2005. *God and Ronald Reagan: A Spiritual Life*. New York: Harper Perennial.

———— 2010. *Dupes: How America's Adversaries Have Manipulated Progressives for a Century*. Wilmington, DE: Intercollegiate Studies Institute.

———— 2012. *The Communist*. New York: Mercury Ink.

———— 2017. *A Pope and a President: John Paul II, Ronald Reagan, and the Extraordinary Untold Story of the 20th Century*. Wilmington, DE: Intercollegiate Studies Institute.

Kennedy, D. James and Jerry Newcombe. 1996. *New Every Morning: A Daily Devotional*. Colorado Springs, CO: Multnomah Publishers.

King, Martin Luther, Jr. 1968. *The Wisdom of Martin Luther King in His Own Words*. New York: Lancer Books.

Knight, Robert. 2010. *Radical Rulers: The White House Elites Who Are Pushing America Toward Socialism*. Fort Lauderdale, FL: Coral Ridge Ministries.

Kramer, Mark, ed. 1999. *The Black Book of Communism*. Cambridge: Harvard University Press.

Lillback, Peter, and Jerry Newcombe. 2006. *George Washington's Sacred Fire*. King of Prussia, PA: Providence Forum Press.

Lutz, Donald S. 1988. *The Origins of American Constitutionalism*. Baton Rouge: LSU Press.

Moore, James P., Jr. 2008. *The Treasury of American Prayers*. New York: Doubleday.

Moore, Johnnie. 2017. *The Martyr's Oath: Living for the Jesus They're Willing to Die For*. Carol Stream: Tyndale House.

Newcombe, Jerry. 2009. *The Book that Made America: How the Bible Formed Our Nation.* Ventura, CA: Nordskog Publishing.

Orwell, George. 1945. *Animal Farm.* London: Secker and Warburg.

Ray, Ronald D. 2013. *Endowed by Their Creator: A Collection of Historic American Military Prayers 1774–Present.* Crestwood, KY: First Principles Press.

Reagan, Ronald. 1984. *Abortion and the Conscience of a Nation.* Nashville: Thomas Nelson Publishers.

Rhodehamel, John. ed. 1997. *George Washington: Writings.* New York: The Library of America.

Ridenour, Amy. 2009. *Shattered Lives: 100 Victims of Government Health Care.* Washington, D.C.: The National Center for Public Policy Research.

Siemon-Netto, Uwe. 2008. *The Acquittal of God: A Theology for Vietnam Veterans.* Eugene, OR: Wipf & Stock Publishers.

St. Augustine. Approximately AD 400. *The Confessions.*

Valladares, Armando. 1986. *Against All Hope: A Memoir of Life in Castro's Gulag.* New York: Alfred A. Knopf, Inc.

Waite, Linda J., and Maggie Gallagher. 2000. *The Case for Marriage: Why Married People Are Happier, Healthier, and Better Off Financially.* New York: Doubleday.

Weikart, Richard, 2004. *From Darwin to Hitler: Evolutionary Ethics, Eugenics, and Racism in Germany.* New York: Palgrave MacMillan.

Witherspoon, John. 1778. *Dominion of Providence over the Passions of Men, A Sermon.* Philadelphia: Fielding and Walker.

Wright, Lawrence. 2006. *The Looming Tower: Al-Qaeda and the Road to 9/11.* New York: Alfred A. Knopf.

INDEX

A

Adams, John, 10, 28, 34, 73–74, 85, 90, 92, 136, 139, 145, 243, 301, 304, 313, 314, 372

Adams, John Quincy, 85, 206

Adams, Samuel, 90, 286, 312, 313, 322, 373

al-Baghdadi, 269

Alexander, Lexi, 94

Alinsky, Saul, 91, 101–3

Alito, Samuel, 232, 260, 261, 262

Alliance Defending Freedom (ADF), 300–301 & n1, 303, 305, 343

American Civil Liberties Union (ACLU), 62, 109 & n1, 276, 278, 297, 310, 321–23, 327, 330

American Family Association (AFA), 33, 221

annuit coeptis, 10

Apatow, Judd, 93

Arnold, Benedict, 75

Arthur, Chester, 86

Articles of Confederation, 118, 313, 368

atheist, atheism, i, xxiii, 7, 45, 71, 85, 88, 109, 111, 114, 184, 201, 211, 226, 269, 273, 274, 277, 285, 286, 293, 298, 329, 330–32, 336, 369

Attkisson, Sharyl, 135 & n3

Augustine, 76, 352–53

B

Bachmann, Michele, 79

Bancroft, George, 3, 25

Barrett, David, 337–38

Barton, David, 56, 183, 221, 274

Batista, Fulgencio, 250

Bauer, Gary, 61, 126 & n2, 213, 229, 242

Bayard, James, 10

Baylor, Greg, 301

Beck, Glenn, 38, 40, 79, 274

Bedard, Paul, 316 & n1

Beevor, Antony, 114

Beliles, Mark, 128, 131–32 & n1, 207, 277, 379

Bennett, William, 145

Bergdahl, Bowe, 107

Berry, Mike, 290

bin Laden, Osama, 334

Blackstone, William, 138, 280, 373–74

Blair, Rev. Paul, 56–57

Blanchard, Jonathan, 69

Blankschaen, Bill, 243

Bloomberg, Michael, 300–1

Bodnar, Jackie, 170

Book of Common Prayer, 39, 321

Bork, Robert, 168, 192, 257

Boykin, Jerry, 218, 224–25, 288

Bradford, William, 13–14, 16, 19

Brejcha, Tom, 327–29 & n1

Brown, Michael (columnist), 344

PUBLISHER'S WORD[1]

Dr. Jerry Newcombe is one of my very favorite authors! We first met in person in 2009 at the National Religious Broadcasters convention in Nashville, Tennessee. I had read many of his writings as coauthor with his late boss, Dr. D. James Kennedy of Coral Ridge Ministries (now D. James Kennedy Ministries), including the magnificent devotional *New Every Morning*.[2] I watched weekly Fort Lauderdale church services on TV featuring the late brilliant pastor and theologian Dr. Kennedy. My wife Gail and I met Jerry as he was taping American leaders for his TV show, and we soon became long-distance friends in Christian ministry.

Within a few rapid-paced months NPI published one of his many books, *The Book that Made America: How the Bible Formed Our Nation*, launched on Independence Day, July 4, 2009. This book has become the most popular of all of our NPI titles. In 2017 the book was translated into Mandarin in China for that nation and for the American Chinese (which include four Chinese children adopted by my wife Gail and me).

We have kindred spirits: Jerry N. and Jerry N. are highly involved in Christianity and Americanism, and now NPI is pleased to publish this newest book that you are reading.

---

1. All Scripture quotations in the Publisher's Word are from *The American Patriot's Bible*, copyright © 2009 by Thomas Nelson, Inc. Notes and articles copyright © 2009 by Richard G. Lee. Scripture taken from the New King James Version®. Copyright © 1982 by Thomas Nelson, Inc. Used by permission. All rights reserved.

2. D. James Kennedy and Jerry Newcombe, *New Every Morning: A Daily Devotional* (Colorado Springs, CO: Multnomah Publishers, 1996).

I have been personally reading these weekly essays by Dr. Newcombe for motivation and for vital information regarding our American culture and its awful deterioration over the last several decades.

We also share a love for the Norse community, as his wife Kirsti is Norwegian-American and I am a product of Scandinavian-Norwegian immigrants from the late 1880s. My grandfather, Andrae Arne Nordskog, was the first general manager of the Hollywood Bowl in the 1920s, about one century ago, and his Nordskog Records was the first music-recording company on the west coast. My dad, Bob Nordskog, was an entrepreneur of many businesses in Los Angeles, and is a Hall of Famer for powerboat racing in the Motorsports Hall of Fame formerly in Novi, Michigan, now moved to Daytona, Florida.

Nordskog Publishing believes this latest of the many Jerry Newcombe books is tremendously important in addressing the current cultural climate in America and in the world. Jerry takes on vital issues of the day and speaks to America's precipitate decline from our foundations as a Christian nation. The Pilgrims undertook their journey to these shores motivated by a vision of Christian liberty, for the "Advancement of the Christian Faith." They wrote the Mayflower Compact on the Mayflower ship before they even disembarked.

Let's read this portion of their Compact with the understanding that these are our roots:

> Having undertaken, for the Glory of God, and advancements of the Christian faith, and the honor of our King and Country, a voyage to plant the first colony in the Northern parts of Virginia; do by these presents, solemnly and mutually, in the presence of God, and one another; covenant and combine ourselves together into a civil body politic. (The Mayflower Compact, November 11, 1620)

This book *American Amnesia* reveals a blind spot in our collective American memory. We have forgotten our beloved history and are largely ignorant about the Pilgrims and Puritans, the founding fathers, the Mayflower Compact, the Battle of Lexington, the Declaration of Independence, the Revolutionary War of Independence, the Articles of Confederation, our U.S. Constitution and Bill of Rights, all the way through to the un-Civil War. And now we see in our more recent history the disastrous and bloody twentieth century and our current twenty-first century characterized by outright disobedience of multitudes of our nation's citizens—the result of our historical amnesia.

Largely to blame is the humanistic public school curriculum of the past century or so. Evil educators and the National Education Association have executed a purposeful dumbing-down and brainwashing of our children and thus our future—ironically paid for by American taxpayers. Thus, humanism, Darwinist evolution, and atheism reign in the U.S. today.

> Humanism is particularly dangerous because, unlike other religion in America, it is endorsed in the public schools and established in every department of the government of the United States. (Kennedy and Newcombe, *New Every Morning*, August 9)

> Cursed is the man who trusts in man and makes flesh his strength. (Jeremiah 17:5)

Churches of America have largely failed to teach and engage their congregants to put legs to their faith! President Ronald Reagan and the U.S. Congress proclaimed 1983 The Year of the Bible. I was privileged to be the Los Angeles County chairman that year. Why have we gone astray only thirty-five years from that proclamation? Could it be due to government corruption, the infection of our school system by left-wing politics, a willingness to compromise the truth, and the failure of the Church to teach constitutional and Biblical precepts?

Too many pastors (churches, Bible colleges, and seminaries) have adopted non-Christian, false, and very serious liberal nonsense that is an anti-Christ virus in today's Body of Believers. Many of our leaders have grown too cowardly to engage the culture of our day.

> For certain men have crept in unnoticed, who long ago were marked out for this condemnation, ungodly men, who turn the grace of our God into lewdness and deny the only Lord God and our Lord Jesus Christ. (Jude 1:4)

> A house divided against itself cannot stand. (President Abraham Lincoln, from Mark 3:25)

Our overarching failure has been that in recent decades *Americans largely have forgotten God,* despite our founding by Christians. Our laws were based upon the British Common Law, which came primarily from the Magna Carta (AD 1215), limiting the power of monarchs. Our founding fathers incorporated it into our United States Constitution. That seminal document begins thus:

> Know that, having regard to God and for the salvation of our soul, and those of all our ancestors and heirs, and unto the honor of God and the advancement of his holy Church and for the rectifying of our realm, we have granted as underwritten by advice of our venerable fathers.... In the first place we have granted to God, and by this our present charter confirmed for us and our heirs forever that the English Church shall be free, and shall have her rights entire, and her liberties inviolate; and we will that it be thus observed.

Our quintessential American love of freedom—particularly religious freedom—is rooted in a Biblically derived sense of intrinsic human self-worth as the bearers of the image of God. We need to return to our King Jesus the Christ and obey Him with reverence, as did those upon whose shoulders we stand as a nation.

Dear reader, look at the whole book of Jude for predictions and warnings about apostates, from Jude, a bondservant of Jesus Christ and brother of James. Yet it ends on a high note:

> Now to Him who is able to keep you from stumbling, And to present you faultless before the presence of His glory with exceeding joy, To God our Savior, Who alone is wise, Be glory and majesty, Dominion and power, Both now and forever. Amen. (Jude 1:24–25)

Let us pray intentionally and with laser-targeted prayers in the months and years ahead for national revival by our Lord God Omnipotent, who loves America, for a new wave of the Holy Spirit, which will require Church repentance nationwide! Pray Christ's power, justice, and love to come upon us in Spirit and in Truth for a new awakening as we leave behind our "American amnesia," and forge ahead in His will and way, remembering the mighty deeds of the Lord over the past four centuries in our land.

...that He might make you know that man shall not live by bread alone; but man lives by every word that proceeds from the mouth of the Lord. (Deuteronomy 8:3)

Additionally, Americans need to pray for the salvation of the un-saved in America and everywhere in the world. God is listening. He knows every hair on our heads, and He wants the world to embrace the King of kings and Lord of lords. God will have His way one day at the end of the age, and every knee will bow and tongue confess that Jesus Christ is Lord. May this book, *American Amnesia*, be a part of the next great move of God—the awakening from amnesia—we all crave to see in our beloved country.

How then shall they call on Him in whom they have not believed? And how shall they believe in Him of whom they have not heard? And how shall they hear without a preacher? And how shall they preach unless they are sent? As it is written: "How beautiful are the feet of those who preach the gospel of peace, Who bring glad tidings of good things!" (Romans 10:14)

But seek first the kingdom of God and His righteousness, and all these things shall be added to you. Therefore do not worry about tomorrow, for tomorrow will worry about its own things. Sufficient for the day is its own trouble. (Matthew 6:33–34)

The Englishman Edmund Burke was right in his timeless warning:

When bad men combine, the good must associate; else they will fall one by one, an unpitied sacrifice in a contemptible struggle. (from *Thoughts on the Cause of the Present Discontents*, 1770)

Dear Reader of American Amnesia, what can you be doing to preserve the free-enterprise system and Christian constitutional American liberty now? The following are quotes from some of America's past patriots and leaders in the holy cause of Liberty. Meditate on these. We are in a season in America during which the Lord is waiting and listening for Christians to rise up and seek Him diligently in prayer—in churches, Bible stud-ies, prayer meetings, and anywhere two or three are gathered together. Prayer (or rather, our Lord God Omnipotent) changes things. America needs a revival. We need to turn back to our Triune Lord—Father, Son, and Holy Spirit. My friend Dr. Marshall Foster, founder and president of the World History Institute, has learned from his historical studies that generally in history (His story), God has initiated revivals and new awakenings about every half century. Pray for our King's new move of the Holy Spirit to sweep throughout our American land.

Here, then, are several select resources from history.

I am apt to believe that it will be celebrated, by succeeding Generations, as the great anniversary Festival. It ought to be commemorated, as the Day of Deliverance by solemn Acts of Devotion to God Almighty. It ought to be solemnized with Pomp and Parade, with Shews, Games, Sports, Guns, Bells, Bonfires and Illuminations from one end of this Continent to the other from this Time forward forever more. (John Adams on the Declaration of Independence, in a letter to his wife Abigail Adams, July 1776)

*

Tyranny, like hell, is not easily conquered; yet we have this consolation with us, that the harder the conflict, the more glorious the triumph. (Thomas Paine, *The American Crisis*, No. 1, December 19, 1776)

*

Sir, we are not weak, if we make a proper use of the means which the God of nature hath placed in our power. Three millions of people, armed in the holy cause of liberty, and in such a country as that which we possess, are invincible by any force which our enemy can send against us. Besides, sir, we shall not fight our battles alone. There is a just God who presides over the destinies of nations, and who will raise friends to fight our battles for us. The battle, sir, is not to the strong alone; it is to the vigilant, the active, the brave.

Besides sir, we have no election. If we were base enough to desire it, it is now too late to retire from the contest. There is no retreat but in submission and slavery! Our chains are forged! Their clanking may be heard on the plains of Boston! The war is inevitable—and let it come! I repeat it, sir, let it come!

It is in vain, sir, to extenuate the matter. Gentlemen may cry, peace, peace—but there is no peace. The war is actually begun! The next gale that sweeps from the north will bring to our ears the clash of resounding arms! Our brethren are already in the field! Why stand we here idle? What is it that gentlemen wish? What would they have? Is life so dear, or peace so sweet, as to be purchased at the price of chains and slavery? Forbid it, Almighty God! I know not what course others may take, but as for me: Give me liberty, or give me death! (Excerpts from "Give Me Liberty or Give Me Death," by Patrick Henry, the first governor of the state of Virginia and member of the First Continental Congress, delivered at St. John's Church the year prior to the signing of the Declaration of Independence. It called for a holy defensive war and was a call to arms against the British oppression, and was passed by the Convention.)

*

All temporal power is of God,
And the magistratal, His institution, laud,
To but advance creaturely happiness aubaud:
Let us then affirm the Source of Liberty.

Ever agreeable to the nature and will,
Of the Supreme and Guardian of all yet still
Employed for our rights and freedom's thrill:
Thus proves the only Source of Liberty.

Through our civil joy is surely expressed
Through hearth, and home, and church manifest,
Yet this too shall be a nation's true test:
To acknowledge the divine Source of Liberty.

(Samuel Adams, "The Divine Source of Liberty." Sam Adams was one of the firebrands of the Revolution and founder of the Committees of Correspondence and the Sons of Liberty. He led the resistance against the tyranny of the King of England following the Boston Massacre.)

*

America's laws are largely derived from English Common Law. They formed the backbone of the American Constitution and our nation's laws.

Sir William Blackstone's *Commentaries on the Laws of England*, published 1765–1769 by Oxford's Clarendon Press, had an immense influence on America's founders, being considered the definitive pre-Revolutionary source of common law by United States courts....

"When the Supreme Being formed the universe, and created matter out of nothing, He impressed certain principles upon that matter, from which it can never depart, and without which it would cease to be....

The Creator is a Being, not only of infinite power, and wisdom, but also of infinite goodness, He has so intimately connected, so inseparably interwoven the laws of eternal justice with the happiness of each individual, that the latter cannot be attained but by observing the former... [a] mutual connection of justice and human felicity....

The doctrines thus delivered we call the revealed or divine law, and they are to be found only in the Holy Scriptures." (Bill Federer's *American Minute*, "Blackstone's Law Commentaries To Finney's Revivals," August 18, 2018)

*

My country 'tis of thee
Sweet land of liberty:
Of thee I sing.
Land where my fathers died
Land of the Pilgrims' pride
From every mountainside
Let freedom ring.

My native country thee
Land of the noble free
Thy name I love:
I love thy rocks and rills
Thy woods and templed hills
My heart with rapture thrills
Like that above.

Let music swell the breeze
And ring from all the trees
Sweet freedom's song
Let all that breathe partake
Let mortal tongues awake
Let rocks their silence break
The sound prolong.

Our fathers' God to thee
Author of liberty
To thee we sing
Long may our land be bright
With freedom's holy light
Protect us by thy might
Great God, our King.
(Samuel Smith, "My Country, 'Tis of Thee")

*

In vain, without the Bible, we increase penal laws and draw entrenchments around our institutions. Bibles are strong entrenchments. Where they abound, men cannot pursue wicked courses, and at the same time enjoy quiet conscience. (Founding father James McHenry, signer of the Constitution)

*

The name of American, which belongs to you in your national capacity, must always exalt the just pride of patriotism more than any appellation derived from local discriminations. With slight shades of difference, you have the same religion, manners, habits, and political principles. You have in a common cause fought and triumphed together. The independence and liberty you possess are the work of joint councils and joint efforts, of common dangers, sufferings, and successes.

But these considerations, however powerfully they address themselves to your sensibility, are greatly outweighed by those which apply more immediately to your interest. Here every portion of our country finds the most commanding motives for carefully guarding and preserving the union of the whole....

Of all the dispositions and habits which lead to political prosperity, religion and morality are indispensable supports. In vain would that man claim the tribute of patriotism who should labor to subvert these great pillars of human happiness, the firmest props of the duties of men and citizens. The mere politician, equally with the pious man, ought to respect and to cherish them.... And let us with caution indulge the supposition that morality can be maintained without religion. Whatever may be conceded to the influence of refined education on minds of peculiar structure, reason and experience both forbid us to expect that national morality can prevail in exclusion of religious principle.

'Tis substantially true that virtue or morality is a necessary spring of popular government. The rule indeed extends with more or less force to every species of free government. . . .

Observe good faith and justice toward all nations. Cultivate peace and harmony with all. Religion and morality enjoin this conduct; and can it be that good policy does not equally enjoin it? It will be worthy of a free, enlightened, and at no distant period, a great nation, to give to mankind the magnanimous and too novel example of a people always guided by an exalted justice and benevolence. Who can doubt that in the course of time and things the fruits of such a plan would richly repay any temporary advantages which might be lost by a steady adherence to it? Can it be that Providence has not connected the permanent felicity of a nation with its virtue? This experiment, at least, is recommended by every sentiment which ennobles human nature. Alas! Is it rendered impossible by its vices?

In the execution of such a plan nothing is more essential than that permanent, inveterate antipathies against particular nations and passionate attachments for others should be cultivated. . . .

Harmony, liberal intercourse with all nations are recommended by policy, humanity, and interest. . . .

I fervently beseech the Almighty to avert or mitigate the evils to which they may tend. I shall also carry with me the hope that my country will never cease to view them with indulgence. . . .

Relying on its kindness in this as in other things, and actuated by that fervent love toward it which is so natural to a man who views in it the native soil of himself and his progenitors for several generations, I anticipate with pleasing expectation that retreat in which I promise myself to realize, without alloy, the sweet enjoyment of partaking, in the midst of my fellow-citizens, the benign influence of good laws under a free government, the ever-favorite object of my heart, and the happy reward, as I trust, of our mutual cares, labors, and dangers. (President George Washington, excerpts from his Farewell Address, 1796. Publisher's Note: I recommend all readers obtain and read with care President George Washington's full Farewell Address and First Inaugural Address.)

*

If we and our posterity shall be true to the Christian religion, if we and they shall live always in the fear of God, and shall respect His commandments, if we and they shall maintain just moral sentiments and such conscientious convictions of duty as shall control the heart and life, we may have the highest hopes of the future fortunes of our country; and if we maintain those institutions of government and that political union, exceeding all praise as much as it exceeds all former examples of political associations, we may be sure of one thing, that while our country furnishes material for a thousand masters of the historic art, it will afford no topic for a Gibbon. It will have no decline and fall. It will go on prospering and to prosper.

But if we and our posterity reject religious institutions and authority, violate the rules of eternal justice, trifle with the injunctions of morality, and recklessly destroy the political constitution which holds us together, no man can tell how sudden a catastrophe may overwhelm us that shall bury all our glory in profound obscurity. (Daniel Webster, statesman, lawyer, and orator, from a speech he gave before the Historical Society of New York in 1852.)

*

The deliberations of the Constitutional Convention of 1787 were held in strict secrecy. Consequently, anxious citizens gathered outside Independence Hall when the proceedings ended in order to learn what had been produced behind closed doors. The answer was provided immediately. A Mrs. Powel of Philadelphia asked Benjamin Franklin, "Well, Doctor, what have we got, a republic or a monarchy?" With no hesitation whatsoever, Franklin responded, "A republic, if you can keep it."[3]

*

America is engaged in a spiritual civil war. With all the evangelical radio and television ministries, you'd think that more Christians would join in the fight, but many Christians haven't committed to do their parts to change our land. Others have heard that Christians shouldn't concern themselves with political and social issues, so they don't even register to vote! We read

---

3. John F. McManus, "'A Republic, if You Can Keep It'," *New American*, November 6, 2000, thenewamerican.com/.

in Genesis 1:26 that God gave humans dominion over everything in the world. This has become known as the Cultural Mandate. To properly fulfill that mandate, we must participate in our local and national elections. (Let me say that I believe it's a sin not to vote.) Have you registered to vote and exercised that avenue to make a difference for Christ? (Kennedy and Newcombe, *New Every Morning*, 1996, November 4)

*

All heaven and earth resound with that subtle and delicately balanced truth that the old paths are the best paths after all. (J. C. Ryle)

*

Ah, Lord God! Behold, You have made the heavens and the earth by Your great power and outstretched arm. There is nothing too hard for You. You show lovingkindness to thousands, and repay the iniquity of the fathers into the bosom of their children after them—the Great, the Mighty God, whose name is the Lord of hosts. (Jeremiah 32:17–18)

GERALD CHRISTIAN NORDSKOG
USA Constitution Day
September 17, 2018

ABOUT THE AUTHOR

Dr. Jerry Newcombe serves as the senior producer, on-air host, and columnist for D. James Kennedy Ministries. Jerry has produced or co-produced more than seventy one-hour television specials broadcast nationwide. He is the author or coauthor of thirty books, including *The Book that Made America: How the Bible Formed Our Nation* (Nordskog Publishing Inc. 2009). At least two of his books have been bestsellers, *George Washington's Sacred Fire* (with Dr. Peter Lillback) and *What If Jesus Had Never Been Born?* (with Dr. Kennedy). Jerry also wrote *Doubting Thomas? The Life and Legacy of Thomas Jefferson* (with Mark Beliles).

Jerry has appeared on numerous talk shows as a guest, including *Politically Incorrect with Bill Maher* (four times), Janet Parshall's radio programs, *Point of View*, the Moody radio network, TBN, the *Fox News Channel*, the *Fox Business Channel*, C-Span2's *Book Notes*, etc. Jerry hosts a weekly radio program called "Vocal Point" on *GraceNetRadio* (GraceNetRadio.com), staging a "meeting of the minds." (The broadcasts are also individually posted at jerrynewcombe.com.)

Jerry Newcombe earned his doctorate in ministry at Knox Theological Seminary, founded by Dr. D. James Kennedy. He is an associate minister at New Presbyterian Church, Wilton Manors, Florida. Jerry is happily married with two children and three grandchildren. The Newcombes reside in South Florida.

For more information on Jerry, visit jerrynewcombe.com.

Also by Jerry Newcombe:

THE BOOK THAT MADE AMERICA:
HOW THE BIBLE FORMED OUR NATION

The Bible is the book that made America. All that is positive in our foundation can be traced back to the Scriptures. Former President Obama once declared that America is not a Christian nation, while *Newsweek* announced the demise of Christian America. This book is the answer to America's critics, with the facts of history.

> "Say that America is a Christian nation and you'll be brought up on hate crime charges—or at least thought an ignoramus. But what are the facts of history? *The Book that Made America* demonstrates that there once was a Book even more integral to this nation than Al Gore's *Earth in the Balance*. I recommend Dr. Newcombe's book highly!"
>
> — Ann Coulter,
> *New York Times* Best-selling Author

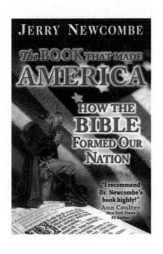

Dedicated to D. James Kennedy
Foreword by Jennifer Kennedy Cassidy
Paperback, 6"×9", 304 pages
Illustrated, indexed
ISBN: 978-0-9824929-0-1 2009
$18.95

The Book that Made America: How the Bible Formed Our Nation is now available in Mandarin.

More on America's Christian roots:

THE BATTLE OF LEXINGTON: A SERMON AND EYEWITNESS NARRATIVE

by Lexington Pastor, Jonas Clark, 1776

"With powerful voice Jonas Clark tells of... the principles of personal, civil, and religious liberty, and the right of resistance. Today our country lacks enough preachers like Clark who gave his congregation courage to stand and make a difference."

—FROM THE INTRODUCTION BY REV. CHRISTOPHER HOOPS

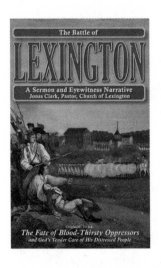

Includes biographical information on Pastor Jonas Clark, facsimile title page from the original 1776 publication, four classic poems commemorating Paul Revere's Ride and the "shot heard 'round the world," and illustrations.

Paperback, 5"×8", 96 pages
ISBN: 978-0-9796736-3-4
2007
$9.95

To see all of our exciting titles, view book contents,
and order e-books, go to:

NordskogPublishing.com

If you like solid and inspiring content,
get our eNewsletter, "The Bell Ringer."

We also invite you to browse many short articles, poems,
and testimonies by various perceptive writers here:

Publisherscorner.NordskogPublishing.com

*Ask the publisher about upcoming titles and e-book versions,
and a discount when you purchase multiple books.*